AF531335

Ramasami and Mr Shaji Baby in collecting material for the book is thankfully acknowledged.

We shall await your valuable suggestions for improving the next edition of this book.

S.A. Abbasi
F.I. Khan

CONTENTS

Chapter - 1

INTRODUCTION AND BRIEF HISTORY OF GREENBELTS

In the context of environmental pollution abatement, a greenbelt may be defined as a strip of trees of such species, and such a geometry, that when planted around a source, would significantly attenuate the air pollution by intercepting and assimilating the pollutants in a sustainable manner.

The concept of greenbelt as a source of pollution abatement was recognised initially by three nations: The USA, Britain and Kenya (Ruth & William, 1994; Gareth et.al. 1992; Andy, 1991 and Parsons, 1990).

Ebenezer Howard, a British social reformer, advanced the concept of greenbelt in 1898, in connection with the planning of "new towns" located outside the periphery of London, which was then sprawling far into the countryside. Howard proposed "garden cities" which would that only be free of pollution but would also be antidote of polluted cities, each of which would be surrounded by an agriculture "country belt". It was British architect and planner Raymond Unwin, a town designer and contemporary of Howard's, who actually coined the term *greenbelt* (Ruth & William, 1994; Gareth et.al. 1992).

In Britain, Howard's concept took two forms: the greenbelts surrounding the new towns in rural Britain (the first of thcsc was

Letchworth, built in 1903); and, beginning in the 1930s, the application of the idea to London itself. The *London Green Belt Act* was passed by the British Parliament in 1938. A more elaborate plan was created in 1944 by Patrick Abercrombie, who proposed a belt, five or more miles wide, consisting of both public open spaces and private holdings, that would be regulated so as to preclude runaway suburban development.

In the United States, the administration of the then President, Franklin Roosevelt, tried to adapt Howard's new town concept as part of its resettlement program. Three such towns were built with Greenbelt, Maryland, being the best known. To this day a partial greenbelt separates the Greenbelt community, now a part of the Washington, D.C. metropolitan area, from its neighbouring subdivisions. The greenbelt concept was also proposed in the plan for Radhurn, New Jersey, a well-known privately financed new town built in the 1920s, but was not fully implemented. Possibly the only fully realised garden city-style greenbelt is in Boulder, Colorado, where a band of publicly purchased land now encircles the city.

In the American concept of greenbelt, relatively wide band of rural land or open space surrounded a town or a city. The term greenbelt meant, generally, any swath of open space separating or interrupting urban development. A land so designated is controlled through regulation or public or quasi-public ownership (such as the Nature Conservancy) to retain its natural character and provide a resemblance of rural ambience in urban or urbanising areas (Ruth & William, 1994; Gareth et.al. 1992).

The central goal of Roosevelt's greenbelt programme, a innovative and radical intervention in American city building, was not to create better urban communities, but rather to generate jobs in a declining national economy. Fortunately, the Resettlement Administration, headed by Rexford G. Tugwell, called on architect/planner Clarence S. Stein to prepare town design guidelines and to serve as planning consultant. Stein settled into an advisory role through which he greatly influenced the character and quality of these communities, especially the best known: Greenbelt Maryland.

After World War II, Stein was instrumental in preserving the towns as examples of socially and environmentally responsible community designs and prototypes for a national new town policy. (Parsons, 1990). He argued vigorously that the establishment, design, and building of new towns should be a principal means of achieving urban decentralisation, congestion-free transportation, sound regional development, and an urban environment that would nurture human growth. During the 1920s and early 1930s Stein had played a central role in developing housing projects and new towns that would serve as the prototypes of the greenbelt towns.

As of now, there are no true greenbelts encircling major American cities are non-existent, although both Boston and San Francisco have citizen-led programs to encourage the formation of London-style greenbelts on a *de facto* basis. In Boston, a "Bay Circuit", proposed in 1929 by Benton Mackaye, a regional planner and father of the Appalachian Trail planner Charles Eliot II, and others, has been struggling to come into being for well over half a century. The circuit is made up of strung-together parks, natural sanctuaries, and historic sites in a 100-mile-long open space corridor around the city. In San Francisco, open space proponents have advocated the establishment of a greenbelt since 1959. The Bay Area Green belt, a hoped-for 3.8 million-acre girdle of parks, watershed lands, farms, rural estates, and ranches was given a boost in public awareness in 1988 by the establishment of a multi-government project to build a "Ridge Trail" through the proposed greenbelt area in the highlands surrounding San Francisco Bay (Parsons, 1990).

In Kenya greenbelt movement has been started through an agro-forestry project founded and run by a womens, association. The movement, started and organised by Professor Wangari Maathi, a lecturer in veterinary medicine, aims to plant trees for a variety of reasons : to stabilise soil, for use as fuel, for landscape improvement and as a source of income for the women taking part in the scheme. Tree nurseries have been established which issue seedlings that are used to produce greenbelts in both rural and urban areas of the country. These seedlings are provided to women's groups which then oversee the planting and raising of the trees. For every tree that survives more than three months outside the nursery, the woman who plants and cares for it is paid equivalent Rs 10/-. Paying female tree-tenders a premium for every seedling that survives not only provides an income for women who would otherwise have none, but has also allowed the Green Belt project to attain a transplant survival rate of around 80 percent. By the end of the 1980s the movement had seen the creation of well over 600 tree nurseries and grown 10 million trees, thanks to the involvement of 50,000 women and children in 3,000 schools (Andy, 1991).

In India there have been public awareness campaigns to plant trees but there is little follow-up after the ceremonial planting of saplings in most cases. This results in very low survival rate and generally poor afforestation eventually. And such initiatives have rarely been directed towards development of greenbelts in the strict sense of the term.

Chapter 2

VEGETATION AS SINK FOR AIR POLLUTANTS

2.1 AIR POLLUTION

The history of air pollution is as old as man's invention of fire. But till a few decades ago the carrying capacity of the global atmosphere was sufficient to assimilate the air pollution that was being generated by anthropogenic activities. This situation has deteriorated very fast during the recent years. Increasing demographic pressure allied with increased developmental activities is generating more copious emission than the air can assimilate (Abbasi, 1998).

The situation in the urban areas is particularly grim and is worsening day by day. This is illustrated in Tables 2.1, 2.2 and 2.3. We see that levels of one of the common air pollutants - particulate matter - in seven out of eight major cities in India are higher than the permissible limits (for residential areas) of 200 mmg/m^3 set by Central Pollution Control Board (Table 2.1). Recent surveys indicate that other air pollutants - SO_x and NO_x - also exceed permissible limits very often (Table 2.2). In a report (The Environmentalist 13 111-115, 1993), R.J. Sinha states that 94% of the traffic constables in Jaipur suffer from one or other disease due to air pollution, especially from vehicular emissions. An astonishingly high incidence (55%) of tuberculosis was found among constables in the 20-30 year age group.

The situation in other cities of the world is also not very pleasant (Table 2.3). Besides the common pollutants listed in Tables 2.1 - 2.3 we also encounter excessive levels of organic and metallic constituents in the air in many locations.

2.2 AIR POLLUTION CONTROL THROUGH URBAN FORESTRY AND GREENBELT

Eventhough urban forestry and greenbelt have a common objective of reducing atmospheric air pollutant load, their definitions and mode of achieving this objectives are widely different. For example, urban forestry is centered around mass human population eg. residential areas, whereas greenbelt is centered around the source of pollution such as industries, power plants, transport system, etc. However the purpose of vegetation in both the cases are same (Rawat and Banerjee, 1996).

Afforestation in urban areas is different from general forestry as trees in urban forestry are not valued for wood or wood products but for ecological, social, and public health importance. Its aim is to provide services rather than goods and to imbibe the principles of ecology into the city. Suitable plantation to form urban forestry stands as the only viable proposition to guard against air pollution.

TABLE 2.1. PARTICULATE MATTER IN THE ATMOSPHERE OF SOME INDIAN CITIES, MMG/M³

City	Suspended Particulate matter (mmg/m³) 1970	1979
Calcutta	341	578
New Delhi	601	481
Nagpur	262	386
Jaipur	446	379
Kanpur	544	344
Hyderabad	146	295
Ahmedabad	307	243
Madras	101	106

Soource : Abbasi (1998)

TABLE 2.2. AIR QUALITY OF INDIAN CITIES (ALL CONCENTRATIONS ARE IN MMG/M^3)

City		SPM		SO_2		NO_2	
		Annual Avg.	Max 24h	Annual Avg.	Max 24h	Annual Avg.	Max 24h
Ahmedabad							
	I	297	1020	23	200	7	39
	C	322	1021	21	316	7	50
	R	214	576	7	121	4	28
Bombay							
	I	174	504	58	268	31	102
	C	207	511	41	475	33	190
	R	223	474	28	276	25	144
Calcutta							
	I	453	2091	47	463	34	175
	C	385	1529	59	529	52	176
	R	268	1588	39	427	30	130
Cochin							
	I	81	184	11	113	6	92
	C	138	288	10	97	11	92
	R	88	204	97	83	4	29
Delhi							
	I	502	1435	35	273	45	266
	C	534	1735	34	281	54	250
	R	371	1480	19	223	41	309
Hyderabad							
	I	87	163	12	190	11	77
	C	189	368	8	112	22	133
	R	156	407	7	63	12	78
Jaipur							
	I	210	1284	7	64	12	87
	C	402	1647	6	58	20	113
	R	243	1329	5	7	13	114
Kanpur							
	I	396	1323	6	76	11	60
	C	369	1147	5	54	10	64
	R	261	892	4	26	9	53

Madras						
I	139	473	15	207	15	60
C	98	217	11	78	18	65
R	78	172	9	78	12	77
Nagpur						
I	168	328	15	1000	14	158
C	244	604	7	60	11	93
R	136	267	8	92	12	78
Standards						
I	500			120		120
R	200			80		80
S	100			30		30

I – Industrial, C – Commercial, R – Residential, S – Sensitive

Source : Abbasi(1998)

TABLE 2.3. EXTENT OF AIR POLLUTION IN SOME METROPOLITAN CITIES 1992*

City	SO_2	NO_2	CO	O_3	Pb	SPM
Bangkok	C	C	C	C	B	A
Beijing	A	C	D	B	C	A
Bombay	C	C	C	D	C	A
Buenos Aires	D	D	A	D	C	B
Cairo	D	D	B	D	A	A
Calcutta	C	C	D	D	C	A
Delhi	C	C	C	D	C	A
Jakarta	C	C	B	B	B	A
Karachi	C	D	D	D	A	A
London	C	C	B	C	C	C
Los Angeles	C	B	B	A	C	B
Manila	C	D	D	D	B	A
Mexico City	A	B	A	A	B	A
Moscow	D	B	B	D	C	B
New York	C	C	B	B	C	C
Rio de Janeiro	B	D	C	D	C	B
Sao Paulo	C	B	B	A	C	B
Seol	A	C	C	C	C	A
Shanghai	B	D	D	D	D	A
Tokyo	C	C	C	A	D	C

Source : Abbasi, (1998)

*- Collected from reports of WHO & UNEP.

A- Serious problem; WHO guidelines exceed by more than a factor of two

B-Moderate to heavy pollution, WHO guidelines exceed by up to a factor of two

C- Low pollution, WHO guidelines normally met with

D - No data available or insufficient data for assessment.

Vegetation acts as CO_2 sink and some species have the capacity to utilise air pollutants effectively. This attribute makes several plants effective biological indicators of air pollution. Several plants have the capacity to collect the dust suspended in the atmosphere and dilute the concentration of toxic and harmful gases like SO_2, CO_2, etc. Of course each and every plant can not be an agent of air pollution control; only those which can tolerate pollutants can act as attenuators. All-in-all, increasing vegetation in the cities, towns, and industrial establishments holds great potential to combat air pollution.

Plants absorb CO_2 from the atmosphere and, in turn, release oxygen in the photosynthetic activity. It is estimated that the total leaf surface of the vegetation on earth is 10 to 20 times greater than the earth's surface (Rawat & Banerjee, 1996). Plants also intercept tonnes of dust, absorb noise, and serve as acoustic screens on busy highways and noisy factory areas (Warren, 1973). Besides, trees are good biological indicators of air pollution since air pollutants produce various kinds of morphological and physiological changes in plants (mansfield and Majernik, 1970).

Trees have been reported to remove air pollutants like hydrogen fluoride, SO_2, and some compounds of photochemical reactions (Brandy, 1973) and collect heavy metals like mercury (Hg) and lead (Pb) from the air (Lin, 1976). After absorbing the air pollutants, trees change them to harmless metabolites through various physiological processes.

2.3 AIR POLLUTANT UPTAKE BY VEGETATION

It has long been recognised that trees filter particulates. Abundant observations appear in the literature and considerable quantitative data are available. It is reasonable to assume that trees can filter particulates at least under certain conditions. The larger the particulate and the more stable the atmospheric conditions, the better the trees screen will operate. With small particulates and increased turbulence, the effectiveness of the screen will decrease.

Long before the scientific concept of gaseous diffusion was formalised, vegetation was known to exchange large quantities of carbon dioxide, oxygen and water vapour with the atmosphere. Hill (1971) reported experiential investigations on uptake of ordinary pollutants: SO_2 & NO_2 by alfalfa canopies.

Based on pollutant uptake experiments on alfalfa canopies it has been estimated that a continuous cover of assimilating alfalfa canopy under conditions equivalent to those of the studies could remove more than 1/4 ton of NO_2 or SO_2 per square mile per day from air containing an average NO_2 concentration of 6 pphm or to the mean SO_4 concentrations measured over a 2000 square mile are of 1-3 pphm (Thakre, 1992).

The sink concept has become ? of interest to atmospheric chemists and meteorologists who are attempting to develop air pollutant budgets. What are the ultimate sinks of air pollutants released by the activities of man? Reports indicate that plants, soils, and soil organisms are effective sinks for gaseous air pollutants under certain conditions. Soils are apparently minor sinks per se, but the microbial constituents of the soils are effective via metabolic activity. Hill and associates using plants grown and exposed under controlled conditions, attempted to quantity pollutant uptake. They developed pollutant uptake values for eight gaseous pollutants from which they calculated the total uptake of each pollutant per acre of alfalfa under given pollutant loads. This work though preliminary, strongly suggests that vegetation is a significant pollutant sink. Bennett et al (1973) have presented a model that simulates pollutant exchange with isolated leaves. The model is able to integrate those factors that are known to affect pollutant uptake rates. Additional techniques and plant species must be considered as we explore the sink capacity of vegetation.

Present data indicates that vegetation could be an important sink for at least the following air pollutants of major importance: HF, SO_2, NO_2, O_3, Cl_2 and to a lesser extent PAN (Thakre, 1992). Undoubtedly, many others such as HCl could be added to the list. Two important pollutants which are known to not be taken up effectively by plants, however, are CO and NO. Soil micro-organisms appear to be a major sink for CO. Nitric oxide, though absorbed slowly by plants, is converted in the atmosphere to other forms which may then be taken up more rapidly.

It is one thing to find that plants are major pollutant sinks and another to extrapolate this information to the development of greenbelts primarily for the purpose of decreasing pollutant concentration. Pollutant uptake by plants involve many factors including the inherent variation in potential for uptake by different plant species, the direct effect of the pollutant on the uptake potential of the plant, the effect of other environmental stresses on the uptake potential of the plant and meteorological factors affecting pollutant distribution (Arthur, 1977).

Pollutant uptake by plants is controlled by the interaction of a number of physical, chemical and biological factors that regulate gas exchange processes and pollutant reaction at the sorbing sites.

Green growing vegetation in removing unwanted gases and aerosols from the air not only cleanses the general atmosphere of these pollutants but influences most markedly their immediate microenvironment.

2.4 REMOVAL PROCESS OF AIR POLLUTANTS

In addition to the soil compartment, the vegetative compartment of forest ecosystems functions as a sink for atmospheric contaminants. As in the case of soils, a complex variety of biological, chemical, and physical processes are involved in the transfer of pollutants from the air to the surfaces of vegetation. For certain contaminants, for example, persistent heavy metal particles, the repository functions of vegetation and soils are intimately linked as a portion of the heavy metals input to the soil are derived from vegetative sources contributing litter to the forest floor (William, 1990). Interest in the ability of plants to remove pollutants from the air has grown considerably in recent years as individuals have become increasingly aware of the amenity functions (Heisler, 1975: Smith, 1970a) of woody plants, particularly in urban and suburban areas. The capability of plants to act as a sink for air contaminants has been addressed by a variety of recent reviews, for example, Aubertin and Aubertin (1981). U.S. Environmental Protection Agency (1976a), Smith and Dochinger (1976), Bennett and Hill (1975), Hanson and Thorne (1972), Hill (1971), Environmental Health Science Center (1975), Keller (1978), and Warren (1973). The surfaces of vegetation provide a major filtration and reaction surface to the atmosphere and importantly function to transfer pollutants from the atmosphere to the biosphere.

Plants also help to remove pollutants from the air in three ways, viz. absorption by the leaves, deposition of particulates and aerosols on leaf surface, and fallout of particulate on the leeward (down wind) side of the vegetation because of the slowing of the air movement (Tewari, 1994).

2.4.1 Removal of Particulate Pollutants

Chamberlain (1967, 1970, 1975), Ingold (1971), Gregory (1973), Slinn (1976), and Albritton et al. (1987) have reviewed the mechanics of deposition of particles on natural surfaces.

Particles are deposited on plant surfaces by three processes (Tewari, 1994): sedimentation under the influence of gravity, impaction under the influence of eddy currents, and deposition under the influence of precipitation. Sedimentation usually results in the deposition of particles on the upper surfaces of plant parts and is most important with large particles. Sedimentation velocity varies with particle density, shape, and other factors. Impaction occurs when air flows fast on obstacle and the air stream divides, but particles in the air tend to continue in a straight path due to their momentum and to strike the obstacle. The efficiency of collection via impaction is the principal means of deposition if (a) particle size is of the order of tens of micrometres or greater, (b) obstacle size is of the order of centimetres or less, (c) approach velocity is of the order of meters per second or more, and (d) the collecting surface is wet, sticky, hairy or otherwise retentive. Ingold (1971) presented data indicating that leaf petioles are considerably more efficient particulate impactors than either twigs (stems) or leaf lamina. For particles of dimension 1-5 μm, impaction is not efficient and interception by fine hairs on vegetation is possibly the most efficient retentive mechanism. The efficiency of washout of particles by rain is high for particles approximately 20-30 μm in size. The capturing efficiency of raindrops falls off very sharply for particles of 5 μm or less.

Following deposition, particles may be retained on vegetative surfaces, they may rebound from the surface, or they may be temporarily retained and subsequently removed. If either the particle or the tree surface is wet or sticky, deposited particles are generally retained. Surficial salt accumulation by plants in marine or north-temperate roadside environments (where deicing chemicals are employed) results, as vegetation acts to trap salt particles. Fluorine, sulfate, and nitrate molecules associated with moisture droplets (fog) in the atmosphere may be distributed to vegetative surfaces with great efficiency (Chamberlain, 1975).

The transfer of particles from the atmosphere to natural surfaces is commonly expressed via deposition velocity. For small particles, for example, condensation aerosols less than 1 μm, deposition velocities are much less than for large particles: for example, spores and pollen 20-40 μm in diameter.

In addition to spores and pollen, particles in the atmosphere larger than 10 μm are frequently the result of mechanical processes, for example grinding or spraying. Soil particles, process dust, industrial combustion products, and marine salt particles are typically between 1 and 10 μm in diameter. Particles in the 0.1-1 μm range frequently represent gases that have condensed to form non-volatile products (William, 1990).

The interaction of these variously sized particles with exceedingly diverse vegetative surfaces under conditions of extremely variable microclimate and particle source characteristics suggests an enormously complex relationship. Since this is the case, field evidence to quantify the amounts of natural or anthropogenic particles removed by trees is very sparse. Numerous investigations have studied detached plant parts or seedlings under wind tunnel, growth chamber, or greenhouse conditions. This is an appropriate and necessary initial step and these studies have yielded considerable qualitative perspective on the capacity of plants to filter air. Nevertheless, the hypothesis that trees are important particulate sinks is supported by evidence obtained from studies dealing with diverse particulate including radioactive, trace element, pollen, spore, salt, precipitation, dust, and other unspecified particles (William, 1990).

2.4.1.1 Radioactive Particles

Because of the considerable interest in the distribution of radioactive material following the use of nuclear weapons or nuclear accidents and because of the case of counting, several investigations have examined the ability of aboveground plant parts to intercept radioactive aerosols (Chamberlain, 1970: Oak Ridge National Laboratory, 1969).

Contamination of tree foliage with radioactive fallout, despite its obvious disconcerting implications, has provided an especially valuable perspective because it has frequently been examined on large trees in natural environments. Romney et.al. (1963) concluded from fallout evidence that Utah juniper foliage principally intercepted particles smaller than 44 μm. Interior canopy elm leaves were shown to be contaminated with elevated levels of radioactivity in selected New England and eastern New York sites following the 1957 atom bomb test series (Bormann et al., 1957). More recently Russell (1974) and Russell and Choquette (1974) have measured concentrations of fission product radionuclides, resulting from megaton range Chinese nuclear explosions in coniferous and deciduous trees in the New England area between 1968 and 1974. Peak contamination was determined to be reached 6-9 months following injection of the stratospheric source the preceding year. It was hypothesised that primary acquirement was due to attachment of rain droplets on leaf surfaces with subsequent diffusion of soluble radionucleides to leaf cuticles, where they were fixed or transported to leaf interiors. Dry deposition was concluded to be relatively unimportant (William, 1990).

2.4.1.2 Trace Metal Particles

Trace metals, especially heavy metals, are most commonly associated with fine particles in contaminated atmospheres. Trace element investigations conducted in roadside, industrial, and urban environments have dramatically demonstrated the impressive burdens of particulate heavy metals that can accumulate on vegetative surfaces (William, 1990).

In the case of lead in the roadside ecosystem, for example, the increased lead burden of plants, largely due to surface deposition, may be 5-20, 5-200, and 100-200 times baseline (nonroadside environment) lead levels for unwashed agricultural crops, grasses and trees, respectively (Smith, 1976). Sink capacity for metal contaminants of a single sugar maple is given in Table 2.4.

Eastern white pine is widely planted in the roadside environment in New England and its capacity to accumulate fine particles (~7 μm diameter; Heichel and Hankin, 1972) has been shown to be substantial (Smith, 1971). Heichel and Hankin (1976) have investigated the distribution of lead deposited on this species in roadsides and have advanced several important observations. The lead burden of older needles and twigs was consistently greater than that of younger organs and was greater in samples taken adjacent to rather than far from the road. These are consistent with observations we made with the same species (Smith, 1971) and are important, as the former indicates that lead accumulates over time on the trees, while the latter argues against the importance of soil uptake as a mechanism of lead acquisition. Heichel and Hankin further concluded that twigs retained particles more effectively than needles throughout the season. This was judged to be due to the roughness of twigs relative to needles. The authors observed that a 12 m tall white pine growing in a dense planting would have about 15 x 155 cm of foliage surface. Although white pine exposed approximately ten fold more foliage than woody surface, the woody surfaces, retained about 20-fold the lead burden of foliage.

TABLE 2.4.
CALCULATED PARTICULATE METAL SINK CAPACITY FOR THE LEAVES AND CURRENT TWIGS OF A SINGLE, 30 CM (12-INCH) DIAMETER URBAN SUGAR MAPLE DURING THE COURSE OF A GROWING SEASON.

Metal contaminant	Growing season removal (mg $tree^{-1}$)
Lead	5800
Nickel	820
Chromium	140
Cadmium	60

Source : Smith (1974)

Like the roadside environment, urban atmospheres also have elevated amounts of particles containing trace metals. In New Haven, Connecticut, scientists/researchers have examined the surfaces of a variety of city trees and have found substantial accumulation of certain metals, particularly lead, zinc, and iron (Smith, 1973; Smith and Staskawicz, 1977). Observations of the leaves of mature London plane trees in New Haven throughout the growing season indicated nickel and zinc foliar surface amounts remained relatively constant. Aluminum, iron, manganese, and lead, on the other hand, appeared to accumulate through the spring and early summer, and decrease during the late summer and fall on this species. This latter decrease and late season decreased particle density indicated by observation with the scanning electron microscope, suggest the particles on foliage are weathered or transported off the leaf. Precipitation, wind, insect activity, and other forces may cause particles to be lost from the leaves and transported by way of the petiole to the twig tissue (William, 1990).

The literature is replete with studies demonstrating significant trace metal particle accumulation on trees in roadside, urban, and industrial situations. Industrial regions, particularly those with metal smelters may excessively contaminate surrounding woody vegetation with particles containing trace metals. A representative study is that conducted by Little and Martin (1972) in the Avonmouth industrial complex, Severnside, England. Close to this complex, elm leaves exhibited 8000, 5000, and 50 $\mu g\ g^{-1}$ zinc, lead, and cadmium, respectively. Page and Chang (1979) and Helmke et al. (1984) have reviewed the trace element contamination of vegetation in the vicinity of coal-fired power plants. Helmke et al. (1984), in their study of vegetation in the vicinity of a coal burning Wisconsin power plant, observed that a significant portion of the dust deposited on local leaf surfaces was fly ash. Wind and rain removal was minimal and fly ash accumulated during the growing season. No detrimental effects of fly ash on the trees were observed (William, 1990).

2.4.1.3 Pollen and Spores

Pollen studies have provided important evidence of vegetative interception of large particles. G.S. Raynor of the Brookhaven National Laboratory, Upton, Long Island, New York, has conducted a series of dispersion experiments employing ragweed pollen emitted from sources at various distances and heights upwind of a forest edge (William, 1990). Pollen loss from the plume occurred in two stages and by two mechanisms, impaction near the forest edge and deposition well within the forest. Pollen loss to the forest was considerably greater than over open terrain (Raynor, 1967; Raynor et al., 1966). Interception of ragweed pollen by a Pennsylvania forest canopy reduced pollen concentration in the forest atmosphere to only 70% of the concentration in a nearby open field (Elder and Hosler,, 1954). Neuberger et al., (1967) measured ragweed pollen concentrations in and out of forests and found that 100m inside a dense coniferous forest over 80% of the pollen had be on subtracted from the atmosphere. Data indicated that deciduous species are less effective than conifers in filtration of pollen (Neuberger et al., 1967; Steubing and Klee, 1970). For these large (~20 μm) particles the dominant transfer to vegetative surfaces is via sedimentation and not impaction (Aylor, 1975).

Fungal spore (size range, 1.5-30μm) interception studies have provided important evidence for understanding particulate capture (Gregory, 1971). Ingold (1971) has concluded that the most efficient plant parts for spore collection are petioles, twigs, and leaf lamina, respectively. Observations of basidiomycete spores in Washington Douglas fir forests have emphasized the extraordinary importance of microclimate and forest stand structure on the distribution and deposition of these particles in the forest. Wind speed, air temperature, inversions, cloud cover, and forest openings all influenced particle movement (Edmonds and Driver, 1974; Fritschen et al., 1970).

2.4.1.4 Salt Particles

Vegetative interception of saline aerosol (primarily NaCl) and nutrient particles has also contributed to our understanding of plant sink function (William, 1990). Particulate deposition of salt particles occurs in roadside environments where deicing salts are employed, in the vicinity of cooling towers, and in maritime regions (Eaton, 1979; Moser, 1979). In coastal ecosystems subject to airborne marine salt, accumulation of salt particles by above ground plant parts injures foliage and twigs (Boyce, 1954; Wells and Shunk, 1938; Oosting, 1945; Oosting and Billings, 1942) and may control species success or failure depending on tolerance to salt loading (Martin, 1959). Clayton (1972) described the trapping of particulate salts by Baccaris brushlands in coastal California. Woodcock (1953) provided evidence that the shape of plant leaves influences the amount of salt deposited. By employing plates of various shapes, he found that long narrow plates accumulated more salt per unit area than did circular plates. Edwards and Claxton (1964) found over four times the deposition of salt on the windward side of a hedgerow compared to the leeward side.

Where foliar capture of marine particulates is below the threshold of foliar injury, particle accumulation may be an important mechanism for nutrient acquisition (Art, 1971; Art et al., 1974). Numerous investigations, reviewed by White and Turner (1970), have indicated that nonmaritime trees also catch airborne nutrient particles. These authors found that a mixed deciduous forest was capable of annually removing 125 kg ha^{-1} sodium, 6 kg ha^{-1} potassium, 4 kg ha^{-1} calcium, 16 kg ha^{-1} magnesium, and 0.1 kg ha^{-1} phosphorus from the atmosphere.

The degree of leaf hairiness was inversely correlated with particle retention. Apparently the small droplets employed had insufficient inertia to penetrate the stable boundary layer created by the hairy leaves. Small diameter branches were more efficient particle collectors than large diameter branches in all species examined.

In their examination of the impact of saline aerosols of cooling tower origin, McCure et al. (1977) emphasised the importance of particle wetness in causing damage to surrounding trees. Dry particles appeared less toxic than hydrated particles. This supports the contention that moist particles are more effectively retained by vegetative surfaces than dry ones.

2.4.1.5 Precipitation, Dust, and Other Particles

Foliar interception of precipitation has been intensively investigated (Zinke, 1967), but the relatively large size of the particles (range, 50-700 μm) makes these data of limited application for considerations of fine particle retention. The enormous importance of rainout in transferring fine particles from the atmosphere to vegetation is recognised (Altshuller, 1984). Numerous precipitation studies support the general observation that conifers intercept more particles than deciduous species, for example, Helvey (1971), who reported canopy interception loss greatest in a spruce-fir-hemlock type, intermediate in pine, and least in broad-leaved deciduous forests.

Numerous additional studies employing dust, synthetic, or unspecified particles have contributed to our understanding of particulate capture by vegetation. Rosinki and Nagamoto (1965) investigated the deposition of 2 μm particles on Rocky Mountain juniper and Douglas fir. At low dosage, particles preferentially accumulated on the windward leaf edge. Eventually a new layer was formed on the previously deposited layer. Thickness increased until equilibrium was reached. Total deposition was increased when wind exposed different leaf areas for deposition. Langer (1965) concluded that dust deposition on coniferous leaves was not significantly influenced by electrostatic effects. Podgorow (1967) investigated the relative effectiveness of pine, birch, and aspen in filtering dust particulates. Pine proved most effective. Interior crown needles accumulated more and retained more dust than exterior needles. Bach (1972) also presented evidence supporting the superior collecting capacity of pines relative to deciduous species. In an Ohio study, Dochinger (1972) examined dustfall and suspended particulate matter in three areas - treeless, deciduous canopy, and conifer canopy - and concluded that trees have the capacity to reduce particulate pollutants in the ambient atmosphere.

Wedding et al. (1975) found, under controlled wind tunnel conditions, that particulate deposition on rough pubescent sunflower leaves was 10 times greater than on smooth, waxy tulip poplar leaves. In a unique study, Graustein (1978) employed the ratio of strontium isotopes in soil dust to determine strontium input to forested watersheds in New Mexico. Most of the atmospherically transported strontium entered the watershed by impaction of soluble particles on spruce foliage. Aspen, also present in the ecosystem, was judged to trap little, if any, dust. The flux of dust-derived strontium to the forest floor was four times greater than the flux to an unforested area (William, 1990).

In an extremely informative set of experiments, Little (1977) exposed freshly collected leaves of several tree species in a wind tunnel to various sizes of polystyrene aerosols labeled with technetium. Particles sized 2, 75, 5.0, and 8.5 μm were tested with leaves from European beech, white poplar, and nettle (*Urtica dioica)*. Surface texture was critical in capture efficiency, with the rough and hairy leaves of nettle more effective than the densely tomentose leaves of popular or the smooth surfaces of beech. For each species there was a strong negative linear correlation between leaf area and deposition velocity, the latter being smallest for the largest leaves. Deposition was heaviest at the leaf tip and along leaf margins, where a turbulent boundary layer was present. Leaves with complex shapes and the largest circumference to area ratio were the most efficient collectors. Both increased wind speed and particle size were reflected in increased deposition velocities. Deposition velocities to petioles and stems were many times greater than deposition velocities to leaf laminas, even though the majority of the total catch was intercepted by the leaf lamina (Table 2.5).

Table 2.5 reveals that nonlaminar catch is significant, however, and Little (1977) suggested that this may cause deposition of atmospheric particles to trees to be relatively high, even during the winter when deciduous species are devoid of leaves.

2.4.2 Studies Conducted for Tree Particulate Sink Capacity of trees

The U.S. Environmental Protection Agency (USEPA) has developed a demonstration plan to explore the capability of urban vegetation to improve air quality (U.S. Environmental Protection Agency, 1976c). This plan, which utilises pollutant fluxes summarised and extrapolated from the literature and air quality and environmental conditions as they existed in the St. Louis, Missouri area, includes an assessment of the particulate removal capacity of selected and hypothetical street trees. It is proposed that trees be planted on both sides of the streets within the city boundaries of St. Louis. The trees would be planted 8.5 m (30 feet) apart. The total street length in St. Louis was determined to be 2316 linear km (6.6 X 10^6 feet), requiring a total of 440,000 trees for complete planting. The three tree species proposed for the street planting included red oak, Norway maple, and linden. An average particulate flux rate of 2.5 X 10^3 mmg, m^{-2} hr^{-1} guesstimated from the literature was employed (USEPA, 1976 b).

Table 2.6 presents the dimensions of the tree species and the estimated quantity of particles that would be removed by the 440,000 street trees. The hypothetical transfer of particles from the atmosphere to the tree surfaces totaled 340 tons annually. The 1980 estimate for total particulate emission in the St. Louis are equaled 126,290 tons. The biological and medical significance of the transfer of the 340 tons from the atmosphere to the vegetation is unclear (William, 1990).

Table 2.5. Average percentage of total catch intercepted by leaf laminas, petioles, and stems of freshly cut european beech, white poplar, and neula exposed in polystyrene particles in a wind tunnel.

Wind speed (*cm sec*$^{-1}$)	Particle size (*μm*)	Plant part	Beech *poplar*	White	Nettle
150	5.0	Leaf laminas	85.01	49.16	90.68
		Petioles	11.18	33.52	4.76
		Stems	3.80	17.32	4.56
250	2.75	Leaf laminas	63.08	73.71	68.30
		Petioles	30.19	11.08	15.56
		Stems	6.73	15.20	16.11
	5.0	Leaf laminas	70.94	57.10	78.59
		Petioles	23.08	26.78	6.66
		Stems	5.99	16.12	7.00
	8.5	Leaf laminas	62.68	45.39	68.30
		Petioles	17.17	29.12	11.29
		Stems	19.61	25.48	20.41
500	2.75	Leaf laminas	63.87	64.81	82.85
		Petioles	28.81	18.81	5.50
		Stems	7.32	16.36	11.06
	5.0	Leaf laminas	73.86	53.39	77.71
		Petioles	14.94	26.12	9.23
		Stems	11.19	20.49	13.06
	8.5	Leaf laminas	90.83	69.27	83.27
		Petioles	3.35	12.58	7.21
		Stems	5.81	18.15	9.82

Source : Little (1977)

TABLE 2.6. ESTIMATION OF THE AMOUNT OF PARTICULATES ABSORBED BY HYPOTHETICAL ST. LOUIS STREET TREES.

1. Number of trees planted

Maple	146,666
Oak	146,667
Linden	146,667
Total	440,000

2. Dimensions of the maple

Height 6 m
Diameter of canopy = 3 m
Total surface areaa tree^{-1} = 36.8 m^2
Total surface area of 146,666 trees = 5.40x10^6 m^2

3. Dimensions of the oak

   Height = 6 m
   Diameter of canopy = 3 m
   Total surface area tree^{-1} = 36.1 m^2
   Total surface area of 146,667 trees = 5.30x10^6 m^2

4. Dimension of the linden

   Height = 5 m
   Diameter of canopy = 2.4 m
   Total surface area tree^{-1} (including undergrowth) = 23.0 m^2
   Total surface area for 146,667 trees = 3.40x10^6 m^2

5. Total surface area for the 440,000 trees = 1.4x10^7 m^2
6. Estimated particulate flux to vegetation = 2.5x10^3 mmg^{-2} hr^{-1}
7. Calculation to determine the amount of particulates absorbed by street trees 1.4x10^7 m^{2}x2.5x10^3 mmg m^{-2} hr^{-1} x gm/10^6 x mmg x lb/453.59 gm x T/2000 lbs x 24 hr/day x 365 days/yr = 3.40 x 10^2 tons particulate yr^{-1}

Source : U.S. Environmental Protection Agency (1976a).
Maple canopy diameter = 3 m
Estimated ground area covered by maple canopy = 7.1 m^2
Area index for maple = 5.18 (Raunder, 1976)
Area index = surface area divided by ground area
5.18 = x / 7.1 m^2
Surface area of maple = 36.8 m^2

Similar studies were also conducted in the vicinity of a coal-fired power station during the conversion of an oil-fired steam generating unit to a coal-fired unit, the Baltimore Gas and Electric Company considered the ability of the ability of trees in the vicinity of the power station to remove particulates from the atmosphere (Jashnani, 1998). The station site was on the Patapsco River, Anne Arundel County, Maryland and the proposed boiler was a 135 megawatt unit.

Based on a literature survey, particulate removal efficiencies for trees were estimated. Assumptions included: particulate average deposition velocity of 1 cm sec^{-1} for trees and 0.8 cm sec^{-1} for grass and weeds, leaf area index of 5.1 for deciduous trees and 2.3 for conifers, and approximately 2 ha of deciduous tree surface and 1 ha of coniferous tree surface ha^{-1} of land area. Given these assumption particulate removal rates and land area required for removal were estimated (Table 2.7).

2.4.3 Removal of Gaseous Pollutants

Substantial evidence is available to support the potential that plants is general (Bennett and Hill, 1975; Hill, 1971; Rasmussen et al., 1975) and trees in particular (Smith, 1979; Smith and Dochinger, 1975, 1976; Roberts, 1971; Warren, 1973) have to function as sinks for gaseous pollutants. The latter are transferred from the atmosphere to vegetation by the combined forces of diffusion and flowing air movement. Once in contact with plants gases may be bound or dissolved on exterior surfaces or be taken up by the plants via stomata. If the surface of the plant is wet and if the gas is water soluble, the former process can be very important. When the plant is dry or in the case of gases with relatively low water solubilities, the latter mechanism is assumed to be the most important.

Plant uptake rates increases as the solubility of the pollutant in water increases. Hydrogen fluoride, sulphur dioxide, nitrogen dioxide, and ozone which are soluble and reactive are readily sorbed pollutants. Nitric oxide and carbon monoxide, which are very insoluble, are absorbed relatively slowly or not at all by vegetation (William, 1990).

2.4.3.1 Removal of Carbon Dioxide, Water Vapour, Other Gases Including Trace Pollutants

The absorption of these pollutants is described by stomatal uptake process. Stomatal pores are small openings, typically approximately 10 μm in length and 2-7 μm in width, in the epidermal surface of leaves through which plants naturally exchange carbon dioxide, oxygen, and water vapour with the atmosphere. The waxy cuticle of leaf surfaces restricts diffusion so that essentially all gas exchange carried out by leaves is via stomatal openings. Even though these openings make up only approximately 1% of the leaf surface area, their orientation and mechanics prove to be nearly optimal for maximum gas diffusion in and out of the leaf (Salisbury and Ross, 1978). Stomatas undergo diurnal opening and closing with the pores of most plants opened within an hour of sunrise and closed by dark. Gas diffusion to and from leaves and the timing and degree of opening of stomatal apertures is strongly influenced by a number of complex environmental factors (Salisbury and Ross, 1978).

During daylight periods when plant leaves are releasing water vapor and taking up carbon dioxide, other gases, including trace pollutant gases, in the vicinity of the leaf will also be taken up through the stomatas (William, 1990).

The rate of pollutant gas transfer from the atmosphere to interior leaf cells is regulated by a series of resistance conveniently thought of as atmospheric, stomatal, and mesophyllic. Factors controlling atmospheric resistance include wind speed, leaf size and geometry, and gas viscosity and diffusivity. Stomatal resistance is regulated by stomatal aperture, which is influenced by water deficit, carbon dioxide concentration,

Table 2.7. Particulate removal rates and land area required for pollutant removal in the vicinity of a 135 megawatt coal burning power station releasing 186 tons of particulates yr^{-1}

	Deciduous	*Conifer*
Particulate removal rate	0.38 tons ha^{-1}	0.14 yr^{-1}
Land area required	486 ha	1336

Source : Jashnani (1988)and light intensity.

Mesophyllic resistance is regulated by gas solubility in water, gas liquid diffusion, and leaf metabolism (Kabel et al. 1976). Because the rate of pollutant uptake is regulated by numerous forces and conditions, the rate of removal under field conditions is highly variable. If leaf characteristics, wind speed, atmospheric moisture, temperature, and light intensity are quantified, however, the pollutant uptake rate can be estimated (Kabel et al., 1976; Bennett et al., 1973).

2.4.3.2 Removal of Hydrogen Fluoride, Sulphur Dioxide, Chlorine, Nitrogen Dioxide, Nitric Oxide, Carbon Monoxide, Ozone, Peroxyacetylnitrate and Other oxidants.

The fundamental investigations of Clyde Hill and Jesse Bennett of the University of Utah lead to several general conclusions, concerning gaseous pollutant uptake (Hill, 1971; Bennet and Hill, 1973, 1975). Their studies have concentrated on alfalfa, oats, barley, and grass. Standard alfalfa canopies removed gaseous pollutants from the atmosphere in rates of the following order: hydrogen fluoride > sulphur dioxide > chlorine > nitrogen dioxide > ozone > peroxyacetylnitrate > nitric oxide > carbon monoxide. In general plant uptake rates increased as the solubility of the pollutant in water increased. Hydrogen fluoride, sulphur dioxide, nitrogen dioxide, and ozone, which are soluble and reactive, were readily absorbed. Nitric oxide and carbon monoxide, which are very insoluble, were absorbed relatively slowly or not at all (Table 2.8). The rate of pollutant removal was found to increase linearly as the concentration of the pollutant was increased over the ranges of concentration that are encountered in ambient air and that were low enough not to cause stomatal closure.

Under growth chamber conditions, wind velocity, canopy height, and light intensity were shown to affect the rate of pollutant removal by vegetation. As previously stressed, light plays a critical role in determining physiological activities of the leaf and stomatal opening, and as such exerts a great influence on foliar removal of pollutants. Under conditions of adequate soil moisture, however, pollutant uptake by vegetation was judged almost constant throughout the day, as the stomata were fully open. Pollutants were absorbed most efficiently by plant foliage near the canopy surface where light-mediated metabolic and pollutant diffusivity rates were greatest. Sulphur and nitrogen dioxides were taken up by respiring leaves in the dark, but uptake rates were greatly reduced relative to rates in the light (William, 1990).

The Removal of sulphur dioxide is also described by tree uptake process. Because of its high solubility in water, large amounts of sulphur dioxide are absorbed to external tree surfaces when they are wet. In the dry condition, sulphur dioxide is readily absorbed by tree leaves and is rapidly oxidised to sulphate in mesophyll cells. At low uptake rates sulphur dioxide is presumed to be oxidised about as rapidly as it is absorbed (Bennett and Hill, 1975).

Roberts (1974) measured sulphur dioxide sorption by single leaves or shoots of several 1 year-old seedlings of numerous woody species. All species examined were capable of reducing high ambient levels within his test chambers (Table 2.9). Because of the large dose employed, 1 ppm (2620 μg m^3) for 1 hr. Roberts reduced the concentration in subsequent trials and examined uptake at concentrations of 0.2 and 0.5 ppm (524 and 1310 μg m^3). At the lower concentration uptake by birch and firethorn was significantly less. It was speculated that higher concentrations of sulphur dioxide may maintain stomatal opening. Under controlled environmental conditions, comparable to those employed by Roberts, Jensen (1975) fumigated hybrid poplar cuttings with sulphur dioxide ranging in concentration from 0.1 to 5 ppm (262-13.1 x 10^3 μg m^3) for periods of 5-80 hr. Uptake was determined by measuring the total sulphur content of the leaves. At low levels of fumigation [0.1 and 0.25 ppm (262 and 655 μgm^{-2})] leaf sulphur initially increased but then declined to unfumigated levels as fumigation continued. This reduction was judged by the author to be due to one or more of the following : reduction in absorption rate, translocation of sulphur out of the leaves, leaching of sulphate from the roots, or release of hydrogen sulphide by the leaves (Jensen, 1975).

The removal of oxidants are also described by the uptake process. Ozone is relatively insoluble in water (0.052 g 100 g^{-1} H_2O at 20°C) but readily diffuses into stomatal cavities (Rich and Turner, 1972; Rich et al., 1970; Thorne and Hansen, 1972; Wood and Davis., 1969). The very reactive nature of this gas undoubtedly causes it to rapidly react on the surface of leaf mesophyll cells.

Table 2.8. Solubility in water and uptake rate of pollutants by Alfalfa

Pollutant	Uptake rate by alfalfa at 1 pphm *(liters min^{-1} m^{-2})*	Equivalent deposition velocity *(cm sec^{-1})*	Solubility at 20°C (cm^3 gas cm^{-3} H_2O)
CO	0.0	0.00	0.02
NO	0.6	0.10	0.05
CO_2	2.0	0.33	0.88
PAN	3.8	0.63	-
O_3	10.0	1.67	0.26
NO_2	11.4	1.90	Decomposes
Cl_2	12.4	2.07	2.30
SO_2	17.0	2.83	39.40
HF	22.6	3.77	446

Source : Hill and Chamberlain (1974)

Table 2.9. Foliar sorption of sulphur dioxide by selected seedlings fumigated at 1.0ppm, (2620 $\mu g\ m^{-3}$) for 1 hour in a controlled environment chamber (27 ± 1°C, 51 ± 7% RH, 1300 ft-c)

	SO_2 uptake	
Species	*mg SO_2 dm^{-2} hr^{-1}*	*mg SO_2 g^{-1} hr^{-1}*
Red maple	0.088	0.260
White birch	0.086	0.268
Sweetgum	0.074	0.267
Firethorn	0.072	0.213
Privet	0.068	0.134
Rhododendron	0.056	0.079
White ash	0.046	0.118
Azalea	0.044	0.072

Source : Roberts (1974)

Under controlled environmental conditions, Townsend (1974) has monitored ozone uptake by a variety of seedling tree species (Table 2.10). Ozone sorption exhibited a linear increase up to 0.5 ppm (980 $\mu g\ m^{-3}$) for both white birch and red maple. These two species were also capable of reducing ambient ozone throughout a prolonged 8-hr exposure (William, 1990).

While tree removal of atmospheric peroxyacetylnitrate has not been reported. Garland and Penkett (1976) have suggested that the deposition velocity of this gas to grass was approximately 0.25 cm sec^{-1}, which is lower than the value for ozone (0.8 cm sec^{-1}) or sulphur dioxide (1 cm sec^{-1}).

For the other gases judged to be significantly removed from the atmosphere by vegetation, hydrogen fluoride and nitrogen dioxide, relatively little work has been reported on trees as sinks. Hydrogen fluoride is very water soluble and very reactive, and can be adsorbed onto plant surfaces and absorbed through stomatas. Leaves exposed to hydrogen fluoride may accumulate fluoride to one million times the ambient concentration. Nitrogen dioxide dissolved in water yields nitrate and nitrate ions in solution. The latter can be reduced to ammonia in leaf cells (Bennett and Hill, 1975). Rogers et al. (1979) have provided nitrogen dioxide uptake rates for loblolly pine and white oak and have suggested deposition velocities of 0.53 and 0.11 cm sec^{-1}, respectively (William, 1990).

2.4.4 Application of Green-belts

Murphy et al. (1977) have modeled the sulphur dioxide uptake of a simulated loblolly pine forest exposed to 50 ppb (131 $\mu g\ m^3$) sulphur dioxide on two clear days in January and June using climate data from a station near Aiken, South Carolina. The simulated uptake compared favorably, but was smaller than the seedling uptake rates reported by Roberts (1974) (Table 2.11). Murphy et al. (1977) also applied their model to regions where forest vegetation was dominant and where actual frequency distributions of sulphur dioxide concentrations were known. At a site on the Savannah River Laboratory with an average sulphur dioxide concentration of 8 ppb (21 $\mu g\ m^{-3}$) during the spring the model predicted an uptake of 11 metric tons day^{-1} over the 778 km^2 area of the southern pine forest site. For Long Island, New York, over an area of 1723 km^2 in June, the model predicted a sulphur dioxide uptake of 10^3 metric tons day^{-1} (SO_2 32 ppb, 84 $\mu g\ m^{-3}$) for a west wind condition. According to the authors the New York estimate was larger due to the larger land area, higher ambient sulphur dioxide, and greater leaf area employed.

Kabel et al. (1976) have argued, and appropriately so, that the uptake rate of sulphur dioxide on a leaf area basis must be extrapolated to a ground area basis in order to predict large area pollutant removal. In addition deposition velocities, or mass transfer coefficients - as these authors prefer (compare Kabel, 1976), - must be given for uptake of stems and branches as well as leaves. Fortunately, Whittaker and Woodwell (1967) have provided generalized area ratios for temperate forest communities (Table 2.12). Kabel et al. (1976) calculated the following deposition velocities using the appropriate ratios: 0.015 m sec^{-1} for dry condition (stomatal plus soil) and 0.21 m sec^{-1} for damp canopy condition, yielding a total deposition velocity of 0.23 m sec^{-1} for a moist forest canopy. Uptake rates were calculated for a model forest (dry condition) downwind from a sulphur dioxide source. Gas concentration profile and uptake rates are presented in Figure 2.1.

Table 2.10

Foliar sorption of ozone by selected seedings fumigated at 0.20 ppm (392 $\mu g\ m^{-3}$) for a few hours in a controlled environment chamber (26 ± 1.5°C, 45 ± 5% RH, 2100 ft-c)

	O_3 uptake	
Species	*mg O_3 dm^{-2} hr^{-1}*	*mg O_3 g^{-1} hr^{-1}*
White oak	0.635	1.318
White birch	0.536	2.347
Coliseum maple	0.502	0.991
Sugar maple	0.371	0.863
Ohio buckeye	0.362	0.927
Redvein maple	0.285	0.911
Sweetgum	0.278	0.854
Red maple	0.272	0.555
White ash	0.239	0.562

Source : Townsend (1974)

Table 2.11. Comparison of simulated sulphur dioxide uptake for a south carolina loblolly pine forest with experimental uptake by deciduous seedlings.

		SO_2 uptake
Species		*kg ha^{-1} hr^{-1} ppb^{-1} by volume*
Loblolly pine (simulated)		
January		
	day 1	1.3×10^{-3}
	day 2	2.2×10^{-4}
	June	
	day 1	2.0×10^{-3}
	day 2	2.0×10^{-4}
Seedlings (experimental)		
Red maple		8.8×10^{-5}
White birch		8.6×10^{-6}
Sweetgum		7.4×10^{-5}
White ash		4.6×10^{-5}

Source : Murphy et al. (1977)

The radioactive measurements of Garland (1977) propose that the deposition velocity for a dry forest canopy varies from 0.001 to 0.006 m sec^{-1}. The Kabel et al. (1976) figure is presumably higher than this due to the inclusion of soil uptake in the latter.

2.4.5 Studies Conducted for Gas Sink Capability of Trees

The ability of trees surrounding the coal fired power station to remove sulphur dioxide and nitrogen oxides was estimated (William, 1990). Using the assumptions previously described, the gaseous removal rates and land area required for removal were calculated (Table 2.13).

As part of the U.S. Environmental Protection Agency's 1976c demonstration plan to explore the capability of urban trees to improve air quality a model forest hectare was developed and employed to estimate gas uptake. The model forest consisted of six species including red oak, Norway maple, linden, popular, birch, and eastern white pine. The arrangement and spacing of the proposed forest is presented in Figure 2.2. The estimations of total tree surface area (canopy plus woody) at five years after planting were as follows:

Maple	(6 m ht)	36.8 m^2
Oak	(6 m ht)	36.1 m^2
Poplar	(6 m ht)	52.5 m^2
Linden	(5 m ht)	23.0 m^2
Birch	(5 m ht)	27.2 m^2
Pine	(3 m ht)	4.2 m^2

The total number of each species planted in the model forest and total vegetative area was as follows:

69	maple	2.54 X 10^3 m^2
69	oak	2.50 X 10^3 m^2
69	poplar	3.63 X 10^3 m^2
68	linden	1.56 X 10^3 m^2
69	birch	1.88 X 10^3 m^2
700	pine	2.90 X 10^3 m^2
Total		15.00 X 10^3 m^2

The soil area of the model forest, not covered by tree trunks, was estimated to be 9.98 X 10^3 m^2. Pollutant flux rates guesstimated from the literature and used in the calculations are presented in Table 2.14. Table 2.15 lists the estimated sink capability. The U.S. Environmental Protection Agency concluded that if 122,517 ha (473 m^2) of the model forest were in place in the St. Louis air quality region studied, this forest could remove 80.5 X 10^6 tons of sulphur dioxide per year and function to maintain the air quality standard for this pollutant (William, 1990).

Table 2.12. Area ratios for forest communities

Stem (bark) to ground surface	
	0.5-0.7 for mature, closed forests
	0.2-0.4 for small, open forests
	0.7-1.0 for dense, Young stands
Branch (bark) to ground surface	
	1.5-1.6 for mature, deciduous forests
	Leaf to ground surface
	4.0-6.0 for closed, deciduous forests
	6.0-7.0 for dense, evergreen forests

Source : Whittaker and Woodwell (1967)

Table 2.13. Gaseous removal rates and land area required for removal in the vicinity of a 135 megawatt coal burning power station releasing 4330 tons yr^{-1} Sulphur Dioxide and 2148 tons yr^{-1} Nitrogen Oxides.

		decidous	conifer
Pollutant removal rate		tons ha^{-1} yr^{-1}	
	SO_2	0.36	0.12
	NO_X	0.69	0.24
Land area required		ha	
	SO_2	11,898	33,995
	NO_X	2,995	8,499

Source: Jashnani (1988)

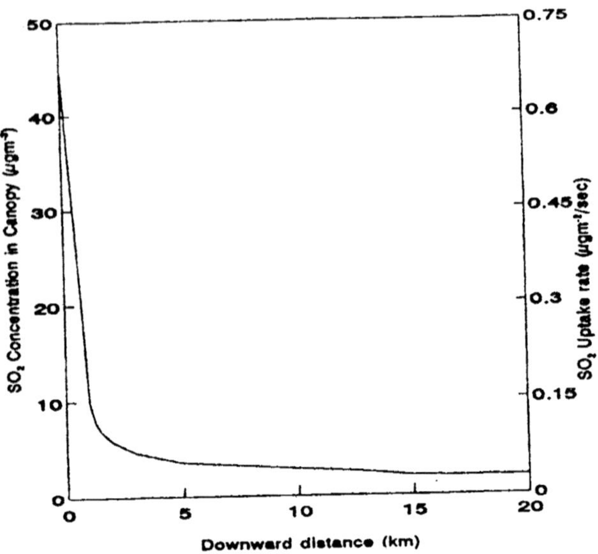

Fig. 2.1: Ground level SO_2 concentration and uptake rate over a model forest with a deposition velocity of 0.015m/sec and eddy diffusivity of 7m2/sec.

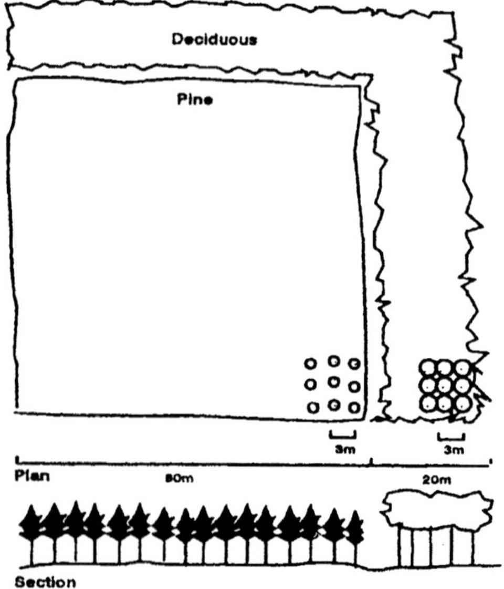

Fig. 2.2: *Model forest hectare developed by the U.S. Environmental Protection Agency to examine the potential of open space to serve as an air quality management strategy Source: U.S. Environmental Protection Agency (1976C)*

Table 2.14. Guesstimated gaseous pollutant flux rates for dry soil and vegetative surfaces

Pollutant	Soil surface ($\mu g\ m^{-2}\ hr^{-1}$)	Vegetative surface ($\mu g\ m^{-2}\ hr^{-1}$)
Carbon monoxide	1.9×10^4	2.6×10^3
Nitrogen oxides	2.0×10^2	2.3×10^3
Ozone	1.0×10^9	6.2×10^4
Peroxyacetylnitrate	-	1.2×10^3
Sulphur dioxide	7.7×10^6	4.1×10^4

Source : U.S. Environmental Protection Agency (1976 b)

Table 2.15. Guesstimated gaseous pollutant removal for model forest hectare.

Pollutant	tons yr^{-1}
Ozone	9.6×10^4
Sulphur dioxide	748
Carbon monoxide	2.2
Nitrogen oxides	0.38
Peroxyacetylnitrate	0.17

Source : U.S. Environmental Protection Agency (1976 c)

Total includes both soil and tree removal, dry condition

2.5 A Few Important Facts Regarding the Scavenging Characteristics of Vegetation, According to William, 1990 :

1. The interception and retention of atmospheric particles by plants is highly variable and is primarily dependent on :
   a. Size, shape, wetness, and surface texture of the particles.
   b. Size, shape, wetness, and surface texture of the intercepting plant part
   c. Micro-and ultramicroclimatic conditions surrounding the plant
1. More is known concerning the physical-mechanical aspects of particle deposition under controlled conditions than is known about the relative capture and retention efficiencies of various plants and different species under natural conditions.

2. Generally, greater leaf surface roughness increases particle capture efficiency for particles approximately 5 μm (and less) in diameter. Smooth leaved species (for example, horse chestnut and yellow poplar) are less efficient than rough leaved species (for example, elm and hazel).
3. Surface roughness acts to decrease the stability of the boundary layer (region of retarded air flow) surrounding the leaf and thus acts to increase particle impaction. Leaf hairs and leaf veins are principal contributors to surface roughness.
4. Smaller leaves are generally more efficient particle collectors than larger leaves.
5. Particle deposition (but probably not retention) is heaviest at the leaf tip and along leaf margins where a turbulent boundary layer is present. Leaves with complex shapes and large circumference/area ratios collect particles most efficiently.
6. Increased wind speeds and increased particle size typically increase particulate deposition velocities.
7. Deposition velocities to petioles and stems are generally many times greater than deposition velocities to leaf laminas. Collection of atmospheric particles by leafless deciduous species in the winter may remain quite high due to twig and shoot impaction.
8. Conifers are generally effective particulate sinks than deciduous species.
9. Mechanisms by which particles are resuspended or otherwise removed from tree surfaces must be investigated more thoroughly.
10. Leaf with abundant trichomes (leaf hairs) are found to be particulate accumulator.

Chapter- 3

TYPES OF GREENBELT AND THEIR APPLICATIONS

3.1 SHELTER BELTS, WIND BREAKS AND FOREST BELTS

3.1.1 Shelter belts and wind breaks

Trees planted in rows can provide several benefits to soils and crops. Such plantings are referred to as 'wind breaks', 'shelter belts', and occasionally 'greenbelts'.

Wind breaks and shelter belts are important soil conservation practices improving the micro-climate for production of crops and protection of rangelands from wind erosion. A wind break is a barrier for protection from winds commonly associated with vegetable gardens, orchards. A shelterbelt is usually a barrier longer than a wind break and consists of a combination of shrubs and trees intended for the protection of field crops and the conservation of soil and water.

In India there is an urgent need to create the cris-cross shelterbelts or windbreaks all over the country to overcome the destructive influence of sand drift and hot dry wind. Such belts are necessary to protect agricultural fields and fertile soil and to improve to some extent the climatic conditions of the region.

India's vast coastal front not only faces wind erosion but also bears the brunt of cyclonic wind and flood, especially in the Bay of Bengal. The Andhra and Orissa coasts annually bear the ordeals of cyclonic storm and water surge which leave thousand dead and property worth crores of rupees damaged. Tamil Nadu and West Bengal coasts also face the same fury though to a lesser extent. At present there is practically no coastal defence. Maritime dune formation is common on the coastal States of Eastern India.

Drifting of sand is becoming a menace on agricultural land around the deserts and in the coastal region. To stabilise such drifting sand various afforestation techniques based on the planting of selected species is necessary. In Indian soil *Casuarina equisitifolia* has been a tremendous success as is *Pinus pinaster* in the south-west coast of France.

For stabilisation of sand drift plating of grass, shrubs and trees (of all sizes) is necessary; but for shelterbelts the contribution of trees of various sizes and some tall shrubs are necessary. No tree planting can be successful unless special measures are first taken to prevent or reduce sand movement.

India particularly needs protective shelter belts in these regions:

1. All round Rajasthan's Thar desert
2. All along Gangetic plains
3. All round Singrauli Thermal Projects.
4. All round Jharia Coal fields
5. All round Raniganj Coal Fields
6. In and around the cities of Calcutta, Bombay, Madras, Bangalore, Vizag, Kanpur, New Delhi.
7. Along eastern coast.

According to Cabron S.M. (1957), when the shelterbelt is impenetrable to wind the flow is deflected upwards over the belt leaving a reduced windzone downward. The pressure on leeward side is lowered, causing a turbulance leeward which reduces the length of the reduced wind zone. An impermeable shelter provides a greater degree of shelter immediately to the leeward but, because of eddying effect, it gives a comparatively shorter zone of *effective* shelter. So a shelterbelt should ideally be-

i. permeable to wind
ii. of proper width and shape
iii. of adequate height.

According to M. Jensen (FAO 1974), windbelt with 35 per cent permeables, affords the greatest shelter and that wind breaks of narrow thickness and of moderate density should be the goal. Trees should be of uniform density from top to bottom (lower branches may not be too open). Lateral gaps should be avoided as even as small gap neutralises the effect of a large section of shelter belt due to wind funelling through the gaps.

On the basis of wind funnel studies the optimum degree of permeability of a (wind tunnel) shelterbelt has been recorded at 35 per cent (FAO 1974).

The factors influencing the effectiveness of windbreaks are: density, height and length. The three systems of windbreaks recognised usually are: permanent, intermediate and temporary. The spacing of windbreaks depends upon the density and angle of windbreaks to the direction of the hazardous wind. The species suitable for a site depend upon the soil type, climate including rainfall, elevation moisture supply etc. The selection of species should be so done that the tallest species should be in the middle row and smallest trees or shrubs in the end rows. A more or less conical cross-section of wind breaks will provide the best protection from wind effects and also increase the zone of protection. The species of various heights should, therefore, be intermingled to obtain such a cross section of the wind break.

Shelter belt screens may preferably be planted at a distance of 20-25 times their height. This would effectively block the impurities in the air by screening out coarse dust and turning away the particles through continuous re-elevation and diversion of the air flow from the object of protection. Best results are achieved when the screen planting has a wind permeability of 40 percent.

The objectives of creating shelterbelts are:

i. to protect agricultural land
ii. to shelter population in a city-from hot wind blast

iii. to arrest particulate matters as much as possible
iv. to shelter live-stock
v. to control sand movement
vi. to provide healthy habitat

It is now well-established that shelterbelts keep heat away, screen the particulate matter in atmosphere and divert air flow. They also diminish wind speed by at least 10 per cent in front of such belts at a height of about five times that of the belt and behind at a height of about twenty five times that of the belt. Best results have been achieved by allowing wind permeability of 40 percent. Experts have shown that a dense formation of the screens does not bring any greater advantage. Shelterbelts act as dust filter especially when laid out at right angles to the main wind direction. At least 10 percent increase in production has been recorded from agricultural field after erection of shelterbelts in several countries. The reduction in wind speeds due to shelterbelts reduces evaporation and raises the carbondioxide percentage of the air with a positive effect on photosynthesis and thus on primary production.

The numerous benefits of shelter belts includes controlling the ravages of wind; improving environmental condition for plants, animals and people; increasing the output from aerable farms and upland grazings; countering salt sea wind, checking fenland and light soils from blowing; reducing the burden of heat losses from houses and green houses; and in some cases yielding timber as well as shelter (Edinberg,1965).

Single row windbreaks can be effective and break the wind as effectively as wider belts but three or more rows allow for greater resilience in the long run. Falling of some species in a multiple row would not create a crisis as in a single row.

Windbreaks near the Sea-Plants have to face strong wind and salt-laiden gales. Species that spread by suckers do well in coastal area. There should be one row of shrub. Trees upto 3 to 5 rows can be effective. Width of each belt may be 10m. An irregular profile is more effective in reducing eddying than more uniform structures.

The use of shelterbelts to improve the productivity of pasture and livestock can be important. These values can be augmented by combining them with other conservation works, such as contour terraces and ditches, so that the tree roots and crowns strengthen and protect the earth work. Shelterbelts, thus, in addition to reducing wind damage-can help runoff, increase percolation of rain water, replenish soil moisture and underground reserve. Stream flow will also be more stable.

3.1.2 Forest Belts

The planning of forest belts has had a long tradition in Hungary. It was started in 1818, by Bachofen-a sylvicultural manager in the frontier area-, who accomplished the binding of the drifting sand area of Deliblat-the "European Salura"-with success. In 1827, forest belts were established in the vicinity of Puszatavacs, their length being nearly 56 kms. The Afforestation Act of the Great Hungarian Plain, in 1923, gave a great impetus to the planting of forest belts and resulted in the planting of approx. 18,205 ha of forest belts and tree groups. Between 1950 and 1961, their extent amounted to some 106, 737 ha.

Owing to its bulk and the structure of the natural tree-stock, forests break the impact of winds. In the case of a well-formed (developed) margin, with tree branches down to the ground, the wind-speed measured in the open area will rapidly decrease towards the centre of the forest and after 150-200 meters, the wind will have almost totally died away. Nevertheless, above the tree canopy, wind will be blowing unabated. This effect of forests is utilized by man to protect settlements, roads, agricultural crops and sandy soils against the wind. The velocity of winds can be successfully broken by only two rows of trees, though a 20-50 m wide forest belt will afford greater protection. In an open area, the effect of protecting forest belt can be observed up to a distance equal to approx. 25 times the height of the trees. In sloping area, the affect of forest belts is less clear cut, as the relief-factors considerably influence their efficiency.

Research and field experience on the shelter belts and wind-breaks have led to useful know-how (Chaudhuri, 1993, and Singarachary, 1997):

a. A wide shelterbelt may not be more effective than a narrow one. It is preferable to have a windbreak as wide as the height of its tallesvt tree.
b. An ideal shelterbelt is permeable, of proper width, shape, and height.

c. According to Jensen (F.A.O. 1974), 35% is the optimum permeability of a (wind tunnel) shelter belt. But in Europe shelter belts upto 60% permeability and in USA up to 80% permeability have been found effective.

d. The trees should be planted to a uniform density from top to bottom, lower branches must not be too open.

e. A report from Govt. of China (1985), shows that a shelterbelt of 8-9 years old can reduce wind velocity and evaporation by 30% and 18% respectively and increase soil moisture and atmospheric humidity by 20% and 9% respectively.

f. Shelter zone on the leeward side extends upto 15-20 times the height;

g. A dense belt provides greater shelter immediately leeward, but the sheltered distance is less, compared to a more permeable belt, and hence a moderately permeable belt is a most preferable.

h. The shelter effect is mainly a function of height and permeability. Width influences the general micro-climate but not the reduction in wind velocity.

i. A belt in which both sides fall abruptly on wind-ward and leeward sides is said to be more effective. The smaller trees and shrubs occupy the interspaces between the tall trees.

j. The maximum effect is obtained if the length is not less than 12 times the height.

k. In a vertical direction, the influence of wind velocity extends to more than four times the height.

l. In respect of soil blow and wind erosion, the protective effort extends to about 30 times the height, the maximum being at about 14 times the height.

m. The fluctuations in ambient temperature are reduced, humidity is increased, and greater dew-fall occurs on the leeward side. The influence on evaporation extends to about ten times the height, the area of greatest protection extends to about ten times the height and the area of protection varying from immediately on leeward side to about 5 times the height depending upon whether wide-dense stand or a permeable narrow belt of trees is the effective barrier.

3.1.3 Design of Shelter Belts and Wind breaks

The design of a shelterbelt will depend on local conditions related to wind direction, speed and characteristics, the essential height and density of the tree species chosen for the shelterbelts, the spacing between the belts, the orientation of the belts, land ownership and so on.

When rows of trees are planted along field borders or around the garden, they help to break or reduce wind velocity and create sheltered zones both leeward and windward. Trees are very effective wind controllers and can minimize occasional loss of property and life. Wind-control can be effected by obstruction, guidance, deflection and filtration (Shukla, 1983). Effect and control varies with species, size, shape, foliage density and retention, actual placement of plant, height, width, row arrangement in the wind-break. Dense planting can reduce wind velocity to 75-85 per cent.

The direction of planting for wind breaks in the north-south meet the wind velocities from south-west and north-east. The wind breaks are raised by planting two close rows of fast growing deciduous species and one parallel row of slow growing or longer living evergreens (Tamarind). As far as possible dense crowned tree species are to be selected (Rao, 1979). Trees suitable for wind breaks are given in Table 3.1.

A shelter belt is more extensive and is a long barrier. It is planted to protect larger area from winds. Shelter belts are commonly planted in a chess board pattern, in which each major field or group of fields is sheltered from every side. Raised sheltered belt should give an effective shelter to an area of a width equal to 20 times the height of its trees. A belt may consist of different species but should have a roughly triangular cross-section. In the centre should be tall trees, short trees in sides; this will ensure maximum impenetrability to wind. The selection of species depends on climate condition and soil types. The plant species like *Prosopis julifera* of low branching and spreading habit are suitable for planting in the outer rows of belts. The planting is done at closer spacing (i.e. 1 metre for shrubs and 2 metres for trees). For effective shelter belt 4-5 rows are sufficient. Trees suitable for shelter belts are given in Table 3.2.

The Andhra Pradesh Forest Department, in collaboration with the Andhra Pradesh Agricultural University, initiated studies at Rajendranagar, Tirupati and Bapatla on the influence of shelter belts and wind breaks on crop fields (Rao, 1983). The shelter belts are 100 m, long and four rows deep. They are aligned at right angles to the South-West monsoon Winds (Table 3.3).

The effectiveness of any barrier would infact depend on the wind velocity and direction, and the shape, width and porosity of the barrier. When the wind blows at right angles to the average tree shelter belts, wind velocity is reduced 70 to 80% near the belt. But no reduction in velocity occurs at a distance equal to 30 to 40 times the belt height. The higher the average wind velocity, the closer shelter belts or other barriers should be spaced to protect the soil from blowing. If the wind velocity is 64.4 km/hr at a 15.25 m height, the following distance may normally be protected from soil erosion by the barriers indicated. Control on croplands : Tree shelterbelts can provide long time protection for cropped fields. Generally two rows of growing, adapted evergreen or deciduous trees, should be planted around farm boundaries. Kinds of trees for this purpose include pine, spruce, mulberry and poplar. Multiflora rose, private and other adapted species of shrub also provide effective protection for vegetable, crops. On most sandy soils, they may be spaced about 91 m. Objections to tree and shrub wind breaks are that they compete with the crop for water and plant nutrients.

The following species appear as per the trail·s conducted at Central Arid Zone Research Institute, Jodhpur:-

Sallow Soils : *Albizzia lebbak, Eucalyptus comaldulensis and Casuraina equisetifolia.*

Semi-rocky areas : *Acacia senegal, Prosopis juliflora Tecomella undulata, Acacia nilotica, Prosopis cineraria.*

i. Rocky areas : *Prosopis juliflora and Acacia senegal.*

ii. Roadside Avenue and Wind Break Planting :

a. *Prosopis juliflora, Azadirachta indica and Albizzia lebbak* were found suitable for low rainfall areas (120-350 mm)

b. *Prosopis juliflora, Azadirachta indica and Albizzia lebbak* were also suitable for low rainfall areas having rainfall of about 350 mm.

Table 3.1 Trees suitable for wind breaks

Dry and arid regions			
1.	Acacia auriculiformis	2.	Ailanthus excelsa
3.	Albizia lebbeck	4.	Anogeissus latifolia
5.	Artocarpus heterophyllus	6.	Azadirachta indica
7.	Causuarina equisetifolia	8.	Dalbergia sissoo
9.	Eucalyptus citriodora	10.	Eucalyptus hybrid
11.	Grevillea robusta	12.	Mangifera hybrid
13.	Melia azedarach	14.	Moringa oleifera
15.	Peltophorum ferruginea	16.	Polyalthia longifolia
17.	Pongamia glabra	18.	Prosopis juliflora
19.	Sesbania grandiflora	20.	Syzygium cumini
21.	Tamarindus indica	22.	Tamarix articulata
Coastal Areas			
1.	Acacia auriculiformis	2.	Ailanthus malabarica
3.	Anacardium occidentale	4.	Calophyllum inophyllum
5.	Cassia Siamea	6.	Casuarina equisetifolia
7.	Grevillea robusta	8.	Mangifera indica
9.	Mesua ferrea	10.	Polyalthia longifolia
11.	Pongamia glabra	12.	Thespesia populnea
Shrubs			
1.	Agave americana	2.	Cassia auriculata
3.	Dodonaea viscosa	4.	Euphorbia teruculli
5.	Gliricidia maculata	6.	Jatropha spp.
7.	Sesbania aculeata	8.	Sesbania aegyptiaca
9.	Thevetia neirifolia	10.	Vitex negundo
Temperature Hill Areas			
1.	Acacia dealbata	2.	Acacia decurrens
3.	Acacia malanoxylon	4.	Alnus nitida
5.	Cupressus macrocarpa	6.	Eucalyptus globulus
7.	Eucalyptus citriodora	8.	Franela rhomboidea
9.	Grevillea robusta	10.	Hakea salinga
11.	Robinia pseudacacia	12.	Ulmus laevigata

Source : Singh, 1986

Table 3.2 Trees suitable for shelter belts.

Suitable Trees and shrubs for shelter belts in dry areas			
1.	Acacia catechu	2.	Acacia leucophloea
3.	Acaccia modesta	4.	Acacia nilotica
5.	Agave species	6.	Ailanthus excelsa
7.	Albizia lebbeck (siris)	8.	Azadirachta indica (neem)
9.	Anacardium occidental	10.	Acacia arabica (babul)
11.	Accacia senegal	12.	Agave spp.
13.	Accacia jacguemontii	14.	Albizzia amara

15. Cassia auriculata
16. Cassia siamea
17. Casuarina equisetifolia
18. Cassia siamea
19. Capparis aphylla
20. Calligonum polygonoides (Phog)
21. Cassia aurticulata
22. Cypresses sp.
23. Dodonea viscosa
24. Dalbergia sissoo (Shishium)
25. Euphorbia terucalli
26. Eucalyptus rostrata
27. Ficus sp.
28. Gliricidia maculata
29. Holoptelea integrifolia
30. Inga diucis (Madras Thorn)
31. Inqa dulcis
32. Jatropha species
33. Kingelia pinnata (Sausage tree)
34. Leucaena leucocephala
35. Mangifera indica
36. Melia azedarach
37. Moringa pterygosperma (Sainija)
38. Opuntia dellenii
39. Prosopis specigera (Kheiri)
40. Peltophorum ferrugineum
41. Pongamia glabra
42. Parkinsonia aculeata (Jerusalem thorn)
43. Prosopis juliflora
44. Prosopis julifera
45. Salvadora oleoides
46. Sesbania aculeata
47. Sesbania aegyptica
48. Syzygium cumini
49. Saccharum munja (Sarkananda)
50. Savladora persica
51. S. oleoides
52. Tamarix articulata (Farash)
53. Tamarindus indica (imli)
54. Thevetia neirifolia
55. Vitex negundo
56. Vitex negundo
57. Zizypus sp.

Suitable species for shelter belts in coastal areas (Humid climate)

1. Ailanthus malabarica
2. Albizia lebbeck
3. Alstonia scholaris
4. Amherstia nobilis
5. Anacardium occidentale
6. Azadirachta indica
7. Bauhinia purpurea
8. Bauhinia variegata
9. Brownea grandiceps
10. Calophyllum inophyllum
11. Cananga odorata
12. Cassia nodosa
13. Casuarina equisetifolia
14. Colvillea racemosa
15. Couroupita guianensis
16. Erythrina cristagalli
17. Gliricidia maculata
18. Lagerstroemia indica
19. Lagerstroemia speciosa
20. Lagerstroemia thorellii
21. Mangifera indica
22. Pongamica glabra
23. Pterospermum acerifolium
24. Putranjiva roxburghii
25. Samanea saman
26. Saraca indica
27. Spathodea companulata
28. Stenocarpus sinuatus
29. Thespesia populnea
30. Terminalia catappa

Suitable species for shelter belts in temperature hill areas

1. Acacia melanoxylon
2. Alnus nitida
3. Cupressus macrocarpa
4. Cupressus torulosa
5. Dodonaea viscosa
6. Eucalptus globulus
7. Franela rhomboidea
8. Grevillea robusta
9. Hakea salinga
10. Robinia pseudacacia
11. Ulmus laevigata

Source : Singh, 1986 and Singarachary, 1997

Table 3.3 Shelterbelt Design

Inter-row spacing (from the win-ward side	Total depth of shelter belt	Composition of species	Inter-row spacing
Centre : (1) Rajendranagar			
I Row		Sitaphal, Phalsa, Agave,	
4.5 m		Phalsa	0.75 m
II Row	18.5 m	Soapnut, Sesbania,	
7.0 m		Emblica, Sesbania.	1.0 m
III Row		Mango, Eucalyptus,	
7.0 m		Wood Apple, Eucalyptus	
		Eucalyptus	1.0 m
IV Row		Bamboo	5.0 m
Centre (2) Tirupati			
I Row		Sitaphal, Phalsa, Agave	
3.0 m		Phalsa	0.75 m
II Row	13.0	Soapnut, Eucalyptus,	
5.0 m		Emblica, Sesbania	1.0 m
III Row		Mango, Eucalyptus,	
5.0 m		Wood Apple, Eucalyptus	
		Eucalyptus, Eucalyptus	
IV Row		Bamboo, Agave, Agave	
		Agave	1.0 m
Centre (3) Bapatla			
I Row		Sitaphal, Phalsa	
3.0 m		Sashewnut, Agave	0.75 m
II Row	13.0	Eucalyptus, Soapnut	1.0 m
5.0 m		Emblica	
III Row		Bamboo	5.0 m

d. Azadirachta indica, Albizzia lebbak and Dalbergia sissoo were 80-90% successful without supplemental irrigation.

iii. Fodder trees : *Prosopis cineraria* is an important forage tree species which grows in cultivated fields. The trees may be 60-80/ha without affecting crop yield. Some of the exotic species with good adaptability in arid regions are *Acacia aneura* (Australia). *Brasilettia mollis* (Venezuela), *Geoffroea decorticans* (Chile), *Prosopis alba* (Argentina), and *Colophospermum mopana* (South Rhodesia).

Of these *Prosopis juliflora, Azadirachta indica and Albizzia lebbak* have been successfully used as three row shelterbelts along the highways in western Rajasthan. Five row shelter belts in pyramidal shape were found to be suitable in desert areas where wind direction changes abruptly. *Acacia tortilis* was found most suitable for air zone afforestation on sand dunes.

Optimal benefits from wind breaks and shelter belts are obtained where mixed plantation consisting of grasses, shrubs and trees are raised. While selection of species may be made according to the experience of local conditions, the following list may be serve as useful as guide (Rao, 1972):-

First Row : *Euphorbia royleana, E. neriifolia, Saccharum munja, Acacia rundodonax, Sesbania acgyptiaca, Lawsonea alba, Agave americana, A. sisalana, Thevetia neriifolia, Tecoma stans, Ipomoea cernua, Vitex negundo, Zizipus nummularia, Calotropis gigantia, Tamarix articulata, Balanites roxburghii, Leucaena glauca, Gliricidia maculata, Ricinus communis, Tephrosia candida, Casuarina equisetifolia,* bamboos.

Second Row : *Zizypus jujuba, Parkinsonia aculeata, Prosopis juliflora, P.spicigera, Acacia arabica, azadirachta indica, Pongamia glabra, Acacia catechu, Cassia siamea, Boswellia serrata, Anacardium occidentale, Acacia mollissima, Casuarina spp., Cocos nucifera, Pionciana alata, Borassus flabellifer.*

Third Row : *Acacia arabica, Albizzia lebbak, Dalbergia sissoo, Eugenia jambolana, Cedrela toona, Tectona grandis, Mangifera indica, Dalbergia latifolia, Tamarindus indica, Hardwickia binata, Terminalia sp., Eucalyptus sp., Grevillea ropusta, Casuarina spp., Anacardium occidentalc, Artocarpus integrifolia* and other palm, bamboos.

Windbreaks may be 80 feet wide and consists of 8 rows depending upon the availability of land (Table 3.4). There should be two rows of long lined broad leafy trees and four rows of hardy conifers. Such a combination affords protection all the year round. A type shelter belt should be like a conical root in cross-section. In the centre, the peak of the roof, there should be tall trees flanked by short trees, confiers and tall shrubs and grasses with low shrubs on the outside.

3.2 AIR POLLUTION CONTROL (GASEOUS, PARTICULATE & AEROSOLS)

Air is poisoned by chimney smoke, exhaust gases of motors, poisonous gases from chemical factories, etc. (Table 3.5). If the individual gases are toxic , the complex effect of various gases containing sulphur, flourine, chlorine, and carbon monoxide, that is dangerous. Of the several air pollutants emitted in India, the most common once are SOx, NOx and SPM. Table 3.6 summarises the 16 hour annual average (arithmetic mean) concentrations of SO_2, NO_2 and SPM, in some indian cities. The ambient air quality standards prescribed in India, for SO_2, SPM, CO and NO_x are given in Table 3.7.

Dense vegetation intercepts incoming and outgoing radiation, precipitation and winds. It has an effect on the micro climate of the area, filters dust from air and collects it. One hectare of spruce (conifer) is often known to collect about 32 tonnes of dust from the atmosphere. One hectare of pine collects 36 tonnes and a hectare of beach collects 68 tonnes of dust until their needles and leaves can retain no more. Shrubs are effective to a smaller extent (Chaudhuri, 1993).

Table 3.4. Plantation order for wind break in agricultural areas

Wind break	Factors determining Protected distance	Remarks
Trees and Shrubs		
Two row (mulberry)	18.2	To find the protected distance, multiply the height of the barrier by the appropriate number in column 2
Fine row (Plum, cedar, mulberry, elm, olive)	15.0	
One row (orange)	12.0	
Three row (cedar, shrub)	11.0	
One row (Siberian elm)	9.5	
Annual crops		
Kochia	12.0	
Sudangrass	7.5	
Grain Sorghum	6.0	
Forage Sorghu	4.0	
Broom corn	1.0	

Table 3.5. Important air pollutants and their sources

Pollutants	Source
Sulfur dioxide	Coal and oil combustion, smelters
Ozone	Photochemical reactions
Oxides of Nitrogen	Fuel consumption
Carbon monoxide	Incomplete fuel consumption
Carbon dioxide	Fossil fuel combustion, metabolic activity
Ammonia	Metabolic activity, cleaning products, and agriculture.
Suspended particulate matter	Resuspension, condensation of vapours, and combustion process
Lead, Manganese	Automobiles, smelters
Calcium, Chloride, Silicon, Cadmium	Soil particulates, Industrial emissions
Organic substances	Petrochemical solvents, vaporisation of unburnt fuels, petroleum products combustion, paint, metabolic action, pesticides, insecticides and fungicides.

Source: United Nations Environmental Programme, (1991).
Urban Air Pollution, UNEP/GEMS Environment library No.4, Nairobi, Kenya

Table 3.6. Air pollutants in selected Indian cities-annual average (16 hours) (value in mg/m^3)

Cities	Pollutants	1987	1988	1989	1990	1991	Five year average
Agra	SO_2	9.3	14.6	12.6	20.9	18.2	15.1
	NO_2	8.2	10.5	6.6	11.6	11.9	9.8
	SPM	329.8	401.6	368.0	465.5	480.0	409.0
Ahamadabad	SO_2	na	na	27.0	20.0	26.0	24.6
	NO_2	na	na	42.7	33.7	33.9	36.8
	SPM	na	na	281.4	289.6	306.3	292.5
Baroda	SO_2	18.41	6.5	19.0	12.9	14.5	16.3
	NO_2	29.0	31.1	14.9	12.5	19.8	21.5
	SPM	225.4	256.0	333.2	296.0	357.0	293.7
Bangalore	SO_2	na	30.3	24.[illegible]	[illegible]6.8	19.9	22.9
	NO_2	na	14.5	14.5	10.3	11.6	12.7
	SPM	na	226.0	141.8	64.3	89.5	110.4
Cochin	SO_2	na	4.3	5.6	7.1	6.1	5.8

{Cont.}...

	NO_2	na	18.5	21.4	14.5	14.3	17.2
	SPM	na	123.8	117.4	121.7	106.4	117.3
Delhi	SO_2	15.5	11.5	8.7	15.6	20.8	14.4
	NO_2	17.9	20.7	17.7	29.3	34.8	24.1
	SPM	576.7	488.2	489.2	389.6	390.0	499.7
Pune	SO_2	3.9	7.4	10.2	14.2	8.26	15.5
	NO_2	20.7	32.9	40.4	37.2	17.9	29.8
	SPM	24.9	216.0	209.5	224.2	306.3	196.2

Source: Compiled from central pollution control board, Delhi, (1994)

Table 3.7. Ambient air quality standards

			mmg pollutant per m³ air sample			
Pollutant averaging time			US			INDIA
		Primary (human Health)	Secondary (all other effects)	Industrial & mixed use areas	Residential & rural areas	Commercial areas
Annual arith. mean		80.0	60.0	80.0* or 0.5mg So_2/100cm²/day*		
SO_2	24-hour max.	365.0	260.0	-	-	-
	8-hour max	-	-	12.0	80.0	30.0
	3-hour max.	-	1,300	-	-	-
SPM	Annual arith mean		75.0	60.0	-	--
	24-hour max.	260.0	150.0	150.0*	-	-
	8-hour max.	-	-	500.0	200.0	100.0
CO	8-hour max.	10,000	10,000	5,000	2,000	1,000
	1-hour max	40,000	40,000	-	-	-
	Oxidant	8-hour max. -	-	-	-	--
	1-hour max.	160.0	160.0	-	-	-
NO_x	Annual arith. mean		100.0	100.0	-	--
	8-hour max.	-	-	120.0	80.0	30.0
Hydor carbons	3-hour max. (6-9 AM)	160.0	160.0	-	-	-

Source: Rao, (1992)

The air quality standard be such at which no significant deterioration of environment occurs.

* NEERI's suggestion

1880 mg/m³ NO_2 = 1ppm NO_2

2620 mg/m² SO_2 = 1ppm SO_2

Even as the focus *vis a vis* air quality has been on air pollutants, the problems concerning the oxygen balance of the atmosphere are also gaining increasing attention. Oxygen is, essential for life. One adult consumes annually one-third of a ton of molecular oxygen and 350 kg of oxygen is required by a motorcar to burn 100 litre petrol. One motorcar owner, who drives 10,000 km annually, consumes the oxygen demand of 10 men (Tables 3.5-3.7). The 6 million inhabitants of Switzerland consume 2 million tons of oxygen in the process of breathing (Krebs 1970). As combustion in industrial furnaces alone requires 28 million tons of oxygen, this amount is equal to the oxygen demand of 84 million men. Apart from this, approximately, 1.4 times this amount, 42 million tons of carbon monoxide, pollutes the air. Apart from air pollution, it will shortly become an especially serious task to satisfy the demand for oxygen in the world. Only green plants, mainly within the canopy of forests are capable of decomposing carbon monoxide in the process of assimilation, with the help of solar energy and of producing free oxygen. A tree with a projected area of 150 m^2, in 100 years, produces as much oxygen as is consumed by one man in the course of 20 years (Kovacs, 1985).

Each tree is a small air-purifying, dust-adsorbing, device and at the same time a small oxygen factory, as well.

Trees act as natural filters as they remove (scavenge) pollutants from the atmosphere and thus improve air quality. Forests act as pollution sinks in two ways - as air filters and as air ventilators. The latter effect is produced because trees cause air currents and eddies that help to ventilate an area that might otherwise have very still air (Kovacs, 1985).

Many measurements have been made of the removal of gases and particulates under natural conditions and a few studies have been performed under artificial conditions. Results indicate that large areas of vegetation remove significant quantities of pollutants and this understanding has supported the use of green belts or shelter belts around urban and industrial areas [(Agarwal and Tiwari, 1997).

Pollutants are removed from the atmosphere by several processes including sedimentation, impaction, and absorption.

Plants can act as "living filter" of air pollutants. Shelter belts and city-lung spaces of pollutant tolerant species of herbs, shrubs and trees in urban industrial areas, help reduce air pollution (Rao, 1980).

a. In Frankfurt, dust levels were found to be three or four times greater in treeless streets, compacted to tree-linked streets.
b. In London's Hyde Park area air pollution is 20 per cent less than other parts of the city.
c. A single tree can offset the pollution effects of one car driven over 96 km.
d. Just to offset pollution there should be three trees for every person on earth.

3.2.1 Particulate Pollutants

Air pollution by particulate matter is attributed to natural conditions as well as to industrial and other activities including power generation plants, transportation, building construction, stone crushing, agriculture and related operations like cement, iron and steel manufacture and forest product processing. The particles going into the atmosphere, depending on their size and weight, may remain in air for varying lengths of time. Those larger than 10 mm in size, settle under forces of gravity on surfaces of vegetation and soil but the smaller ones remain suspended in air for longer periods of time and in accordance with the gas laws get dispersed, distributed and diffused by wind motion and eddy currents (Rao, 1992). The suspended particulate matter (SPM) gradually gather mass through agglomeration, coalescence and water vapour deposition and eventually settles down on surfaces or may be waned down by rain. The concentration of suspended dust may vary from less than 30 mmg/m^3 air volume in rural areas to over 200 mmg/m^3 air volume in urban areas (Rao, 1992).

From Ambient Air Quality Data published by the National Environmental Engineering Research Institute (NEERI), Nagpur for the year 1979, it is apparent that the SPM and dust fall levels are significantly high in Indian Cities (Table 3.8). The ambient air quality reference level set by NEERI is 150 mmg/m^3 for 24 hr period (Ahmed et al., 1989).

Bose et al. (1983) measured the seasonal values of SPM and settled dust in different activity zones of Jharia Coal Field Complex and highlighted the seriousness of dust problem in mining cum industrial areas of the country (Table 3.9).

Sudhakar and Agrawal (1978) studying the particulate pollution load in Kanpur textile factories observed that maximum mg/m^3 concentration of particulate matter was 70.0 in a jute mill, 11.4 in a cotton mill and 64.0 in a woollen mill, the hazard of pollution being maximum in jute mills, where almost all workers usually suffer from respiratory ailments.

The dust laden wind blows into vegetation and deposits dust on the leaves, branches and stems which act as barrier. The wind loses much of its velocity on account of these mechanical obstacles resulting in the precipitation (or sedimentation) of dust (suspended particles) in an increased extent. The dust is washed down to the ground with the onset of rain and due to moisture, it loses its flying capacity and gets bound. This is called active filtering. Dense tree stands through which the wind cannot penetrate have positive effect on the purification of the air. The winds ascent in front and descent behind the obstacle, create air currents, jams and vertices leading to increased sedimentation of dust. This is called 'passive protection' (Chaudhuri, 1993).

Extensive afforestation has been done in the lignite districts of the Rhine land in Germany and in Neyveli (Tamilnadu, India) lignite mines have given effective results.

The leaves and needles of trees in a forest absorb upto 50 percent of the collected radio iodine and thus a dense vegetation protects man against radioactive dust, saving the people from the effects of radio-activity contaminated nutrition.

Hyde-Park,a green area of about 1.5km2 in the centre of London,reduces smoke concentration by 27% (Meetham, 1964). Vegetation can reduce suspended particulate matter of 120 mmg/m^3 over a distance of 200m. From a study in Soviet Union, it is estimated that Lilac, Maple, Lindon, and Poplar trees can filter 2.33, 1.11, 0.61 and 0.26 mg dust/m^2 leaf surface, respectively (Bach, 1972).

According to Yunus et al. (1983), the dust collecting effectiveness of plants mostly depends on the morphological traits of leaves. Such as epidermal and cuticular features, surface geometry, phyllotaxy, orientation, size and area of leaf, etc (Table 3.10).

The planting of trees and shrubs was recommended as a way to combat dust pollution in Russian cities by Novoderzhkina et al. (1966), who reported a 2-3 times reduction in dust fall by plants on a meter wide green belt between the roads and buildings. Dochinger (1972), who examined the ability of the plants to abate particulate pollutants, reported a reduction of up to 42% in overall dust fall by a canopy of coniferous plants in the urban areas of Ohio, U.S.A. Bach (1972), who studied the dust collecting potential of some plants, observed interesting relationship between certain leaf surface parameters and their dust trapping potential. In India some preliminary studies have been carried out by Shetye & Chaphekar (1980) in Bombay, Das (1981) in Calcutta, Rao at Varanasi and Varshney and his associates in New Delhi. According to an estimate dust pollutants comprise around 40% of the total air pollution problem in India.

Table 3.8. Annual summary of air quality for 1979 with reference to suspended particulate matter (SPM) and dust fall (DF) for certain Indian cities (after NEERI Report, 1980-81)

City	SPM mmg/m^3	DF (MT/Km^2/month)
Bombay	197 - 285	8 - 19
Calcutta	413 - 5172	21 - 37
Delhi	296 - 481	12 - 30
Hyderabad	255 - 295	12 - 30
Jaipur	222 - 379	12 - 16
Kanpur	206 - 344	24 - 36
Madras	106 - 169	8 - 12
Nagpur	159 - 386	8 - 88

Source : Ahmed et al., (1989)

Table 3.9. Average dust fall and ambient concentration of suspended particulate matter indifferent activity zones of Jharia Coalfield Complex (modified after Bose et al., 1983).

Activity Zone	*Dusfall (tons/km²/month)* Summer	Rain	Winter	*SPM (mmg/m³)* Summer	Rain	Winter
Mining commercial residential	23.02	11.26	15.44	380	181	398
Mining industrial	29.61	7.44	17.57	-	-	-
Industrial resdential traffic	25.78	8.23	18.20	-	161	387
Industrial residential	27.78	12.51	16.64	-	224	321
Mining industrial residential	30.47	13.14	18.00	401	254	436

Source: Bose et at., (1983)

Table 3.10. Leaf area and epidermal characteristics versus dust collection efficiency of certain plant species (modified after Yunus 1983)

Plant	Leaf area (cm²)	Epidermal characteristics (Adaxial surface) Trichome Frequency/ (mm)	Trichome size	Veinislet/ mm² (mg/cm2)	Dust load
Calotropis procera	70	47	226	65	8.8102
Ipomoea fistulosa	92	19	34	38	3.2757
Catharanthus roseus	6	-	-	24	1.4105
Bougainvillea glabra	17	15	156	7	1.1464
Eucalyptus globulus	33	-	-	8	0.5498

Source : Yunus et al., (1983)

Studies carried out on common avenue trees and road-side shrubs in various localities of Lucknow have indicated a relationship between the morphological traits of plants and the amount of dust captured by them. The morphological characteristics which have been found to play significant role in the interception of air particulates are : orientation of surface (smooth/striate), presence or absence of trichomes and morphology and frequency of trichomes, exudates, wax deposition, etc. Based on extensive field observations and laboratory investigations, and using above mentioned criteria, a few species of plants have been identified which posses higher dust filtering capacity (Table 3.11). These species may be raised in green belts around industrial and urban areas to lessen the dust load of the environment (Ahmed et al., 1989).

Shetye and Chaphekar (1980) compared the dust collecting efficiency of leaves of mature trees of *Erythrina indica, Thespesia populnea and polyalthia longifolia*. They found *Mangifera and Thespesta*, which are evergreen plants with horizontally oriented leaves, to be good dust catchers and deciduous *Erythrina* and evergreen *Polyalthia*, with vertically suspended glabrous leaves, to be very poor dust collectors. At any given time and place, they found *M.indica* to be much more efficient for this purpose than *T.populnea*.

A study (Das et al., 1981) at the pollution Research Laboratory, College of Agriculture, University of Calcutta revealed that evergreen trees with smooth or hairy leaf surface, like mango or fig, are better dust collectors than deciduous trees with compound leaf, like neem (*Azadirachta indica*) or Indian laburnum (*Cassia fistula*).

As summarised in Table 3.12, the dust collecting efficiency of some important Indian trees has been measured by Das (1981) and Das et al (1981). It is clear that evergreen trees with simple leaves, having rough and pilose (hairy) surface are better dust collectors than deciduous trees with compound leaves having glabrous(smooth) surface;; that *Ficus, Mangifera, Tectona* and *Polyalthia* species are better dust collectors than *Cassia, Poinciana* and *Sesbania sp;* that the upper leaf surface collects most of the dust particles but the lower leaf surface also plays an important role.

The dust collecting efficiency of trees with compound leaves or needles, as in pine tress, is rather poor. But these may also exert a significant filtering effect when air current passes through their dense growth. They act like sieves separating the suspended particulate matter of the air current by providing physical barriers.

Trees having compact branching, closely arranged leaves, broad leaves of simple elliptical and hairy structure, shiny or waxy leaves, and high praline content are suitable.

It is found that 8m wide greenbelts between roads and buildings can reduce the dust fall by 2-3 times. Conifers can reduce the dust fall upto 42% in temperate urban areas.

For dust abatement purposes, the tree species should be fast growing, hardy and pollution tolerant. Rao (1971) observed that Pithecolobium dulce (Jungal jalebi) possesses the essential characteristics of such a tree. It is a fast growing perennial and evergreen plant with a limited water requirement and it remains generally ungrazed. For obtaining maximum dust collecting and wind breaking effect, a compact hedge of P.dulce may be developed by planting 4 to 5 plants side by side in a row. This plant can attain a height of 18-20 meters within a period of 4 to 5 years (Rao, 1992).

Table 3.11 Plant species with better dust filtering capacity

1. Calotropis procera R. Br.
2. Ficus benghalensis L.
3. F. infectoria Roxb.
4. Holoptelea integrifolia Planch.
5. Ipomoea fistulosa Mart. Ex Choisy
6. Lagerstroemia sp.
7. Nyctanthes arbortristis L.
8. Peltophorum pterocarpum
9. Tectona grandis L.
10. Terminalia arjuna W. & A.
11. Thevetia nerifolia Juss.

Source : Ahmed et al., (1983).

Table 3.12. Dust collecting (filtering) efficiency of some avenue trees at Indian Botanic garden, Shibpur, Howrah. Calcutta (after Das et. Al., 1981)

Tree species	*Dust per sq. m* On upper leaf surface (g/m²)	*Dust per sq. m* on lower leaf surface (g/m²)	*Total dust per* sq. m on leaf surface (g/m²)
Simple leaved			
Ficus religiosa (Peepal)	2.56	1.59	4.15
Ficus infectoria (Pakur)	2.64	1.45	4.09
Ficus benghalensis (Banyan)	2.71	0.88	3.59
Tectona gradis (Teak)	4.10	1.55	5.35
Shorea roubsta (Sal)	3.40	1.10	4.50
Terminolia arjuna (Arjuna)	3.25	1.24	4.49
Polyalthia longifolia (Ashoka)	3.92	0.64	4.56
Mangifera indica (Mango)	2.50	1.55	4.05
Lagerstroemia flosregeinal (Jarul)	2.82	1.22	4.04
Bauhinia purpuria (Kanchnar)	2.70	1.20	3.90
Anthocephalus cadamba (Kadamba)	2.42	1.15	3.57
Thespesia populnca (Tulip)	2.82	0.71	3.53
Compound leaved			
Saraca indica (Sita Ashoka)	2.56	1.22	3.78
Butea frondosa (Palas)	2.20	0.85	3.05
Azadirachta indica (Neem)	2.20	0.72	2.92
Cassia fislula (Amaltas)	1.82	0.42	2.24
Tamarindus indica (Tamarind)	1.56	0.52	2.08
Poinciana regia (Gul mohar)	1.12	0.62	1.44

Source : India Today

A special mention may be made here of *Argyreia speciosa* (samudrashok), a convolvulaceous hardy and fast growing garden climber, which can thrive luxuriantly in highly dust and polluted areas. Its cordate leaves are large (more than 15cm long and 10 cm wide) hairy, thick and horizontally oriented so as to catch maximum quantity of dust from the air. Being perennial and evergreen with golden green leaves, it is an ideal plant which combines both ornamental and dust abatement qualities. It can be easily grown by cuttings on fences, wire nets and boundary walls of residences, office complexes and other private and public building. The author has found this plant to be an excelled protection cover for green houses and nurseries situated in dust polluted areas. Also trees having stratified canopy with branching system, such as *Leucaena leucocephala* (Subabul) can act as a good wind breaker and efficient dust filter in urban and industrial areas (Rao, 1992).

The study of Das et al. (1981) indicates that species of advanced plant families like *Gramineae, Orchidaceae,* etc., during the course of evolution, have developed built-in-mechanism for absorbing chemicals from air borne particulate pollutants to their advantage. The air in fact, acts as a supplementary sources of nutrition to them (Rao, 1992).

3.2.2 Gaseous Pollutants

All gases and particles smaller than about 100 mmm are transported to surfaces by turbulent transfer processes, and, as atmospheric particles are in this size category, dry deposition tends to be interchangeable with tuberlent deposition. In contrast, the relatively small fraction, by mass, of large particles (those with diameters > 10 mmm) and appreciable terminal velocities and deposited under the influence of gravity (D.Flowler in "Trees and the deposition of atmospheric pollutants" (Chaudhuri, 1993).

Most of the primary air pollutants SO_2, O_3, NO_x and HF are reactive gases which or their secondary and tertiary reaction products react with the protective layers of coniferous needles. The large particles (diameter > 1 mmm) are transported through the sub-layer by their own inertia and by gravitational forces, whereas particles appreciably smaller than 0.1 mmm are transported by Brownian diffusion. In between, in the size range of 0.1 to 1 mmm, particles do not have an effective vehicle for transfer through this boundary layer and consequently their deposition rates are minimal" (Chemberlain, A.C., 1975). Most sulphur containing particles are in the sizes range 0.1-1.0 mmm and inevitably, deposition velocities are small and is linked with small ambient concentrations of Sulphur particles, 2 to 8mmm m^{-3}, makes the measurement of their fluxes in a forest very difficult, although there is now a prospect of success using an eddy correlation techniques (Brown).

Giridhar and Chaphekar (1983) have studied pollution absorption and removal capacity of plants as related to the quality of foliar surfaces. They have reported that *solanum melongena* and *Cyamopsis tetragonoloba* effectively remove SO_2 when exposed to 0.1 to 1 ppm concentration. The rate of SO_2 removal was found to be related to leaf area.

Studies carried out in New Delhi by (Varshney and co-workers) have (Varshney 1992) brought out the role of tree bark in promoting surface deposition of sulphur pollution. Leaf analysis of *Nerium idicum* plants along the ring road have clearly demonstrated the scavenging property of this plant which has not been found to suffer from any visible injury (Varshney, 1992).

Coniferous trees are particularly effective in filtering out gaseous pollutants from overlying air. Parts of the trees and the underlying soils absorb the toxic materials that are scavenged. After heavy rains the sulphur particles that have collected on leaves are washed off on to underlying soils and into adjacent streams and lakes. Coniferous trees can also intercept acid mists (Chaudhuri, 1993).

A continuous cover of assimilating Alfalfa can remove more than a ton of NO_2 or SO_2 per square mile per day from air (Hill, 1977).

3.2.3 Pollution Based on Source & Types of Pollutants

a. Automobile exhaust pollutants

Automobile exhaust pollutants are the primary cause of air pollution in the urban areas (60%) followed by industries (20-30%) and fossil fuel (Sivasamy & Srinevasam, 1996).

According to an estimate automobiles emit over 1.8 million tonnes of pollutants, of which more than 80% are released in cities. Because of their mobility and wide distribution, automobiles often cause more serious hazards than those caused by stationary sources. The major pollutants emitted by automobiles are: lead, carbon monoxide, oxides of nitrogen, unsaturated hydrocarbons and oxides of sulphur (Abbasi 1998).

With a view to investigate a possible correlation between motorised vehicular traffic and sulphate and lead accumulation in foliage and avenue trees, a study was undertaken in Lucknow during January 1989 (Ahmed et al, 1989). Ten road transactions spread over different parts of the city and varying traffic densities were selected for this purpose. Samples of mature and healthy leaves of the following plant species were collected from all the ten sites for comparative studies: *Ailanthus excelsa* Roxb., *Antigonon leptopus* Hook., *Azadirachta indica* A. Juss., *Bougainvilles* sp., *Callistemon lanceolatun* R. Br., *Calotraopis procera* R. Br., *Cassia fistula* L., *Clerodendron splendense* Linn., *Dalbergia sissoo* Roxb., *Delonix regia* Rafin., *Eucalyptus citriodora* Hook., *Ficus religiosa* L., *Holoptelea integrifolia* Planch., *Lantana camara* L., *Moringa oleifera* Lam., *Pithecolobium dulce* Benth., *Polyalthia longifolia* Benth. & Hook., *Pongamia glabra* vent., *Ricinus commnuis* L., *Tabernaemontana coronaria* willd. and *Thevetia nerifolia* Juss.

Air quality monitoring for sulphur dioxide (SO_2), suspended particulate matter (SPM), collection of leaf samples and counting of traffic density were carried out at Lucknow cities during peak traffic hours (9.00 A.M. to 11.00 A.M.) on normal working days.

The levels of sulphate (SO_4) and lead (Pb) were estimated in the foliage of plants collected from the investigated sites. The study showed maximum levels of SO_4 and Pb in the foliage of plants growing along the road with maximum traffic density and the minimum levels of SOx and Pb burdens in plants collected with minimum traffic load (Ahmed et al., 1989).

Due to the increasing trend of vehicular transport in the cities, the situation is becoming progressively alarming. Some of the species effective against automobile exhaust pollution are *Ficus bengalensis, Holoptelea integrifolia, Ailanthus excelsa, Albizzia lebbeck, Alstonia scholaris, Azadirachta indica, Dalbergia sissoo, Syzygium cumini, and Nerium indicum* (Rawat & Bamerjee, 1996).

b. Thermal power stations & coal fired industries

Power plants emit into the atmosphere several pollutants, specially fly ash, dust, SO_2, CO, and heavy metals.

Thermal power plants burn coal and release enormous amounts of sulphur dioxide (on an average, Indian coal contains 0.2 to 1.4% sulphur), oxides of nitrogen (NO_x), fly ash and particulates. According to an estimate coal based power generation units in India add about thirteen million tonnes of fly ash (major constituents; silica 52%; iron oxide 26%; alumina 16.26%); eight million tonnes of particulates; 4,80,000 tonnes of SO_2; 2,80,000 tonnes of NO_x; 16,000 tonnes of CO and 5,000 tonnes of hydrocarbons to the atmosphere annually (Ahmed et al., 1989).

It is, therefore, imperative to develop a green belts in and around thermal power plants to guard against the deleterious effects of air polluants emissions. Some of the suitable species are: *Acacia nilotica, Aegle marmelos, Ailanthus excelsa, Albizzia lebbeck, Alstonia scholaris, Azzadirachta indica, Darbergia sissoo, and Bourgain villea spectabills* (Rawat and Banèrgee, 1986).

c. Urban and industrial polluants

The dust load in urban and industrial areas is increasing steadily due to more and more industrial, metal refining, construction, transportation and residential activities. Rao and Pal (1979) observed that the cumulative deposition of particulate can be significantly high (Table 3.13).

For environmental quality control, it has been suggested that suspended particulate matter concentration of 60 mmg/m^3 and settled dust of 10 $tons/km^2/month$ may be taken as natural background level of dust for an area and the concentration above this may be considered as hazardous on injurious to life. It may be mentioned here that the settled dust level in Chembur, Bombay, seven years ago was found to be 25 tons/ $km^2/month$ (Rao, 1992).

As shown in Table 3.14, the urban dust may be considered as a mixture of heterogeneous particulate matter consisting of heavy metal particles, tarry deposits and other kinds of particles related to the day-to-day activities in the area (Das and Bhaumik., 1980). Species such as *Ficus bengalensis, Holoptelea integrifolia, Nyctanthes arbortristis, and Lagerstroemia spp*, have been reported to be effective in mitigrating the harmful effects of particulate matter (Rawat and Banerjee, 1996).

d. Coal dust and fly ash

Coal is formed from partly decayed vegetable matter under great pressure in the earth and it is composed mostly of carbon (Table 3.15). The quantity of settled coal dust on soil surface ranges from 900 to 190,000 kg/km^2/month; the deposition being less calm and wet periods turbulent and dry periods.

Fly-ash comprises finely divided particles of ash entrained in flue gases arising from combustion of coal. The size of fly-ash particles may vary from 0.02 mm to over 300 mm. It contains completely burned coal. The carbon content of fly-ash may vary from 5-20%, although some samples may contain as high as 50%. Also, as given in Table 3.16, a large number of minerals, originally present in the coal, may occur in fly-ash (Bhatia 1978). The concentrations of 17 elements in coal and corresponding fly-ash, collected from stack precipitators of power plants, are presented in Table 3.17 (Kamath, 1979).

e. Cement dust

Cement dust emanating from cement factories, building construction sites, etc. contains varying quantities of oxides of Ca, K and Na with lesser amounts of Si, Al, Fe, Mn, and S (Rao, 1992). Its composition depends entirely upon the nature of raw material used, but CaO predominates in all kinds of cement dust (Table 3.18). The size of cement particles may range from 0.1 to 100 mm. Parthasarthy et al (1975) measured the variations in the rate of cement deposition on foliar surfaces of maize plants in relation to the distance from kiln and found that fourth and fifth leaves from the stem tip had more dust deposition on them than that on upper three leaves and that the cement covered plants showed reduction in leaf size, plant height as well as decreases in number and size of cobs with respect to control plants growing in non-polluted fields (Table 3.19 and Table 3.20).

Table 3.13. Levels of particulate matter settling on soil and leaf surfaces at various distances North-East of the aluminium factories at Renukoot

Distance from factory (km)	*Particulate deposits* Soil surface ($mg/m^2/day$)	Leaf surface (mg/m^2)
0.5	265	120,000
0.7	178	74,000
1.0	95	31,800
1.5	40	12,300
2.0	-	-
2.5	-	8,800
3.5	-	4,000
4.0 (Control)	-	-

Source: Rao and Pal, (1979)

Table 3.14. Quantitative analysis of different elements present in the dust sample near Calcutta

Element	*Percent*
Carbon	5.19
Nitrogen	0.63
Phosphorus	0.30
Potassium	0.41
Iron	2.20
Manganese	0.04
Copper	0.02
Zinc	0.14
Calcium	3.40
Magnesium	0.40
Silicon	22.0
Cadmium, Lead, Arsenic etc.	Trace

Souce: Das and Bhaumik, (1980)

Table 3.15 Composition of Indian coals (% in unit coal, after Indian standards)

Group Volatilies	Range of organic (% at 925°C)	C	H	H	S*	O_2
Anthracite	(Anthracite (A_1)3-10	3	3-4	1	0.5	1-2
	semianthracite (A_2)10-15	93-92	3-4	1	0.5	1-2
Bituminous	Low volatile (B_2) 15-20	92-91	4.4-4.6	1.5	0.5	1-2
	Medium volatile(B_2)20-32	91-87	4.5-5.3	1.5	0.5	2-6
	High volatile(B_3) 32* (caking)	87-84	5.0-5.8	2	0.5	5-8
	High volatile (B_4) 32* (semi caking)	84-82	5.0-5.5	2.5	0.5	8-11
	High volatile (B_5) (non caking)		4.5-5.5	2.5	0.5	10-15
Sub bituminous	noncaking (B_6) 32* slacking on weathering	80-78	4.5-5.0	2	0.5	15-17
Lignites or brown coals	Normal lignite(L_1) 45-55	78-65	4.5-5.5	1	1	20-30
	Canneloid (L_2) 55-65 Lignite	75-65	5.0-6.0	1	1	20-30
Peat		60-65	5.5-6.5	1-3	0.5	30-40

Source: Rao, (1992)

* Some (tertiary) coals from Assam contain upto 4% of organic sulphur

Table 3.16. Composition of fly-ash from Indraprastha Power Plant, New Delhi (after Bhatia 1978)

Components	*Percentage*
SiO_2	58
Al_2O_3	24
Fe_2O_3	7
CaO	4
MgO	2
SO_3	1
$K_2O + N_2O$	1.5
P_2O_5	0.6
SnO_2	0.5
Ni, Be, V, Hg, Se, Mn	Traces

Source: Bhatia (1978)

Table 3.17. Comparison of elements in coal and fly-ash: determined with neutron activation analysis

Element	Ppm concentration		Element	ppm concentration	
	Coal	fly-ash		Coal	fly-ash
Na	289	1,299	Se	22.1	10.6
K	2,075	18,275	Zn	5539	2027
La	47.6	238	Fe	20,888	1,06,665
Ce	30.2	145	Te	1.53	5.05
Hg	11.0	48	Co	33.4	12.8
Tb	1.83	8.87	Eu	0.95	5.6
Th	5.34	25.0	Sm	0.65	1.99
Cr	62.8	40.4	Au	0.06	0.69
Hf	7.1	32.6			

Source: Kamath, (1979)

Table 3.18 Chemical composition of cement manufactured at the churk cement factory (data provided by the factory authorities)

Constituent	Weight(%)
SiO_2	22.0 - 24.0
Fe_2O_3	2.5 - 3.0
Al_2O_3	5.0 - 7.0
CaO	62.5 - 64.0
MgO	3.0 - 4.0
K_2O	NA
SO_3	2.0 - 2.5
	1.0 - 3.0 (Ignition loss)

Source: Rao, (1992)

f. Petro coke.

The Petro coke particles emanate from the coaking in oil refineries. These particles may contain upto 90% fixed carbon and upto 10% volatile matter along with sulphur and other minerals (Table 3.21) (Rao, 1992).

g. Combined gaseous pollutants

Some of the species found effective in checking the harmful effects of air pollutant mixtures are *Emblica officinalis, Polyalthia longifolia, Acacia nilotica, Ficus bengalensis, Zizyphus mauritiana, Alstonia scholaris, Eucalyptus citriodora, Psidium guajava, Syzygium cumini, Casuarina equisetifolia, Pithecolobium dulce, Anthocephalus chinensis, Artocarpus heterophyllus, Ailanthus excelsa, Madhuca indica, Mimusops elengi, Azadirachta indica, Ficus infectoria, Butea monosperma, Holoptelia integrifolia, Ficus religiosa, Lagerstroemia indica, Prosopis juliflora, Dalbergia sissoo, Albizzia lebbeck, and Tamarindus indica.*

3.2.4 Tolerance Level & Air Pollution Tolerance Index

The extent of plant injury due to air pollution's may vary from species to species depending on their tolerance to pollutants. *Tolerance* is defined as the capacity of plants to withstand the effects of pollutants without significant reduction in quality or quantity of yield. Species with low tolerance to a specific pollutant are often called *sensitive* and these can serve as biological indicators of that pollutant (Rao, 1992).

The concept of using certain plant species as environmental indicators and resistant species is fairly well established in the field of ecology. Selection of species for a given situation is of utmost importance. Using results of the experiments and various other available data, trees have been categorised into *sensitive, intermediate* and *pollution resistant* species. Table 3.23 suggests the degree of sensitivity of some tree species to different air pollutants. In western United States certain species have been used as indicators of biotia and soil (Table 3.22). This has followed the publication of the significant work of Fedric E. Clements (1920) on "Plant Indicators". Technically there is no satisfactory definition of a '*pollutant indicator*' or '*bioindicator*'. It may be stated that in functional sense an indicator plant is one which exhibits injury or stress symptoms when exposed to phytotoxic concentration of a pollutant or a combination of pollutants. In general, the plants which have been suggested to have indicator values are listed in Table 3.22.

Singh and Rao (1983) have recently made an attempt of proposing a method of determining air pollution tolerance index (APTI) by synthesising the values of four different biochemical parameters. The four parameters used in the APTI are leaf extract pH, ascorbic acid, total chlorophyll and relative water contents (RWC). The value of APTI is computed as follows:-

$$APTI = \frac{[A(T + P)] + R}{10}$$

where, A is the ascorbic acid content, T is the total chlorophyll, P is the leaf extract pH and R is the relative water content of the leaf. On the basis of these studies Singh and Rao (1983) have made analysis of deciduous evergreen and herbaceous plants in and around Varanasi and have ascribed APTI values which appear in Tables 3.24-3.26.

Table 3.19. Cement dust deposition in the vicinity of a cement factory

Deposit	Distance from factory (km)	
	(mg/cm²/day)	*Tons/ha/30 days*
0.35	0.9181	3.7543
0.50	1.0870	3.2610
0.74	0.2506	0.7518
1.00	0.0231	0.0693
Average	0.5697	1.7091

Source: Parthasarthy et al., (1975)

Table 3.20: Cement dust deposited on maize leaves from top downwards in ten vicinity factory

Particulars	*Total deposit (g/leaf)*
First leaf	0.071
Second leaf	1.860
Third leaf	2.381
Fourth leaf	3.016
Fifth leaf	2.156

Source: Parthasarthy et al., (1975)

Table 3.21: Characteristics of petrococke particals (based on data provided by quality controls, Baranui Oil Refineries)

Characteristics	*Weight(%)*
Fixed Carbon	87-90
Volatile matter	8-10
Shulphur	0.8
Ash	0.2
Average particle size(mm)	51.0
Bulk density (g/ml)	0.7

Pollution resistant trees have been found to tolerate air pollutants, show good growth rate, mitigate the bad effects of air pollution effectively, and also check the physical flow of fly ash into the neighboring human settlements. Cultivation of air pollution resistant trees can be undertaken in the areas outlined in Table 3.27. Selection of species should be done on the basis of type of pollution and site condition. Whenever possible, plants may be raised as stands rather than growing them in isolation and their management has to reflect the concern for maintaining and improving the quality of environment.

Table 3.22 : Degree of sensitivity of some trees species to different air pollutants

Pollution	Sensitivity species	Intermediate species	Resistant species
Sulphur dioxide	*Callistemon viminalis,*	*Tilia americana,*	*Thuja occidentalis,*
	Cassia fistula,	Ricinus communis,	Citrus sinenses,
	Ulmus americana,	Prunus virginiana,	Eucalyptus globulus,
	Ulmus parvifolia,	Prunus ceragifera,	Sesbania aegyptica,
	Delonx regia,	Populaus deltoides,	Prosopis juliflora,
	Ficus glomerata,	Ulmus americana,	Tilia cordata,
	Var. typica,	Hibiscus rosasinensis	Plantanus acerifloria,
	Sygium cumini,	Azadiracha indica,	
	Pongamia pinnata,	Terminalia tomentosa,	
	Petrospermum acerifolium,	Populaus baisamifera	
	Morus microphylla,		
	Morus alba,		
	Pyrus communs,		
	Ficus religiosa,		
	Populus nigra,		
	Heavea brasiliensis		
Flouridea	***Prunus persica,***	***Prunus americana,***	***Ulmus americana,***
	Pinus mugho,	Thuja occidentalis,	Tilia americana,
	Prunus domestica,	Prunus avium,	Pyrus communis,
	Tilia cordata,	Prunus virgiana,	Plantanus acerifolia,
	Morus rubra,	Prunus cerasitera,	
	Citrus sinensis,	Ailanthus altissima	
	Rhus galbra,		
	Juglans nigra,		

Mercury vapours	Juglans regia, *Taxus cuspidata* ***Lingustrum vulgare*** Prunus persica, Diospyros virginiana, *Ligustrum vulgare*	***Acer palmatum,***	—
Hydrogen sulphate	—	***Ricinus communts***	***Malva parvitlora,*** Prunus serotina *Prunus persica*
Nitrous oxide	***Melaleuca teucadendron,*** *Hibiscus rosasinensis*	*Citrus sinensis*	*Carissa sarandas*
Ethylene	***Prunus persica,*** *Ligustrum vulgare*	***Thuja occidentalis,*** *Gardenia radicans*	—
2,4 Dichloro phenoxy acetic acid	***Ailanthus altissima*** ***Morus alba***	***Prunus virginiana,***	*Pyrus communts*
Chlorine	***Aesculus hippocastanum,*** Ligustrum vulgare, Ailanthus altissima	***Prunus serotina,*** Nyssa syvatica, Prunus persica	—
Hydrogen Chloride	***Betula verrucosa,*** ***Corylus avellana,*** Larix europea, *Larix leptolepis*	***Aesculus hippocastanum,*** ***Robinia pseudoacacia,*** Pinus sylvestris, *Sorbus intermedia*	***Juniperus comunts,*** ***Quercus penduculata,*** Pyrus communts
Ozone	***Spiraea prunifolia,*** Gledtschia tricanthos, Lingustrum vulgare, Plantanus occidentalis		

Source: Rawat & Banerjee, (1996)

Table 3.23: List of plant indicators of Air pollution

SO_2 INDICATOR

Non - flowering plants

- Alternaria tenuis
- Aspergillus niger
- Fusarium moniliformi
- Penicilium nigricans
- Rhizopus nigricans

Flowering plants

Annual	Herb	Shrub	Trees
Amaranthus virdis,	Carthanmus tinctorius,	Nerium indicum	Adenia cordifolia,
Abelmoschus	Gossypium sp.		Buchananialanzan
esculantus, Archis	Helianthus annus,		Butea monosperma,
hyhoger, Brassica	Hibiscus esculentus		Diospyros
nigra, Cymaopsis	Hordeum sp.		meleanaxylon,
tetragonoloba, Glycine	Lactuca sativa,		Mangifera indica,
max, hordeum vulgare,	Medicago sativa,		Pyrus malus,
Ipomoca crassicauli,	Spinacea oleracea		Pinus sp.
Medicage			
sativa,			
Medicage aureus,			
Phaseolus aureus,			
Phoenix :ylverstris,			
Phaseolus radiatus,			
Pisum sativum,			
Raphaus sativus, Solanum megalongena,			
Spinacca oleracea,			

Triticum aestivum			
FLUORIDE INDICATOR			
Cyanodon dactylon,	—	—	—
CEMENT DUST INDICATOR			
Glycine max, Triticum aestivum	Calotropis procera Withania sominifera	—	Cassia fistula Dalbergia sissoo
FLY-ASH INDICATOR			
Triticum aestivum	—	—	—
PETRO-COKE INDICATOR			
Phaseolus aureus	—	—	—
SMOKE INDICATOR			
—	—	—	Azadiracta indica
DUST INDICATOR			
Triticum aestivum			
HERBICIDE INDICATOR			
Cicer arictinum,	Helianthus annus	— Mangifera Polyalthia Thespesia populnea	Erythrina indica, indica, longifolia,
COMBINATION OF POLLUTANTS			
Brassica oleracea, Chenopdium album, Cicer arictinum, Commelina benghalensis, Dolichos lablab, Glycine max, Helianthus annus, Medicago saliva, Sonchus asper	Croton sparsiflorum, Withania sominifera	Lantana camara, Nerium, Odoratum, Tobernaemontana, Coronaria	Aegle marmelos, Diosyros melanoxylon, Mangiferaindica, Melia indica, Tectona grandis

Source : Varshney, (1992)

Table 3.24 Deciduous trees arranged in decreasing order of their air pollution tolerance index(APTI) determined on the basis of leaf extract pH, ascorbic acid, total chlorophyll and relative water contents (RWC)

Plant species	*Total* chlorophyll (mg/g dry wt)	pH	*Ascorbic* acid (mg/g dry wt)	RWC	APTI %
Ficus religosa	15.21	8.2	10.65	87	34x2
Albizzia lebbik	8.22	6.2	18.44	47	31x2
Cassia fistula	7.01	5.9	15.44	63	27x2
Phyllunthus distichus	8.59	5.7	17.07	27	23x2
Zizyphus jujuba	9.95	6.0	9.89	74	19x2
Azadirachta indica	7.05	6.2	12.21	74	19x2
Phyllanthus emblica	9.37	6.2	8.27	64	19x2
Sapindus mukorassi	5.27	7.0	8.21	68	16x2
Tamarindus indica	6.85	4.0	6.00	86	15x2
Psidium guyava	6.22	6.2	5.10	73	14x2
Morus alba	2.96	5.4	6.08	64	12x2
Moringa oleifera	6.08	6.1	2.66	68	12x2
Anthocephalus cadamba	7.92	5.1	2.95	81	12x2
Bombax ceiba	3.79	6.2	2.66	68	10x2
Madhuca indica	4.73	5.6	2.51	67	9x2
Aegle marmelos	3.05	6.0	1.62	74	9x2
Feronia elephantum	2.02	5.8	1.34	75	9x2
Cordia myxa	5.51	8.3	2.54	42	8x2
Delonix regia	5.96	6.2	2.55	34	7x2
Bambusa banbos	12.16	6.7	1.41	30	6x2
Butea frondosa	4.72	6.3	1.61	34	5x2
Tectona grandis	5.59	7.2	0.35	48	5x2
Dalbergia sissoo	5.13	6.6	0.94	18	3x2

Source: Rao, (1992)

Table 3.25: Evergreen trees arrangedin the decreasing order of their air pollution tolerance index(APTI) determined on the basis of leaf extract pH, ascrobic acid, total chlorophyll and relative water contents (RWC)

Plant species	*Total* chlorophyll *(mg/g dry wt)*	pH	*Ascorbic* acid *(mg/g dry wt)*	RWC	APTI %
Ficus glomerata	18.89	8.4	9.41	71	32
Pithecelobium dulce	17.21	6.0	8.35	87	28
Polyalthia longifolia	6.56	6.0	8.75	78	19
Ficus infectoria	6.58	7.9	7.51	76	9
Nerium odorum	2.39	6.0	8.17	84	15
Eucalypthus citriodora	4.59	5.2	6.61	85	15
Ficus infectoria	7.81	7.2	5.12	68	15
Leucaena leucocephala	10.41	5.7	4.42	72	14
Mangifera indica	3.89	5.2	4.12	72	11
Anona squamosa	4.66	5.4	4.11	60	10
Syzyglium jambolana	7.07	4.5	2.86	68	10
Acacia arabica	2.54	6.1	3.94	54	9
Artocarpus heterophyllus	6.30	6.2	3.12	48	9
Astonia scholaris	3.68	6.5	2.89	64	9
Grewia asiatica	1.85	5.6	2.10	74	9
Casuarina equisetifolia	0.75	5.3	1.79	56	7
Nyctanthes arbortristis	6.96	6.8	1.46	34	5
Litchi chinensis	1.74	6.1	0.70	40	5

Source : Rao, (1992)

Table 3.26 Shrubs and Herbs, arranged in decreasing order of their air pollution tolerance index(APTI) determine on the basis of leaf extract pH, ascorbic acid, total cholorphyll and relative water content (RWC)

Plant species	Total chlorophyll (mg/g dry wt)	pH	Ascorbic acid (mg/g dry wt)	RWC	APTI %
*Shrub Bougainvillea spectabilis*1	2.64	6.0	13.36	70	32
Calotropis gigantea pinsettia	13.58	6.3	9.34	63	25
Poinsttia pulcherrima	17.63	5.9	7.41	77	25
Ricinus communis	18.80	6.0	5.35	83	25
Rosa indica	4.75	5.6	9.25	71	17
Calotropis procera	5.07	6.1	8.64	61	16
Durania plumieri	8.00	5.7	6.10	69	15

{Cont.}....

Murraya exotica	6.67	6.1	4.23	72	13
Lantana indica	5.52	7.5	2.33	33	6
Lagerrstroemia indica	2.56	4.3	0.34	42	4
Carissa carandas	2.52	5.7	0.80	63	3
Herb. Vinca rosa	9.43	5.8	19.50	75	37
Croton tiglium	12.29	6.0	9.33	78	25
Argemone mexicama	22.48	6.2	5.14	63	21
Ageratum conyzodes	23.81	6.6	3.33	64	17
Phyllanthus niruri	5.68	5.5	7.96	78	17
Clerodendron infortunatum	6.57	5.7	9.34	48	16
Ocimum bascilicum	6.21	6.1	4.50	73	13
Cynodon dactylon	11.55	6.2	1.50	66	9
Leucas aspera	5.98	6.9	2.93	54	9
Musa sapienttum	2.33	6.4	3.14	57	9
Ipomoea correa	8.54	6.2	1.76	68	9
Euphorbia hirta	12.25	5.9	1.90	55	9
Dichanthium annulatum	10.43	6.2	0.91	50	7
Chrozophor sp.	5.57	5.9	0.31	38	4

Data from Singh and Rao (1983)

3.3 NOISE POLLUTION ATTENUATION

Robinette (1969) pointed out that plants are efficient absorbers of noise especially of high frequency. Border planting along highways and streets can be effective if plantings are lower towards the noise and higher towards the hearer, thus not only absorbing but deflecting the noise upward. The '*Ashok*' and '*Neem*' trees are regarded as the best sound absorbers. They can be planted infront of residential and industrial buildings as well as along the road sides (Bhutani, 1992).

When the sound wave hits an obstacle it is bent, reflected or absorbed. Trees reduce noise either by absorbing or suppressing it. The wood of deciduous trees, being of laminar structure, rather absorbs and transmits sonic waves, though in the meantime, by adsorption, they also reduce their intensity. The cylindrical needles of conifers rather distribute sonic waves and these by mutual interference are reduced. A 30m wide, mixed deciduous and coniferous, dense forest belt reduces noise by 60-80% (Meister 1959).

The Minneapolis St. Paul Metropolitan Airports Commission and Ontario Hydro, a power company, have attempted to reduce noise disturbance to the acceptable level with the help of green belts (Sharma & Kaur, 1995). The Indian standards for noise levels in different zones are mentioned in Table 3.28.

David Egan (1988) has dealt with the problems of noise on the highways and how to reduce its intensity by erection of barrier of solid wood followed by shrub planting. The system proposed by him reduced highway traffic noise of 80 dBA at the site. He found planting of thorny *Elaeagnus purgens* at both slopes absorbed sound appreciably. Dense planting of trees and shrubs atleast 100 feet deep can provide 7 to 11 dB of sound attenuation (Chaudhuri, 1993). The attenuation from trees according to him, is mainly due to branches and leaves (sound energy near the ground will not be significantly reduced) and deciduous trees will provide almost no attenuation during the months when their leaves have fallen. A single row of trees has no value as an accoustal barrier. Paradoxically, where a single row of trees is added to solve an existing noise problem, the situation may seem worse because listeners tend to overestimate loudness when the view of the noise source is blocked. Many rows of trees have some value as an acoustical barrier. However, attenuations from dense plantings more than 100 feet deep will be limited by the flanking of sound energy over the top of the canopy of trees. He, however, is of opinion that the vegetation planted for this purpose should be evergreen, the canopy should be closed, belt should be sufficiently long, dense, foliage must extend to the ground. About earth barms he says that when completely converted by grass and other sound absorbing plant material it can be effective isolators, reducing noise by 5 to 10 dBA. They can be as effective as reflective thin wall barriers or low barms which have this wall barriers along this top. The effectiveness of earth barms can be reduced by reflective top surface (asphalt or concrete path) and deciduous trees which can scatter sound energy, thus reducing attenuation by 5 dB or more (Chaudhure, 1993).

Table 3.27: Potential areas for planting in cities

Areas for planting	Silvicultural characteristics	Suggested species
Factories and industrial premises	Ability to grow adverse site and collect the dust, fly ashes etc.,	*Acacia nilotica, Aegla marmelos, Ailanthus excelsa, Albizzia lebbeck, Alstonia scholaris, Azadirachta indica, Dalbergia sissoo, and Bougainvillea spp.*
Mined area around the Cities	Ability to build-up adequate capital of organic matter in the newly formed soil	*Prosopis juliflora, Acacia nilotica, Dalbergia sissoo.*
Road side plantations	Air pollution resistant tree species with good crown and foliage, to provide shade and to cater the aesthetic values	*Ficus bengalensis, Azadriachta indica, Alstonia scholanis, Tamarindus indica, Aegla marmelos, Ailanthus excelsa, Albizzia lebbeck, Holoptelea integrifolia, Lagerstroemia indica, Syzygium cumini, Nerium indicum etc.,*
Lands assigned for development activities	Fast-growing short-rotation species	*Prosopis juliflora, Acacia nilotica, Sesbania grandiflora, Populus deltoides, etc.*
Premises of educational and training institutions	Intermediate pollution resistant trees and shrubs with beautiful flowers and foliage	*Dalbergia sissoo, D.latifolia, Jacaranda mimosifolia, Swietenia mahogany, S. macrophylla, Peltoforum ferruginosum, Samanea saman, Spathodiacampanulata, Millettia ovalifolia, Lagerstoemia indiac, Erythrina indica, Hibiscus rosasinensis, Murraya*

		exotica, Cassia biflora.
Compound of residence, public buildings, and park and gardens	Tolerance to environmental stressness and catering the aesthetic values.	*Achras sapota, Artocarpus integrifolia, Dwarf varieties of mango, Citrus species, Nycthanthes arbortristis, Michelia champaka, Ixora coccinia, Murraya paniculata, Gardenia spp. Anona squamosa, etc.,*
Premises of saced place	Intermediate pollution resistant trees and shrubs with beautiful flowers and foliage	*Michelia champaka, Nyctanthes arbortristis, Hibiscus rosasinens, Plumeria acertifolia, Nerium indicum, Lxora coccinia, Gardenia jasminoides, Jasminum spp.,etc*
High-tension lines	Small shrubs should not touch wires	*Oscium sancrtrum, Mentha spicata, Solanum nigrum, Catharanthus tinctorius, Withania somnifera etc.,*
Drainage channels	Ability to absorb foul smells, heavy metals and other pollutants	*Salix tetrasperma, Phragimites Arundo donax, Lpomaea pescarprae, Datura inoxia, etc.,*

Source : Rao, (1992)

Table 3.28. Indian standards for noise levels in different zones

Area	Noise limits Leq dB(A)	
	Day Time	Night Time
Silence zone	50	45
Residential area	55	45
Commercial area	65	55
Industrial area	75	65

Aylor (1971) studied the effects of leaf area, stem diameter and density, and ground conditions on the transmission of sound between a source and receiver the reports that foliage reduces sound transmission, especially at higher frequencies with increase in leaf area density and should increase with increase in leaf area thickness. When foliage is absent or much reduced, the stems reduce the high frequency sound. Attenuation by vegetation and ground decreases with increasing distance from the source, the efficiency of a band of ground or vegetation decreases with increasing width of the band.

As large spaces may not always be available, it seems appropriate to opt for vegetative mufflers rather than large open areas to achieve the same degree attenuation. For example, the loudness of a 1000 Hz tone is reduced by a little more half by one hundred feet of dense corn to achieve the same attenuation without the vegetation cover, the distance between the point source and receiver has to be than doubled (Abbasi, 1998).

A comparative study of noise attenuation by bushes and hedges (Table 3.29) shows that hedges serve as better sound absorbers than bushes. The attenuation by hedge increases with its (density) thickness and also with its proximity to the road. Thus, thick and dense hedges with low reflectivity, serve as good attenuators of sound (Padmanabhamurthy & Satapathy, 1995). Suitable hardy and perennial local varieties can attain sufficient height, density and thickness if utilised for hedges serve most as noise mitigators in the streets (Table 3.30).

The characteristics and structure of vegetation which plays an important role in noise pollution attenuation are:

Table 3.29. SPL (sound protection level) attenuation by different vegetation

Site	*Characteristics of the* bushes/ hedge attenuation,dB	*Average* (Delhi Area)
SPL attenuation by bushes		
Seikh Sarai	Height: 210 cm, thickness: 175 cm Distance from Road : 225m	2.0
Bhikaji cama place	Height: 210 cm, thickness: 176 cm Distance from the road: 68 m	2.0
India Gate	Height: 210 cm, thickness:175 cm. Distance from the Road: 380 m	2.0
I.I.T. Gate	Height: 210 cm, thickness: 175 cm Distance from the road: 100 m	2.0
SPL attenuation by hedges		
Seikh Sarai	Height: 228 cm, thickness: 145 cm Distance from the road 226 m	3.0
Bhikaji cama place	Height: 90 cm, thickness:97 cm Distance from the road: 68 m	2.0
India Gate	Height: 150 cm, thickness: 55 cm Distance from the road: 4m	
I.I.T. Gate	Height: 210 cm, thickness: 175 cm Distance from the road: 190 m	4.0

Source: Padmanabhamurthy & Satapathy, (1995)

i. Trees having thick and fleshy leaves with flexible petioles having capacity to withstand vibration are suitable. Heavier branches and trunk of the trees also deflect or refract the sound waves (Sivasamy & Srinivasam, 1995).

ii. For noise reduction (in screen planting), plant leaves should be as big as possible and strong and hard in structure; the leaves should overlap scale-wise and their position should preferably be perpendicular to the angle of incidence of the noise; foliage density is also necessary in the inner vegetation zone; deciduous trees which help dead foliage on their branches in winter (hornbeam, oaks) are more effective than others which screen mainly in summer months; evergreen conifers, though usually believed suitable generally produce but little effective. Some researchers feel that noise reduction of 5-15 dB depending on species is possible planting trees or shrubs (Chaudhuri, 1993)..

Table 3.30. Plants suitable for Noise pollution attenuation are mentioned below :

1. Alstonia scholaris
2. Azadirachia, indica
3. Butea monosperma
4. Erythrina variegala
5. Grevillea robusta
6. Pterospermum acerifolium
7. Tamarindus indica
8. Terminalia arjuna
9. Acer negunda
10. Alnus indica
11. Betula pendula
12. Cornus alba
13. Juniperus chinensis
14. Populus ferolinensis
15. Syringa vulgaris
16. Viburnum lantana.

Source: Sivasamy & Srinivasan, (1995)

iii. Trees, shrubs and tall grass configurations have been shown to reduce sound level by 1/3 to 1/2 of the measured readings recorded over equivalent distances of open surfaces. (Cook, D.I. and Van Haverbeke D.F. - "Trees and Shrubs for Noise abatement" U.S. Forest Service).

The sound absorbing capacity of the plants depend on its structure. The denser the underground and the ground vegetation, and canopied nature of forest, the greater is its vertical closure, and higher is its sound absorbing capacity. A dense belt of 50m width of trees of different heights (vertical mixture) reduces the traffic noise by 20 to 30 decibels, and provides indirect protection against noise.

iv. A combination of tall trees and shrubs 9-13 inch wide is effective in controlling highway noise and this can be further improved when planting is combined with earth buffers that is mounding (Chaudhuri, 1993)..

v. Belts 36m wide and 16m high can reduce highway noise by nearly 50 percent. Different patterns of planting are adopted according to the speed of the vehicles. greenbelts of (small and large) 18 to 30m width, 15 to 27m from traffic lanes with central rows of atleast 13.5m tall are necessary for high speed vehicles, while for moderate speed vehicles, greenbelts (small & large) of 6 to 15m width within the edge of belts from 6 to 15m from the centre of the nearest traffic lane. Shrubs of 1.8 to 4m high should be planted next to traffic lane followed by backup rows of trees 4.5 to 9m tall. (Sivasamy & Srinivasan, 1995)

3.4. ABATEMENT OF GREEN HOUSE EFFECT AND GLOBAL WARMING.

Two of the most serious environmental problems the world is facing today are greenhouse effect and global warming. Both these problems have been caused by the rapidly rising concentrations if air pollutants in the atmosphere (Abbasi et al 1999).

The main factor culprit among the gaseous pollutants introducing green house effect and global warming is carbon dioxide. Carbon dioxide forms 0.03 percent of our atmosphere. Prior to Industrial Revolution, there were 280 parts per million of carbon-dioxide in the atmosphere. By now this has increased are 350 parts per million and a 1.5 parts per million and being added each year (Chaudhuri, 1993).

Thus, over the years, CO_2 content in the air has increased from 0.03% in 1860 to 0.336% presently and is contributing substantially towards greenhouse effect. The atmosphere is getting warmed up beyond the natural levels leading to undesirable consequences. Some of the facets of this phenomena are:-

(a) Carbon dioxide is odourless and transparent gas to be identified visually. About 5 billion tonnes of Carbon dioxide are emitted into the world's atmosphere each year from the burning of fuel from industry and personal activities. Another 1.6 billion tonnes are emitted through burning of tropical forests.

(b) As the population increases, the carbon dioxide levels increase. 3 million years ago there were small, scattered groups of people earth. 250 years ago the world population was 600 million. Today, there are 8 billion people on earth; at some places the population density is 20,000 per square kilometre.

c) A fast growing tree absorbs upto 22 kilograms of Carbondioxide per year, that is, about 10 tonnes per acre of tree is enough to offset the carbondioxide produced by driving a car 34,000 km.

d) Comparing a single rural tree with a single urban tree, scientists at Lawrence Berkeley Laboratory, California, estimate that the urban tree is 15 times more valuable in limiting carbon dioxide build up. The survival ratio of green plants to animals/human is 99:1, that is in order to maintain the existence of one part of the animal population, 99 parts of green plants should be maintained.

Green belts provide for regeneration of the atmosphere not only through removal of pollutants but also through utilisation of CO_2 by vegetation, production of water and oxygen, and modulation of temperature and wind. Trees use carbon dioxide in photosynthesis. Throughout the world growing plants soak up some 120 billion tons of carbon a year - more than 20 times the amount of carbon released by burning fossil fuels. It has been calculated that planting an area of trees twice the size of France would absorb 660 million tons of carbon each year for the next three decades until the trees became mature-about ten per cent of net carbon emissions. It has been said that if the tree cover of land in Britain is doubled from the present 10 per cent to 20 per per cent, and broadleaved trees planted, that would absorb some 3 million tons of carbon each year. Similar impacts can be achieved in India (Chaudhuri, 1993).

It is interesting to note that one of the great 'sinks' for carbon dioxide in the oceans is the plant life. It is estimated that ten billion tons of carbon dioxide are 'fixed' each year as a result of photosynthesis by plant life in the oceans. Sea weeds use some 10 per cent of it and the rest is used by the various types of plankton. Of the carbon dioxide which disappears into the oceans about half dissolves into the water and the other half is taken by the plankton. So it has been suggested that if the growth of plankton can be increased, large portions of carbon dioxide from air can be captured (Chaudhuri, 1993).

- The capacity (per hour) of a 100 year old beach tree for carbon dioxide intake is 2352 gram (from 4800 m^3 of air), water intake 960 gram, sugar production 1600 gram and oxygen output 1712 gram. Converting these figures for green area with trees, shrubs and turf means that 1 ha whose leaf surface is 5 ha in it's full grown state draws 900 kg carbon dioxide from air in 12 hours and releases 600 kg of oxygen. The behaviour of CO_2 and O_2 gases with respect to man's utility is explained as follows: (Chaudhuri, 1993):
- A man's oxygen needs are met from oxygen production of 150 m^2 of leaf surface per year.
- The maximum CO_2, (hourly) intake amounts to 150 mg per day per m^2 of leaf surface under optimum condition in terms of light, water supply, temperature and artificial increase of Carbon dioxide contents in air to 1 volume per cent.
- About 2.7 billion acres of new forest plantation would be required to absorb the Carbon-dioxide generated by fossil fuel combustion at the rate prevailing in 1962.
- Oxygen release from a tree of 25 m height, 15 m crown diameter, 2700 m^3 crown volume, 160 m^2 crown cover, outer leaf surface 1600 m^2, inner leaf area (sum of intercellular walls) 160,000 m^2, wood volume 15 m^3, dry substances of wood 12000 kg. tied up carbon 6000 kg. CO_2 intake 2352 gr/hour, water intake 960 gm/hour, sugar production 1600 gm/hour, is 1.7 kg or 1712 gm/hour (CO_2 consumption is 2.35 kg) (Chaudhuri, 1993).

3.5. IMPROVING MICRO-CLIMATE, IMPROVING WATER RETENTION POTENTIAL AND SOIL CONSERVATION.

A dense vegetation significantly affects the micro-climate of the area. This is turn affects soils, plant-life and water -balance (Singh, 1986).

Plants reduce extremes of climate. A large number of deaths are reported in our country due to sun-stroke (loo) and severe cold waves in the plains of India. This malady can be controlled to a great extent by planting trees; trees lower the temperature by controlling solar radiation. However, their effectiveness depends on the density of foliage, leaf shape, branching pattern etc. It is said that a single isolated tree transpires approximately 40 litres of water per day. However, this depends on plant species, their habitat, climatic conditions, soil type, etc.: when the relative humidity increases in the vicinity of tree-planted block, people living near by get relief from the glaring sun shine. Their working efficiency is increased because of better comfort level (Singh, 1986).

There is ample interception and filtration of solar radiation through trees. They inhibit wind flow and reduce evaporation of soil moisture by their crowns above and a thick layer of fallen leaves create a mulching layer on the ground. Thus, beneath the canopy of the trees humidity is usually higher and evaporation rates are lower. Temperature become low during the day and warm during the evening than the surrounding area. At night tree canopy minimises the loss of heat (Singh, 1986).

Forests also have indirect effects on water availability by interception, stem flow, transpiration etc. (Sarkar and Kelkar, 1977). Trees help in making winters comparatively warmer and the summers cooler.

Tree control temperature following means (Chaudhuri, 1993) :

(a) Trees planted around homes, along streets, in parking lots, parks and green belts can break up the 'heat islands' that develop around urban communities.
(b) Masses of trees are needed throughout a city rathar than isolated trees.
(c) Heat surrounding a tree is removed by evaporating water, 4.2 kilo joules of heat is removed from the air from each gram of water which is converted from liquid into vapour. This cooling effect could reduce air conditioning costs from 10 to 50 percent.
(d) In winter, even large deciduous trees eddy the straight line winds which cause chilling.

The climate beneath the tree crown shows reduced temperature (annual, monthly and diurnal), increased minimum temperatures. Negative departures (lower minimum in the forest than in the open) have also been recorded. Studies by Krishnaswamy, Debral and Prem Nath's (1957) In plantations of *Pinus raxburghii, Butea monosperma, Casuarina equisitifolia* and *cupressus torulosa,* have indicated that

(i) temperature under the crown was less than in open,

(ii) *Pinus roxburghii* plantations were coldest during summer and hottest during winter

(iii) the diurnal fluctuations in temperature have been significantly higher in the open than under forest conditions iv) bare ground got heated more repidly than the ground under vegetation cover v) least variation between temperatures in the open and under plantation was observed during July and

(iv) temperatures at ground level and at 152 cm above it were higher under a forest canopy than at similar levels in the open during winter nights. Similar work has been done in an *Araucaaria cumninghamii* plantation, in New Forest, Dehradun (Singh, 1986).

Debral, Rao and Qureshi (1969) made a study of extreme weather elements (temperature, its diurnal range and humidity) inside forest plantations of *Pinus roxburghii* and *Dendrocalamus strictus*. They found that air temperature was modified by the sheltering as well as blanketing effects of vegetation cover. Fair weather conditions (winter) induced the maximum differences in the temperature pattern (Rao, 1979).

Debral and Premnath (1972) reported the results of microclimatic studies (air temperatures and vapour pressure) under a *Tectona grandis* plantation where the forest cover modified the air temperatures, the effects being more pronounced during the winter season. Under the plantations inversion took place during day time which generally occured at night in the open.

Seth and Debral (1959) observed the ameliorative effects of forests canopy on climatic extremes during first period and have attributed same to (i) warmth of the ground and subsoil and (ii) very little temperatures inversion.

Reduction of wind velocity in forested area is very well known. Forests exert a profound influence on the hydrological regime of a locality (Rao, 1979).

Vegetational soils in comparison with grassland soils, have greater porosity. They tend to encourage infiltration and absorption of water and thus enrich under ground water supplies. Well stocked vegetational with deep rooted trees have a moisture storage capacity varying 50,000 to 2,00,000 m^3 of water per sq.km (Shukla, 1983).

Rain falling on a treeless watershed strikes the unprotected ground with the full force of the storm. Individual drops hit like bombs, gonging, beating and battering the soil, lifting and spashing it back and forth, chirmy it into a pasty mud that rapidly fills and clogs the pores and passages through which water might enter the soil. Soon the badly compacted ground can no longer absorb the overflow which now collects on the surface and if the surface is sloping as is usually the case, races down hill in million of little currents (Singh, 1986).

Plants check flood havoc during rainy season. They also help in regulating the water supply in rivers during winter and summer. Tree belts act in lessening the hazards of floods in high rainfall areas. They impede and reduce the velocity of rain-water rushing into the rivers. They reduce the excessive silting of the river beds thereby increasing their carrying capacity (Singh, 1986).

In drought affected areas vegetation cover reduces the drought hazards because trees are more hardy than agricultural crops. Planting of trees improve water level in wells.

Planting of trees (Table 3.31) in the catchment areas near dams, water reservoirs, canals and rivers will prevent the erosion of the top soil to a great extent, and will reduce the problem of siltation of reservoirs by reducing the velocity of rushing rain water full of mud. The comprehensive studies conducted at the soil Conservation Research Institute, Dehra Dun reported the possibility of reducing the sedimentation load from 80.5 tonnes per hectare per year to 7.4 tonnes per hectare in a period of four years by plantation of trees and construction of gully plugs, check dams and debris basins (Tejwani, 1977). Planting of trees intercepts rainwater resulting in the reduction of run-off and increasing downward movement of rain water into the soil. Thus, under ground storage of water increases. This water, which is of better quality can easily be lifted artificially for drinking and for irrigation of crops for longer periods (Singh, 1986).

3.6. AESTHETICS, RECREATION AND HEALTH

In recent years some State Governments in India have attempted beautifying various Towns and Cities. For example, The Department of Forests, West Bengal has a wing designated as "Parks and Gardens".

It is against this background that the raising of shrubs (and of course the trees and herbs) in various sites such as school and college premises, club premises, road sides, industrial sites, city parks, port areas, garbage dump sites, residential quarters sites should be considered essential both for aesthetic and environmental requirements (Rao, 1983). Even as aesthetics and important, the choice of species should aim at value addition including by fruit trees (Mango, Jack fruit , Jaman, Tamarind, Bael, Litche, etc.)(Chaudhuri, 1993).

Table 3.31 Species suitable for catchment areas

1. Acacia catechu	2. Acacia ferruginea
3. Acacia leucophloea	4. Acacia modesta
5. Acacia nilotica	6. Acacia planifrons
7. Acacia sundra	8. Anacardium occidentale
9. Azadirachta indica	10. Choloroxylon swietina
11. Cassia siamea	12. Dalbergia sissoo
13. Dodonaea viscosa	14. Eucalyptus hybrid
15. Hardwickia binata	16. Lannea grandis
17. Prosopis juliflora	18. Pterocarpus marsupium
19. Pterocarpus santalinus	20. Syzyglum cumini
21. Tamarindus indica	22. Tamarix articulata
23. Terminalia arjuna	24. Terminalia belerica
25. Zizyphus mauritiana	

Source : Singh, (1986)

While choosing a species for landscape, the size, form of crown, height of tree, flowering season, period of leaflesseness, etc. have to be kept in view. Plants selected for planting close to buildings must have the qualities of light crown, fragrant flowers, small to medium size trees. Species chosen must be of assorted varieties which is necessary to get flowers at different times and to get flowers of various colours. As such phenological and anti-ecological qualities of a species both the short term as well as long term effect of planting of a particular species are to be kept in mind. In choosing a species the moisture and soil type requirement are very important. A mosaic of different aged stand of trees gives great beauty as well as the widest range of habitats. Mixed age, mixed species planting is often desirable. Sometimes a pure stand of a single species can have a beauty and character of their own; light crowned trees sometimes are preferable to thick and dark crowned trees (Chaudhuri, 1993).

If the Indian landscape designers for tree planting study the vast number of Indian species in the forests, they will have a wide range of choice. India has a rich repertoire of species to choose for particular soil or climate. Some species have been introduced long back which have attractive crown and flower; such as:

Spathodea campanulata
Coroupita guinensis
Cresentia cajute
Acacia millissima
Eucalyptus globulus
E. tereticornis
Oreodoxa regia
Indigofera tasmaniana

It is possible to chose species to screen dust, absorb sound, provide shade, besides proving beautiful foliage and fragrant flowers (Table 3.32). Trees are an important part of the townscape. There are purely visual pleasures to be derived from looking at isolated trees. In urban scenes, it is often the visual play of a mass of natural foliage contrasted with the built forms which is important and which adds upto a sum that in total is greater than that of its parts. Trees provide contrast of colours, texture and form in a built environment, introducing shapes, colours and feeling for nature into the man-made geometric pattern of roads and building (Shukla, 1983).

In the change of colour with the passing of the seasons, trees provide endless variety and delight, with fresh greenery and gay blossoms in spring, swollen crowns of foliage casting heavy shade in summer, ripening fruit and seed and vivid autumn colours. Even in winter, those which shed their leaves still provide visual pleasure in the delicate sculpture of naked branches casting intricate shadows on brick or concrete walls and pavings or silhouettes against the sky (Clouston 1990) (Chaudhuri, 1993).

Trees and green surroundings are vital for human existence especially in the cities where the natural rhythm of life processes is disturbed. In modern day's landscaping choice of species must in most of the cases is influenced by ecological facts. The species should naturally adapt to the site, should be aesthetic in their forms.

The smell of the flowers, sight of colourful petals, ripening fruit or dying leaves all have association with nature and temper the artificial appearance of urban surroundings.

Trees provide a sense of Belonging: Milwankee in Wisconsin, USA, is often quoted as a model for other cities. Over 300 people are employed to care for over 300,000 street trees. Along the boulevards more than 60 species of trees are used, interspersed with shrubs and beds of annuals. Each tree is chosen to fit into the architectural

Table 3.32: List of Graceful and Shade trees.

Graceful Trees	
1. Salix babylonica	2. Callisteoon viminalis
3. Melaleuca teucodendron	4. Alstonia scholaris
5. Terminalia catapa	6. Saraca asoka
7. Brownea hybrida	8. Polyalthia longifolia var pendula
9. Ficus benjamina	10. Ficus comosa
11. Poputus ciliata	12. Dillenia indica
13. Dysaxylum hamiltonii	14. Filicium decipiens
15. Nephalium longana	16. Pyrus sp.
17. Prunus sp.	18. Exbucklandia populnea
19. Anogeissus pendula	20. Sonneretia apetala
21. Brassiopsis hainla	22. B. alphina
23. Holarrhena antidysenteric	24. Leucaena leucocephala
25. Terminalia catapa	26. Tecoma undulata
27. Santalum album	28. sapium baccalum sapium
29. Euphorbia tirucalli	
Shade Trees	
1. Samarea saman	2. Ficus bengalensis
3. Pterocarpus indicus	4. Swietenia mahogony
5. Swietenia macnerophylla	6. Syzigium cumii
7. Terminalia belerica	8. Heritiera macrophylla
9. Mangifera indica	10. Elaeodendron glaucum
11. Ficus benjamina	12. F. comosa
13. F. infectoria	14. Meliosma dilleniaefoia
15. M. thomsonii	16. Mimusops elengi
17. Engethardha specaus	18. Artocarpus heterophylla
19. Peltophorum plterocarpum	20. Diosphyros embryopeties

Source : Chaudhuri, (1993).elements to give visual interest as well as its ability to resist disease and insect damage. They work hard to get the right tree in right place (Chaudhuri, 1993).

Trees are Habitat for birds and animals which further add to the aesthetic values. Generally, birds like to make their habitat, nests, on trees. Further, trees provide shade and hidding places to the wide life. A few trees like banyan, pipal (*Ficus spp.*), neem (*Azadirachta indica*) and semal (*Bombax ceiba*) attract birds by their flower and fruits, and provide a very suitable shelter to a large number of birds. Block planting of trees become an attraction place for bird habitat. Similarly, a large number of wild animals find their suitable habitat under dense plantation. The song of birds, the murmering brook, the rusuling of leaves and branches-all these sounds have a calming effect (Singh, 1986).

GREENWAYS

Greenways are corridors of undeveloped land that link developed areas to outdoor recreational areas. The greenway concept has developed most completely since the 1970s as a synthesis of two earlier landscape designs known as the greenbelt and the parkway (Ruth and William, 1994). Thus, greenways are intended to combine the greenbelt idea of separating developed areas with undeveloped tracts of land and the parkway plan of providing for wooded or landscaped thoroughfares. Designed as linear open spaces, greenways are often established along natural corridors such as river valleys and ridgelines, or along scenic roads, historic trails, and railroad rights-of-way that have been modified for recreational use (Ruth and William, 1994).

Two of the primary purposes of greenways are to add to the quality of life in developed areas and to provide for the maintenance of important ecological functions. They typically connect otherwise isolated parks to areas of development and to one another, allowing urban dwellers to take advantage of a greater area for recreation. Some greenway projects have succeeded in attracting business ventures in outdoor recreation. The linear configuration of greenways has aesthetic as well as practical value. They create the illusion of depth and expansiveness without covering large areas of land. In keeping natural corridors free from extensive development, greenways help to preserve natural ecosystems. Although intended primarily for human use, many greenways also serve as routes for wildlife migration (Ruth and William, 1994).

Landscape projects that fit to the flexible definition of greenways can be found around the U.S. Notable areas include the Willamette River Greenway in Oregon, the Bay and Ridge Trails in the San Francisco Bay area, Boston's Bay Circuit (a part of that city's "Emerald Necklace"), and the greenway project of Boulder, Colorado. The Canopy Roads Linear Parkway in Tallahassee, Florida, is a modern version of a corridor of higharching trees originally built by Creek Indians. The Brooklyn-Queens Greenway connects over forty miles of parks and parkways in the New York City area (Ruth and William, 1994).

The radiation of the sun has thermal, chemical and physical effects on humans. In thick vegetation these are present in a very favourable mixture because of the alteration of glades and lower and higher stock of trees. For all living beings, oxygen is very essential without which life is impossible. Plants supply this to the entire animal kingdom and plant kingdom. Not only this, plants utilize carbon dioxide and in return they release oxygen thereby keeping the environment clean. Plants help in maintaining the balance of gasses in environment. For this very purpose plants act as cleaner of the environment (Kovacs, 1983).

The vegetation produces large quantities of oxygen. It is true that it consumes almost the same quantity for the decomposition of dead matter, but greenary air is still exceptionally rich in oxygen. Vegetational air contains large quantities of volatile oils (terpenes). These deepen respiratory intensity. Some scientists call it "air-vitamins" which have a favourable effect on the human organs.

Some interesting facts (Chaudhuri, 1993):

(a) A person inhales 23,000 times a day, absorbing 16 kilogram of oxygen; it takes about seven trees to provide this amount of oxygen.
(b) 50 tonnes tree produces at least 1 tonne of oxygen per year.
(c) Each year an acre of trees can produce enough oxygen to keep 18 persons alive.
(d) An 18 hole golf course supplies enough oxygen for 6,000 to 8,000 people.

Trees contribution to personal Health :

(a) Rodger Ulrich of the University of Dalaware has reported that hospital patients who could look at trees following surgery had 85 per cent less time in hospital and took fewer pain killing drugs compared to similar patients who had brick walls for views.

(b) He also found that student's exam stress, such as muscle tension, blood pressure, headaches and pulse rates, could be beneficially reduced when the students were shown natural landscape scenes.

(c) American researchers are now considering the calming, recuperative effects that plant have on human health. Some employers are planning green court yards for employees. The New York Police Department has a campaign under way to improve the environment as a mean of diminishing criminal behaviour.

(d) In Australia some rehabilitation programmes for young people run in green environments.

(e) Sport scientists have suggested that an appropriate activity for the prevention of Cardiovascular disease could be improving the quantity and quality of plants in a domestic garden, that is 'pumping green' as might be better for urben health than jogging along our roads or pumping iron in a gymn.

(f) Even the smell of plants can have beneficial effects on human health. Smell is a powerful link to our emotions and memory. Pleasant fragrances brought on pleasant memories while the nasty smells evoked unpleasant memories. There are many books now available on the subjects of aromatherapy (the therapeutic use of aromatic oil from plants) and Osmotheraphy (the Science of smell).

Chapter - 4

APPROACH TO GREENBELT DESIGN

4.1 INTRODUCTION

As we have elaborated in the preceding chapter, a large number of gaseous and particulate air pollutants are emitted in the air environment. The physical and chemical properties and effects of these pollutants vary a great deal individually and synergistically. The nature and quantum of pollutant depends on the type of industry and the kind of raw material and energy used in its operation.

The development of green belts, by using pollution tolerant plants, can significantly towards air quality improvement. This involves selecting suitable plant species, determining climatic and adaphic parameters, studying wind and temperature profiles, nature of pollutants to be ameliorated, and general landscape of the locality. The design of the green belt and its composition may vary from place to place and industry to industry. A general social forestry of plantation type approach will not be of much help in industrial plantations (Rao, 1992).

The planning of green-belt, shelter-belt, or pollution-sinks also involves facets of bioaesthetics. Accordingly the selection of plant species may involve plant characteristics tolerance, canopy structure, foliage form, height of plant and its overall flowering and production potential. This involves, careful scrutiny of plants in nature as well as in horticultural conditions, in order to assess their suitability and performance in a stressed ecological situation of polluted environment.

Plantations also generate recurring hidden profits in terms of better health and happiness of its workers which in turn leads to better harmony and increased production vis-a-vis profit in quantified figures.

It has been seen that the pollutants emanating from thermal power plants, cement factories, metal processing plants, lime and brick kilns, pulp and paper factories, fertilizer plants, mining area and quarries, oil refineries, etc., though varying in their physical and chemical properties, are identical with respect to their effects on plant, animal and human life (Rao, 1992).

The physical state of pollutants may be particulate or gaseous. The particulate ones may be either settleable or suspended (SPM). In either cases, they may eventually fallout on surfaces of materials, plants and animals. The gaseous pollutants also get absorbed on surfaces. The effect of the pollutant on the impinging surface, is a function of the degree of toxicity of the pollutant.

The pollutants thus falling out may remain suspended for some time in the air-shed but these eventually get deposited either as wet deposition or dry deposition on surfaces of vegetation, soil, water, buildings and other properties. These may also be deposited on outer surfaces of animal bodies or inhaled into their lungs.

The effect of these pollutants, either adsorbed on the surface or absorbed inside the system of plants and animals or of inanimate objects will depend on the surface characteristics of the impinging surface and chemistry of the pollutant. In case of plants all those external and internal factors which affect the stomatal aperture will also affect the levei of pollution interacting on plants (William, 1990).

The control of air pollutants can be affected at the emission source only. Once the pollutants enter into the air environment, their effect can only be reduced through detoxification, oxidation, or absorption/adsorption on to surfaces.

Several methods have been developed to evaluate the suitability of plants for using them for purposes mentioned above. Biomonitoring of air pollutants through the use of plants, microbes and animals has now become a standard procedure in the study of air pollution ecology (Varshney, 1992).

In case of plants the visible symptoms are easily deciphered as chlorotic or necrotic foliar injuries symptoms but the subtle ones can be identified with the help of microscopic examination and physiological experimentation, which necessitate elaborate laboratory facilities. These changes in plants are quick to appear in the pollutant-sensitive species which help in the identification of pollutants in the field. The less sensitive or tolerant plants are able to withstand pollution for longer times. They have the capacity to detoxify the pollutants and use them as a raw material in their metabolic processes or just accumulate them in their system (Varshney, 1992).

Innes (1990) has stated "Tree barriers between Industrial and residential areas can also reduce air pollution considerably. A plantation of 30 m depth gives almost complete dust interception and significant reductions in gaseous pollutant concentrations. Even a single row of trees can reduce pollution levels markedly if it is planted on green verges with or without an underlay of shrubs. One row can lead to 25 per cent reduction of dust concentration observed in tree-lined streets. Free circulation of air within the canopy of a tree barrier also helps to promote the filtering of pollutants. He noise is significantly reduced by tree barriers of less than 30 m depth and the cosmetic and psychological benefits of plantings are considerable" . (Chaudhuri, 1993).

Innes further states, "planting techniques such as contouring can help to reduce the impact of pollution on the area surrounding each source. The landscape architect can thus assist local planning authorities and industry by slitoulating lands coping schemes around industrial and residential sites that will help to ameliorate the level of air pollution. Grass swards absorb twice as much of some pollutants as does bare soil. The scavenging effect increases with the inclusion of shrubs and trees. Thus, the average concentration of a pollutant in the atmosphere declines with increasing proportions of well planted open space in industrial and urban areas".

4.2 OBJECTIVES OF GREENBELT DESIGN

Greenbelt (GB) development envisages a multiplicity of objectives encompassing the microlevel air pollution abatement to enhancement of socio-economic value of the region:

i) The prime objectives of GB is attenuation of air and noise pollution. It comes to the immediate rescue during accidental release/explosion minimising the risk to a considerable level. The accidental release are mostly at ground levels for example Bhopal tragedy and Shriram Mills, New Delhi episodes. The GBs in such cases are the only alternative to stop/arrest further dispersion of pollutants.

ii) GB can serve as a measure for soil protection for erosion losses, enhance the aesthetic value and beautify the landscapes. Waste water and solid waste generated can be best utilised for GB maintenance after due treatment for converting them in manure's (Thakre, 1994).

iii) Development of GB can help generate employment avenues and thus involve the mass participation in environmental protection activity. This will increase the socio-economic standards of habitants and also help maintain the harmonious structuring of the human living areas and industries and other anthropogenic activities.

A greenbelt should fulfill the following objectives:

i. Detection of fugitive release of pollutants into the environment (using sensitive plant species).
ii. Adequate dilution of accidental releases / pollutants.
iii. Noise pollution control.
iv. Wastewater reuse.
v. Make plants as pollutant sink.
vi. Balancing of ambient oxygen and carbon dioxide levels.
vii. Mitigation of fugitive emissions including odour.
viii. Balancing Eco-environment.
ix. Aesthetics.
x. Optimum use of waste land and environmental conservation.

4.3 FACTORS INFLUENCING GREENBELT DESIGN

Green belt development mainly depends upon:

i. Nature and extent of pollution load
ii. Assimilative capacity of the ecosystem

iii. Climatic factors
iv. Soil and water quality

For optimisation of width of green belt, the prime considerations are :

i. Height and canopy area of trees
ii. Mean wind velocity and direction
iii. Distance from source/Location of sources of pollutants
iv. Pollutant concentration
v. Nature of pollutants
vi. Dry deposition velocity of plants (specific to pollutants and plants)
vii. Topography and size of the land available.

4.4 CRITERIA FOR GB DEVELOPMENT

Government of India has made it mandatory to have GB areas around the new as well as existing industries. However, no specific norms regarding the width of GB and pollution potential activity have been promulgated so far.

The classification of industries as per the international norms depends on the following aspects (Thakre, 1994):

- Area of industrial complex
- Total work-force
- Situation and distance from town centre/housing areas
- Transport facilities required
- Raw materials and products to be transported/handled and manufactured
- Nuisance produced
  - air pollution
  - noise
  - hazards

The width and the floral composition of a GB would vary from industry to industry. In Germany and Netherlands, there are fixed criteria for width of GB to be developed around the identified activity zone depending on the source strength (Tables 4.1 & 4.2). Thus, in Germany the width of GB varies from 100 meters around commercial centres to 2000 meters around heavy industries, of specially situated in isolation because of their heavy pollution potential. In Netherlands, the required

GB width varies from more than 500 m for heavy industry to 50 meters for light and non-polluting industries.

In India, many governmental and private, sector agencies are recommending GB development around industrial complexes. But the know-how for scientifically designing greenbelts to achieve optimum benefits is not available. This work aims are developing such a know-how.

4.5 DESIGNING OF GREENBELT

Designing of a very specialised task. This needs careful consideration of the local agro-climatic conditions, source and type of pollutants and selection of right types of tree species. Planning is to be done in such a way that greenbelt is developed within a short period and remains effective over the years.

The effectiveness of a GB for interception and retention of atmospheric particles depends on several factors viz. shape, size, wetness, surface texture and nature (Solubility and insolubility) of the particles/pollutants as well as intercepting plant parts (Ingold, 1971). Damp surface of the plants enhances pollutant removal rate by 10% because under such conditions stem, branches, twigs and leaves are engaged in absorption process. Light has also got a pronounced effect in foliar removal of pollutants by influencing physiological activities and stomatal opening (Mansfield, 1973; Smith, 1981). Under urban environment, moisture restricts absorption of gaseous pollutants by limiting stomatal opening (Ahmad et al, 1991).

A reduction of overall dust fall up to 42% by conifers in urban areas of temperate zone has been reported. Removal of particulates from atmosphere by shady trees showed that conifers were more effective than deciduous hardwood trees (Dochinger, 1972). According to Ahmad et al. (1991), the dust trapping ability of plants depends on certain morphological characters viz. branching habit, arrangement of leaves, its size, shape, surface (smooth/striate), presence or absence of trichomes and their frequency, exudates and wax deposition. Beach (1972) and Wedding et al. (1975) also observed relationship of leaf surface parameters and dust trapping potential of trees.

4.6 CONSIDERATION OF IMPORTANT ATTRIBUTES IN GREENBELT DESIGN:

Important parameters that govern the complete design of greenbelts are distance form the pollution sources, siting of industries, the typc of industries, type of pollutants, atmospheric conditions, etc. The green belt should be so located that its edge coincides with the point from where the zone of maximum ground level concentration of the air pollutant starts. As explained in Chapter 5-7, this zone does not begin immediately from the point at which the pollutants are released from a stack (chimny) but rather occurs some distance away; this distance depending on the temperature of exiting gases, their densities, and the meteorological conditions prevailing at that time. Also, the greenbelts should be wider in the directions where the wind velocities and frequencies are higher. The greenbelts, thus shall rarely have an axially symmetrical geometry but would rather have an irregular shape as depicted in Figures 4.1 and 4.2.

Table 4.1. Width of buffer zones: urban areas in Germany

Class Zone (m)	Width of Buffer Siting	Possibilities of
1.	0	Residential area
2.	100	Centres of Urban areas
3.	200 to 300	Industrial areas for light
4.	——	industry with no nuisance
5.	600	Industrial areas for
6.	800	industries that produce
7.	1500	nuisance
8.	2000	Special industries
9.	2000	in isolated locations
10.	2000	

Source : Thakre, (1994)

Table 4.2. Green belt criteria : Netherlands

Class	Industry	Width of GB(m)
I	Heavy industry with high potential of air pollution	> 500
II	Heavy industry with low potential of air pollution	200 to 500
III	A. Medium heavy industry with high potential of air pollution	100 to 200
	B. Medium heavy industry with low potential of air pollution	100 to 200
IV	A. Light industry with high potential of air pollution	50 to 100
	B. Light industry with low potential of air pollution	50 to 100
V	Service industry	10 to 50
VI	Workshops, handicrafts etc.	1 to 10

Source : Thakre, (1994)

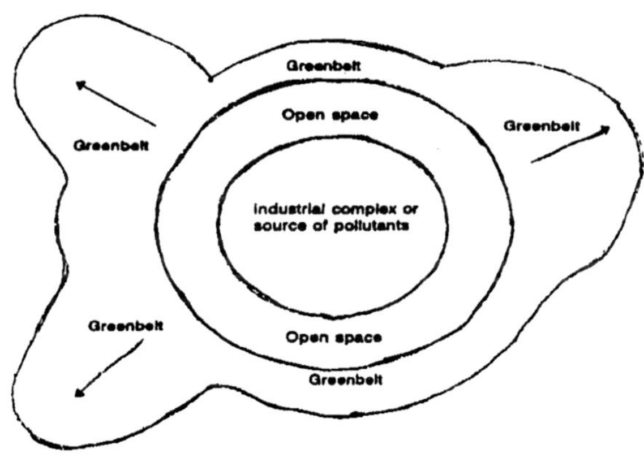

Fig. 4.1: Typical layout of greenbelt

4.6.1 Distance consideration

The recommendations made by the National Symposium on Industrial Location, Urban Planning and the Environment organised by SOCLEEN (Society for Clean Environment, Bombay) in 1985, and the Department of Environment Working Group Report (1986) with regard to the distance between industry and surrounding areas are as follows (Trivedi and Goel, 1995) :

1. There should be a distance of at least 25 km between pollution causing industry and the ecologically or otherwise sensitive areas. The areas identified under the category are presented in Table 4.3.
2. The distance between industries and high-tide line of coastal areas should be at least 500 m.
3. Industry should be at least 500 m away from flood plain of the riverine system or modified flood plain affected by dam in the upstream or by flood control systems.
4. Industry should be at least 500 m away from the Highway and 2 km from the railway.
5. Various distances from 5 km to 50 km should be maintained between the population centres (population 3,00,000 or more) and the industry based on the toxicity of pollutants released from the industry. An exclusive zone of 1 km. to 4 km radius free from habitation and a "sterilized" zone of 5km radius should be left.

4.6.2 Sitting of industries

In the selected area for sitting of industries, following criteria should be taken care of (Trivedi and Goel, 1995) :

- For sustaining the industry no forest area should be converted into non-forest activity.
- No prime agricultural land should be used for siting the industry.
- In the selected site, industry should be at the lowest level so as to be away from the general sight.
- Sufficient land should be acquired by the industry to accommodate sites for waste treatment plant. The treated water should be used for raising green belt, creating waterbody for aesthetics or aquaculture (if suitable). For the odorous industry, the thickness of the green belt should be at least 1 km.

Table 4.3. Ecological and otherwise sensitive areas to be protected from pollution

1. Religious and Historic places
2. Archaeological monuments
3. Scenic areas
4. Hill resorts
5. Beach resorts
6. Health resorts
7. Coastal areas rich in corals, mangroves
8. Estuaries rich in mangroves, breeding ground of specific species
9. Gulf areas
10. Biosphere reserves
11. National parks and sanctuaries
12. Natural lakes swamps
13. Seismic zones
14. Tribal settlements
15. Areas of scientific and geological interest
16. Defence installation, specially those of security importance and sensitive to pollution
17. Border Areas (International)
18. Air Ports

Source: DOE working group report (1986)

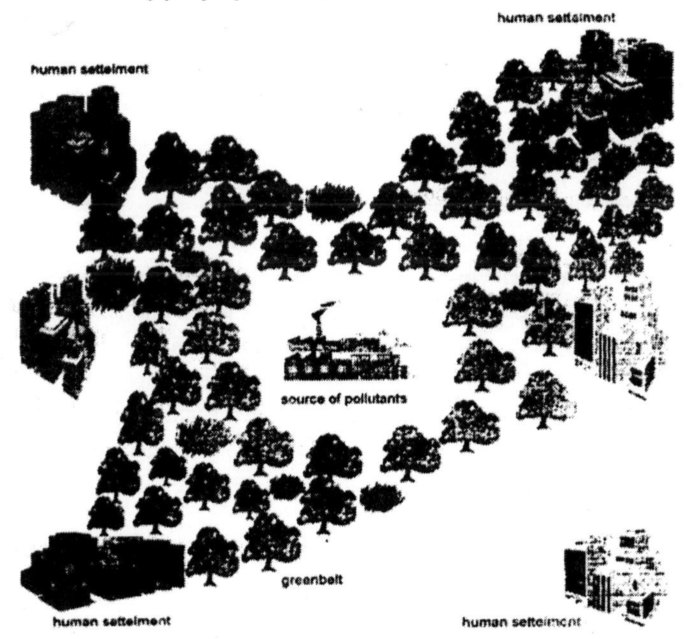

Fig. 4.2: Shcematic diagram showing industries, greenbelt and urban population

- Green belt should be provided between two adjacent industries.
- Adequate space should provided for storing solid wastes.
- Industry layout should be such that it should not affect the scenic features of the landscape.
- Associated township of the industry should have a physiographic barrier between it and the industry.
- There are a number of industries which are potentially harmful in causing environmental degradation. Twenty industrial groups have been identified by Department of Industrial Development of India (Table 4.4) those require to follow the specific guidelines with regard to their siting. Some of the areas with specific land uses, and some natural life-sustaining systems are extremely sensitive to pollution and require a safe distance from the pollution causing industry. Meteorological and micrometeorological considerations are also important for siting an industry because of the fact that in certain climatic and weather conditions the air pollutants tend to accumulate in the atmosphere and are finally brought down to the ground level.

A tentative classification of industries (Table 4.5) in relation to air pollution and siting is provided by Maas (1976). It is based mainly on the severity of the effects of industry on the human population. Adequate buffer zones of various thickness are recommended for the different groups of the industry. These buffer zones are to be provided with green belts which are helpful in cleaning the environment.

4.6.3 Meteorological Considerations

Meteorological conditions are very important in regulating the transport, dispersion and fate of air pollutants in the atmosphere. Stable atmospheric layers with frequent inversions are the unfavourable meteorological conditions as they help in accumulation of pollutants in a localised area. On the other hand, atmosphere instability and turbulence promote greater dispersal of pollutants thus helping in reducing the adverse impacts of toxic emissions.

For highly polluting industries, a site in the zones of frequent unstable layers shall be most appropriate for preventing the accumulation of air pollutants in atmosphere. However, an industry cannot be located on the consideration of macroclimatic data alone as the micro-meteorological features may be also be influential in deciding the fate of pollutants in a particular area. For example, the direction and velocity of the local winds and topography may be important factors in deciding whether the air pollutants shall accumulate in the atmosphere near the ground level or shall be dispersed away. Residential areas should not be allowed to develop downwind of the industries to avoid a direct transport of the pollutants to the population.

Table 4.4. List of polluting industries required to obtain environmental clearance for siting

1. Primary metallurgical producing industries viz. zinc, lead, copper, aluminium and steel
2. Paper, pulp and newsprint
3. Pesticides/insecticides
4. Refineries
5. Fertilisers
6. Paints
7. Dyes
8. Leather tanning
9. Rayon
10. Sodium/potassium cyanide
11. Basic drugs
12. Foundry
13. Storage batteries (lead acid type)
14. Acids/Alkalise
15. Elastics
16. Rubber/synthetic
17. Cement
18. Asbestos
19. Fermentation industry
20. Electroplating industry

Source: DOE working group report (1986)

For proper understanding of air pollution problems, an overview of ecological principles and concepts must be considered first. There are several natural systems which operate continuously maintaining a balance of a variety of actions and reactions involved. The driving force of all the activities in nature is the sun which provides the energy for meteorological operations and also to the earth surface.

Table 4.5. Classification of Industries with Regard to their siting and thickness and type of greenbelts

Type	Industry	Examples	Situation & distance town centrof housing areas	Nuisance produced			Buffer zone	
				Air pollution	Noise	Hazards	Type	Width
1.	Heavy Industries	Oil refiners chemical works, metallurgical & seaport indus	Outside the Urban area (>3200m)	SO_2 H_2S H_2SO_4,HF NH_3 yield, isolatioc greenary	Moderate fire risk economic	Explosion and produce an	Forests to	>2 km
	Heavy Industries	Machine manufacture, ship building Big harbour industries, power stations	Outside the Urban are (1600 to 3200m)	CO, SO_2	Maybe consider able, includes traffic noise	Explosion and fire risk	As above but including parks and sports fields	1km
3A	Medium-heavy industry with much air pollution	Manufacture of straw board, artificial fibres, ceramics &	Urban area (1600 to 3200m)	Not very much (SO2, HF, dust but may include	Consider traffic	Fire risk	Screening parkland	500 or more

		cement work		malodorous emissions				
3B	Medium-heavy industry with little air pollution	Manufacture of car lamps, foods textiles	Urban area (1600m)	As in 3A	As in 3A	As in 3A	As in 3A,	200m or more
4A	Light industry with small air pollution industries	Tannaries, textile & food	Near Town in fringe areas (400-1600m) malodorous emissions	Not very much but include	Moderate	Fire risk plants (mainly for 4m) trees of a decorative naturefor screening parkland	Screening	50-100m
4B	Light industry with little air pollution domestic machines	Manufacture electronic apparatus and	As in 4A	As in 4A	As in 4A	As in 4A	As in 4A	As in 4A
5	Service Industry laboratires	Printing works bakeries, film	Near Town (<800m)	Little	Little plants parkland	None	Decorative	<100m
6	Workshops handicrafts	Fashion studies, photoprinting shops, potteries	Near Town (<400m)	None	Little plants	None	Decorative	<50m

Source: Maas, (1976)

The pollutants which are added into the air environment are greatly affected both in quantity and quality by the meteorological parameters prevailing in the area. solar radiation, rainfall, temperature, humidity, wind direction and speed and conditions of temperature inversion. Besides these , topography of the area plays an important role in dispersion, diffusion, dilution and general transport and fallout of the pollutants. A given concentration of a pollutant may attain different ambient concentrations after a lapse of time under different meteorological conditions. Therefore, emission rate being the same, ambient concentration of pollutants may differ from area to area because of varying climatic conditions (Rao, 1992).

The meteorological parameters also play a significant role in determining the pattern and level of response of organisms to pollutants. The incidence of temperature inversion plays a major role in pollutant-organism reaction. Topography - valley or flat terrain influences the spatial dispersion of pollutants and the pollutant injury to life. As different places differ in their climatic and topographic conditions, the effect of pollutants may not be alike for all geographical regions in a country.

4.6.4 Micro-meteorological variables

Exchange of air pollutants between the air and the vegetation surfaces depends upon factors which affect pollutant transfer and the properties of the sources and sinks.

Atmospheric pollutants with negligible settling velocities are reversibly transferred to and from surface vegetation by a combination of diffusion and flowing air movement (Table 4.6). Except when winds are very light, the atmosphere is typically turbulent. Atmospheric turbulence is created primarily as a result of chaotic airflow over rough surfaces and rising air currents caused by solar heating of the ground layer. Gushiness, which everyone has experienced, is a manifestation of atmospheric turbulence. Turbulence is highly important in effecting air mixing. Randomly moving air parcels (turbulence elements or eddies) can transport their contents rapidly from place to place. The stability of the atmosphere, basically its tendency to suppress vertical air motion, is related to wind shear and vertical temperature structure. Vertical temperature structure, described by the atmospheric temperature lapse rate (rate of temperature decrease with height), has often been sued as an indicator of atmospheric stability. A stable atmospheric layer over an area in which the temperature increases with height (called an inversion layer) suppresses connective turbulence and mixing. This condition limits dispersion and is thus of special interest in localities subjected to local build-up of air pollution. Although the temperature lapse rate is commonly used as an index of stability, since chaotic winds over rough surfaces affect vertical mixing in the surface layer, the index should reflect the wind and ground roughness as well as the lapse rate. A number of useful parameters, that describe the dynamics of fluid systems, have been used to assess the transport of matter and energy and to quantitatively indicate the development of turbulence (Thakre, 1994). Some parameters are given in Tables 4.7 and 4.8.

Table 4.6. Micro-Meteorological variables

* Aerodynamic roughness	: Mass transfer	(a) Particles
(b) Gases		
	: Head	
* Momentum	: Atmospheric stability	
	: Diffusion Effect of Canopy	
	- Diurnal variation	
	- Fetch	
* Flow Separation	: Above Canopy	
	: Below Canopy	
* Friction Velocity		
* Inversion layer		* Turbulence
* Pollutant Concentration		* Wind Velocity
* Relative humidity		*Zeroplane displacements
* Seasonal Variation	: Mass transfer	(a) Particles
		(b) Gases
* Surface Heating	: Heat	
* Temperature	: Momentum	
* Terrain	: Uniform	
	: Non Uniform	

Airflow within and immediately above vegetation couples plant and air pollutant sources, receptors, and sinks with the atmosphere. It is within this surface layer scale that interactions discussed in the following sections are concerned. Air pollutant coupling and other interactions in vegetation-atmospheric systems require interdisciplinary study.

Micrometeorological conditions influence plant and atmosphere energetics, the rates at which air pollutants and other matter and energy are exchanged in the plant-atmosphere system, and to some extent pollutant residence times on or in the plants and plant parts. The chemical and physical forms of the pollutants along with morphological, physiological, and biochemical states of plants (regulated largely by the energy and chemical balance in the plant microenvironment) determine to what extent pollutants can be sorbed or emitted by the vegetation as well as effects of a particular pollutant exposure dosage on the plants (Trivedi, 1992).

Inoue (1963) has discussed airflow adjacent and within simple crop canopies and separated the air layers into three characteristics parts : (1) a logarithmic wind profile layer (boundary layer) above the canopy surface, (2) an exponential canopy-eddy layer, and (3) lowest part of the plant air layer in which plants and ground surface influence the wind profile. A logarithmic profile exists very close to the ground with the wind speed decreasing to zero at ground level. In the immediate vicinity of individual leaves gaseous pollutant transfer to the leafs external and internal surfaces occurs by molecular diffusion through the leaf-air boundary layers adhering to each leaf (where a portion may react with surface substances), through the leaf epidermis (via stomata, breaks), and through the mesophyll free air spaces within the leaves. Since mesophyll cells are bathed in aqueous media and are highly structured, the pollutants solubility and reactive properties, the transport of solutes within leaves, and the reaction sites influence cellular sink potentials and consequent effects on the cells. The concentration profile of various gaseous pollutants dispersing through the stand of green plants is directly proportional to the solubility of gas.

4.6.5 Land availability and greenbelt designing

Land availability becomes a major constraint in GB development around a source of pollution. The sources can be point, line or area and in every case the criteria for GB development will vary depending on the source strength.

Quantitative assessment for the land requirement for GB development has to be on systematic and scientific basis so that the authorities responsible can be convinced and at the same time optimum returns are obtained through the developmental activities.

Table 4.7. Depositing material

Particles	*Gases*
* Agglomeration	* Chemical activities
* Diameter	* Diffusion : Brownian : Eddy
* Density	
* Diffusion : Brownian with surface solubility	* Partial pressure in equilibrium
* Eddy equal is (a) Particles (b) Momentum (c) Heat	
- Effect of Canopy on Diffusion phoresis Electrostatic effects	
- Attraction	
- Repulsion	
* Gravitational Settling	
* Hygroscopicity	
* Impaction	
* Interception	
* Momentum	
* Physical properties	
* Resuspension	
* Shape	
* Size	
* Solubility	
* Thermosphoresis	

Source : Thakre, (1994)

Table 4.8. Surface variables

* Accommodations
    - Exudates
    - Trichomes
    - Pubescence
    - Waste
* Biotic Surface
* Canopy Growth
    - Normal
    - Expanding
* Canopy Structure
    - Areas Density
    - Bark
    - Bole

{cont.}...

- Leaves - Porosity - Productive Structure - Soils - Stem - Type	
	* Pollutant penetration & distribution in canopy prior deposition loading
* Electrostatic Properties * Leaf-Vegetation - Boundary layer - Change at high winds - Flutter - Stomatal resistance * Non biotic surface - pH effects on : - Reaction - Solubility	* Water

Source : Thakre, (1994)4.6.6. Pollution attenuation coefficient concept for greenbelt

Thakre (1994) has provided following factors for the design of effective GB.

For the design of GB around pollution source certain basic algorithms are used from Gaussian Plume diffusion approach and settling rate concepts for air pollutants.

When a parcel of pollutant travels through a green belt it obeys the exponential law for dry removals.

$$Q_x = Q_c * \exp^{(-1|x)}$$

where,

Q_x = Pollution travelling through greenbelt at distance, x

Q_c = Mass flux entering the greenbelt

= Pollution attenuation coefficient

$= K\, V_d \,/\, U_c$

V_d = Dry deposition velocity of pollutant for vegetative canoipy, ms^{1}

P_c = Foliage surface area of a single tree

P_t = Foliage surface area density of tree

Attenuation factor Af is a measure of effectiveness of green belt and can be defined as the ratio of mass flux traveling the same distance in absence of GB (QWB) and through GB (QB)

$$A_f = Q_{WB}/Q_B$$

$$A_f = \frac{F_D\ (X_1 + X_2)}{F_D X_1\ [\mathrm{erf}\{h_e/\ddot{O}\ddot{O}26z(X_1)\}\ e^{-l^1} X_2] + \mathrm{prfc}\ \{h_e/\ddot{O}\ddot{O}26z(X_1)\}\ F'_D.X_2}$$

where,

X_2 = Width of GB (m)

h_e = Effective height of GB (m)

= Pollution attenuation coefficient (m^{-1})

X_1 = Distance between pollution source and GB (m)

$F_D\ (X_1 + X_2)$ & $F'_D\ (X_1)$ are the plume depletion factors due to dry deposition of pollutant on natural surface.

$F'_D\ X_2$ = Plume depletion factor for the distance above GB

Parameters considered for computation of optimum width of GB along with their symbols in equation are given in Table 4.9.

Atmospheric conditions specially wind speed and the solar radiation are the major factors both for the spread of air pollutants as well as their uptake by green foliage during gaseous exchange activity taking place during photosynthesis. Based on the wind speed and day and night conditions, six stability classes have been categorised as shown in the Table 4.10.

Class 'A' indicates greatest amount of spreading and most unstable atmospheric stability conditions and class 'F' indicates least spreading and most stable atmospheric conditions.

The wind speed a governing factor in carrying air pollutant parcel from one point to other is drastically influenced while passing over the GB and within the GB and also differs from one atmospheric stability class to other (Thakre, 1994). The most accepted wind speed values to be used during the optimum Green Belt width calculation are given in Table 4.11.

4.6.7 Selection of trees for green belt

As elaborated in preceding chapters, the effectiveness of the green belt depends on the selection of the right type of the tree species tolerant to the particular pollutants of that area. An ideal tree for planting in the green belt should have following characters (Roy and Sharma, 1997) :

- Fast growth rate for quick development of canopy
- Strong branches for durable canopy to withstand storm
- Large leaf size for more retention of pollutants
- Dense foliage for better trapping of pollutants
- Long life span for extended life of the green belt

It is necessary to know the pollution tolerance level of the trees before selecting them for planting in green belt. Singh and Rao (1983) have worked out a formula of Air Pollution Tolerance Index (APTI) on the basis of leaf parameters to evaluate the tolerance level of the trees (please see section 3.2.4, Chapter 3). It is suggested that trees having high APTI value are to be planted in the green belt for minimising gaseous pollutants (Table 4.12). On the other hand, for minimising dust pollution trees having high dust trapping ability are to be selected (Table 4.12).

Further, depending upon the topo-climatological conditions and regional ecological status selection of appropriate plant species for this purpose should Depending upon the topo-climatological conditions, type of available land and cure the scheme for tree plantation should to be vigorously implemented.

Table 4.9. Parameters considered for computation of optimum width of Green belts

Symbols	*Parameters*
Separation distance between source & Green Belt (m)	X_1
Width of Green Belt (m)	X_2
Height of Green Belt (m)	h
Pollution attenuation coefficient (Af)	
Dry deposition velocity (ms^{-1}) in absence of Green Belt	Vdp
Deposition velocity onto plant canopy	Vdg

Table 4.10. Atmospheric stability classes

Surface wind speed at 10m height (m sec^{-1})	Insolation Stability Class				
	Day			Night	
	Strong	Moderate	Slight	Thinly over cast or > 1/2 cloud	clear to < 1/2 cloud
* < 2	A	A-B	-	-	-
* 2-3	A-B	B	C	E	F
* 3-5	B	B-C	C	D	E
* 5-6	C	C-D	D	D	D
* > 6	C	D	D	D	D

Insolation = Amount of sunshine

Table 4.11. Value of wind speed under various stability categories

Parameters	*Stability Class*				
	A	B	C	D	E
U (ms^{-1})	2.0	2.0	4.0	5.5	3.0
Uc (ms^{-1})	0.5	0.5	0.8	1.0	0.6

U = Wind Speed outside Green Belt
Uc = Wind Speed inside Green Belt

Table 4.12. Trees suitable for planting in the Green belt along with salient features (After Das, 1981; Singh & Rao 1983, Nayar 1985, Sharma et al 1991 & Boralkar, 1994)

Name of the plant species	Height	anopy Architecture efficiency	Dust Collecting Index (APTI)	Air Pollution Tolerance
Albizzia lebbek	Tall	Round	Moderate	***
Azadirachta indica	Tall	Semi-erect	Fair	**
Pithecolobium dulce	Tall	Round	Moderate	***
Ficus glomerata	Tall	Round	Moderate	***
Ficus infectoria	Tall	Round	Moderate	***
Polyalthia longitolia	Tall	Erect	Moderate	**
Tectona grandis	Tall	Erect	Moderate	**
Terminalia arjuna	Tall	Erect	Moderate	**
Bauhinia purpurea	Medium	Semi erect	Good	**
Butea Monosperma	Medium	Semi-erect	Good	*
Cassia fistula	Medium	Round	Fair	***
Lagerstroemia flosreginae	Medium	Semi-erect	Moderate	**
Saraca indica	Medium	Round	Fair	*
Thespesia populnea	Medium	Round	Moderate	**
Acacia arabica	Dwarf	Round	Good	**
Diospyros embryopteris	Dwarf	Round	Moderate	***
Thevetia nerifolia	Dwarf	Round	Fair	*
Parkinsonia aculeta	Dwarf	Semi-erect	Good	

*** High, ** Medium, * Low

Soucre: Das, (1981); Singh & Rao, (1993); Nayar, (1985); Sharma et al., (1991) & Boralkar, (1994)be based upon the following criteria : the plants should be

i. fast growing
ii. with thick canopy cover
iii. preferably perennial and evergreen
iv. with large leaf area index
v. indigenous
vi. resistant to specific air pollutants
vii. able to maintain the ecological and hydrological balance of the region

4.6.8 Planting and management of the green belt:

Healthy and established saplings having 1 m height for planting in the greenbelt should be selected in order to avoid mortality. Pits measuring 1m x 1m x 1m are to be dug up at desired points in triangular pattern. For planting tall shrubs and dwarf trees 4.5m spacing between plants and rows is sufficient while medium and tall trees in middle and rear rows are to be planted 6-7m and 8-10m apart respectively depending upon the space available. Close planting is recommended for accommodating more number of trees per unit area resulting in more leaf surface. Excavated soil should be sun dried thoroughly and to be mixed with F.Y.M in 2:1 ratio alongwith BHC (10% dust) @ 50 gm/pit for controlling soil borne insects and pests. Planting of sapling should be done during monsoon. Replanting should be done without delay if there is casualty. Proper care and maintenance of the saplings at the initial stage for 2-3 years is essential. It helps quick development of canopy which is very much required for the green belt (Roy and Sharma, 1997).

Close planting with three tier system keeping dwarf trees with round canopy exposed to the source of emission followed by medium and tall trees with cylindrical canopy is ideal design for the industrial area because all plants are exposed to the pollutants (Anonymous 1976, Sharma et al., 1994). This helps to divert the emissions upward as plants act as a physical barrier.

Close planting also results in taller trees with deeper roots and ultimately yields more bio-mass per unit area and more efficient absorption of pollutants (Patel, 1982). Planting of trees in staggering arrangement in multiple rows across the direction of the wind is recommended for better trapping and absorption of the pollutants. Trees of the front rows act as absorptive layer while the core area (rear rows) cleans the air. The width of the outer area of the plantation should be 3-4 times wider than the core area depending upon the availability of the space (Nayar, 1985). For designing green belt as city lungs in urban areas, the pattern of planting should be a little different from industrial areas. Dwarf trees and shrubs in multiple rows should be planted all along the periphery, flanked by medium and tall trees gradually towards centre so that all the plants can intercept from different directions.

Chapter 5

GREENBELT DESIGN BASED ON MATHEMATICAL MODELLING

5.1 INTRODUCTION

In the preceding chapter we have discussed in detail how trees, and the 'greenbelts' based on trees, can perform numerous useful functions. Such greenbelts can serve as wind breaks and shelter beds, to assist in crop production and reducing soil loss. They can serve as aesthetically pleasing yet effective controllers of dust, noise, and other forms of atmospheric pollution. They can improve the micrometeorology of the area by cushioning temperature fluctuations, and helping in rainfall capture. They can provide habitats for birds, and other forms of colourful wildlife. And they can yield food, fuel, and fibre.

If developed around industrial and commercial complexes, greenbelts can significantly reduce ambient noise and other forms of atmospheric pollution. Even more important, such greenbelts can serve as crucial damage control buffers when runaway industrial accidents – involving explosions, fires, and toxic releases – occur. As the frequency of such industrial accidents is continually increasing (Abbasi and Khan 1998), so is the need to have effective greenbelts.

Effective greenbelts. We have emphasised the word 'effective' because until a greenbelt is designed on the basis of precise scientific study – taking into account the nature of pollutant sources, the wind directions and other meteorological factors, and the way pollutants shall be dispersed during different seasons - it may not be effective.

It is a popular misconception that pollution emanating from an industry can be reduced *effectively* just by surrounding the industry with a greenbelt. In reality a great deal of sophistication, based on mathematical modelling and validation, is needed to design *effective* greenbelts because the gaseous pollutants do *not* uniformly and radially disperse from the source of emission but travel in certain directions dictated by various factors including, among others:

a) density, exit temperature and exit height of the pollutant gases,
b) meteorology of the area,
c) terrain characteristics, etc.

Gases emanating from an industry may not come close to the ground till several thousand meters from the point of emission. If a greenbelt is developed just close to such an industry (and if it ends before the pollutant plume comes close to the ground), the greenbelt may serve no purpose at all. Likewise a greenbelt need not be a strip of uniform width – indeed in most situations it would be a strip of *varying width* the geometry of which would be dictated by factors such as the ones enumerated above.

Furthermore the species of trees and other vegetation that a greenbelt should contain is again dictated by several factors of which local soil/ water conditions are but one set of guiding parameters. The type of pollutants that are to be controlled is a key governing aspect.

It thus becomes necessary to have a tool based on gaseous dispersion modelling to help us decide the geometry of the greenbelt *and* its effective location. It is equally necessary to have knowledge-based systems developed on the premises of such specialised information as pollutant assimilation pathways (physical, chemical, biological, and biochemical), pollutant deposition pathways (dry *deposition*, wet deposition), and impacts of factors such as canopy density and plant anatomy on the control of different types of pollutants.

5.2 GREENBELT DESIGN BASED ON MATHEMATICAL MODELLING

This involves the following three main steps:

i) stability characterisation,
ii) dispersion estimation and,
iii) estimation of greenbelt design parameters.

Each aspect is modelled independently, the outputs of each steps are inputs to the next step(s). The complete process of greenbelt modelling is shown in Figure 5.1. Each step of the process of greenbelt design is detailed in the following sections.

5.2.1 Characterisation of atmospheric stability

Characterisation of atmospheric stability is the most important issue related to the dispersion of the pollutants and subsequently their attenuation (Abbasi 1998, Khan and Abbasi 1997, 1998; Roy and Sharma, 1997). There have been many schemes proposed to estimate the atmospheric stability. Among them, stability characterisation using Mohn-Obukhov length is the one most frequently used by the researchers, as it predicts results with better accuracy, and the parameters used in the estimation are easily measurable (and are frequently available). Further it is applicable to most of the site characteristics (semi-urban, coastal, etc).

We have also opted for Mohn-Obukhov stability characterisation model with coastal effects. In this model (Figure 5.2) the stability is classified using Mohn-Obukhov length and Mohn-Obukhov coefficient, which are defined as (Pasquill and Smith, 1983):

$$L = U_x^3 \, Cp \, rr \, T / Kg \, H,$$

Where H is vertical heat flux (w/m^2)

U_x is friction velocity
Cp is specific heat
rr is Density = P/RT
T is absolute temp
g is gravitational force
K is conductivity

$$xx = Z / L,$$

Where xx is Mohn-Obukhov coefficient

H can be estimated using empirical equation:

$$H = 0.4(s - 100)$$

Otherwise using Bowen ratio, Bo

$$H = Bo * Le * E$$

Where

Le = Latent heat of evaporation

E = evaporation rate

U_x is friction velocity is either measured or estimated.

Relationship between Pasquill stability categories and Mohn-Obukhov stability criterion is summarised below.

Pasquill stability criterion	*Mohn-Obukhov Length, L*	*Physical significance*
A	-2 to 3	1.1.1.1 Very unstable
B	-4 to -5	Moderately unstable
C	-12 to -15	Slightly unstable
D	∞	Neutral
E	35 to 75	Moderately stable
F		
	0 to 35	Very stable

Relationship between Turner stability category and Mohn-Obukhov length:

Turner stability criterion	*Mohn-Obukhov criterion*
A	$\leq$ -0.087
B	$-0.007 \leq 1/L \leq -0.020$
C	$-0.020 \leq 1/L \leq -0.005$
D	$-0.005 \leq 1/L$

5.2.2 Modelling of pollutant dispersion

Once the stability of the atmosphere has been classified, the next step is to estimate the dispersion of air pollutants released from various sources. This includes the estimation of plume path, plume geometry, and concentration of pollutants at various locations. Numerous models have been proposed for this purpose. These models fall in three main categories:

i. Analytical models,
ii. Numerical models, and
iii. Statistical models.

The first class of models are of particular interest for the present application. The others can also be used, but they require higher computational load without producing proportionality better results in terms of precision or accuracy.

After a detailed study of the available models, and their limitations, we have zeroed on the modified gaussion model (Pasquill and Smith, 1983; Schmel, 1980) in which we have done further modifications appropriate to the application in coastal areas. The set of steps involved in the estimation of dispersion characteristics of pollutant by this model are presented in Figure 5.3. The equations to be used for concentration estimation are as follows:

$$C(x, y, z) = (Q / 2PP\sigma_y\sigma_z u) * \exp(-y^2 / 2\sigma_y^2) * [\exp[-(z-h)^2 / 2\sigma_z^2] + \exp[-(z+h)^2 / 2\sigma_z^2]]$$

Where $\sigma_{y,}$ σ_z are dispersion coefficient (standard deviation of concentration in y and z direction), and are estimated using recently proposed scheme of Erbrink (1995); u is wind speed; x, y, z are the co-ordinates, and h is the height of the source.

The other related characteristics of dispersion are estimated as:

Concentration at cloud axis on ground level.

$$C_{cloud} = [Q / PP\sigma_y\sigma_z u] * \exp[-h^2 / 2\sigma_z^2]$$

5.2.3 Maximum ground level concentration,

$$C_{mgl} = [2Q / ePPuh^2] * [\sigma_z / \sigma_y]$$

The ground level concentration can also be estimated as:

$$C_{max} = K (Q / h^2)$$

Where K is constant, $\sigma_z = 0.707$ h

5.2.4 Maximum ground level concentration would occur at

$$\sigma_z = 0.707\ h$$

$$\sigma_z = h / 2^{1/2}$$

5.3 MODIFICATIONS INCORPORATED TO SUIT LONG-TERM APPLICATION IN PONDICHERRY AND MANALI (CHENNAI) WHICH ARE BOTH COASTAL AREAS:

5.3.1 Longer duration

Generally the horizontal dispersion coefficient (σ_y) is modelled for 10 to 15 minutes of release. But we have wished to develop a model

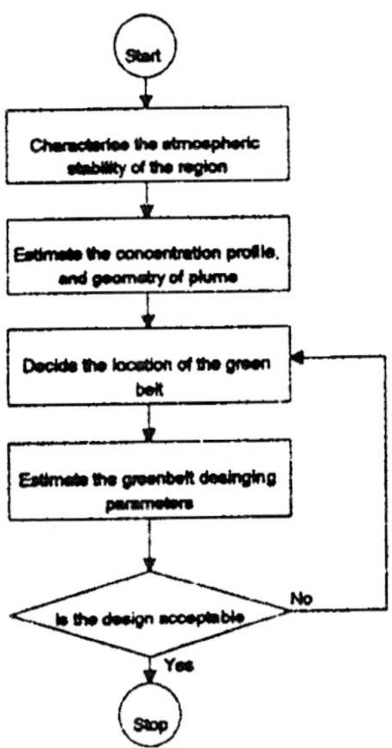

Fig. 5.1: Complete Process of the Greenbelt Design

which can be applicable for long durations (a full day, a month, even a year). To incorporate this effect a new factor σ_{ywz} has been defined. This factor modifies the original value of ss_y as:

$$\sigma_y^2 = \sigma_y^2 + \sigma_{ywz}^2$$

Where the σ_{ywz} is defined as $\sigma_{ywz} = 0.065 * (7t/u)^{½} x$

Where t is the duration of release (h)

x is downwind distance (m)

u is wind speed (m/s)

5.3.2 Coastal area effect :

The original model discussed above is generally applicable to flat terrains of nearly constant roughness. Application of this model to the highly urban areas, valley, or coastal areas may give erroneous results. Therefore, we have modified the model to account for the coastline effect in dispersion estimation. This effect has been accounted using lateral and vertical dispersion coefficient. They are modified as:

$$\sigma_y = \sigma_y (R) [x / R] a^a$$

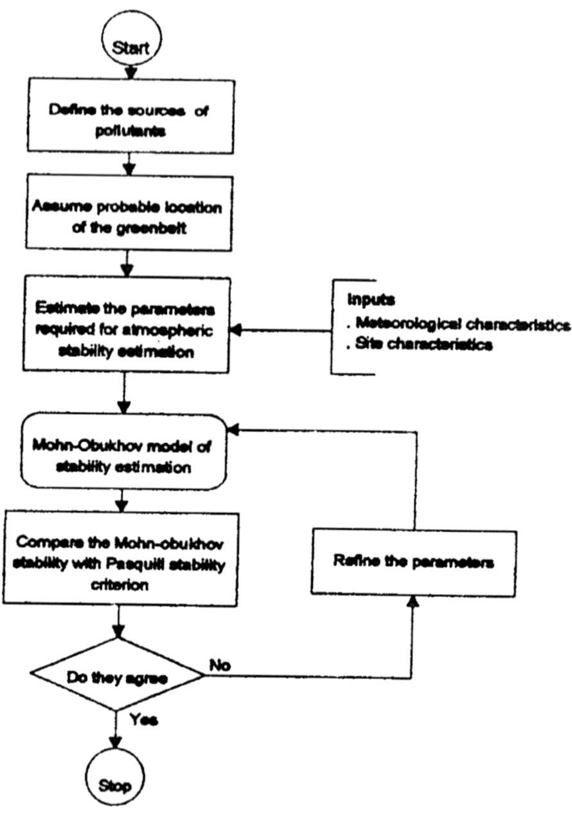

Fig. 5.2: Steps Involve in Characterising Atmospheric Stability

$$\sigma_z = \sigma_z (R) [x / R] b^b$$

Where, $ss_y(R)$ and $ss_z(R)$ are the values of ss_y and ss_z at the reference distance R (= 100m), aa and bb are indices.

Indices	*Water* (α)	*Land*	*Water* (*b*)	*Land*	σ_y *(R) water*	σ_y *(R) land*	σ_z *(R) water*	σ_z *(R) land*
B	0.75	1.00	0.75	1.00	25.0	19.0	10.0	11.0
C	0.70	1.00	0.70	0.90	20.0	12.5	8.0	7.5
D	0.69	0.90	0.65	0.85	15.1	8.0	3.2	4.5
E	0.65	0.80	0.62	0.80	16.1	6.0	1.8	3.5

5.4 POLLUTANTS ATTENUATION

5.4.1 Deposition process :

Pollutants are attenuated by two different processes: dry deposition and wet deposition (detailed in previous chapters). A brief description on estimation of deposition rate and other parameters such as attenuation coefficients, attenuation factor, greenbelt width, density of pollution is presented below.

- Dry deposition and wet deposition are of comparable importance in the ease of SO_x. Dry deposition is most significant where ground level concentration are high, in other words close to the sources.
- Another mechanism of deposition is when fog or cloud droplets are removed directly to the ground or to the vegetation. This is termed as 'occult deposition'.

Wet scavenging is defined as the natural process by which atmospheric pollutants are attached to and dissolved in cloud and pollution droplets or droplets. The amount of compounds thus received per unit of surface area is defined as wet deposition.

Washout (wet deposition) is an efficient removal mechanism for solvable gases.

The higher the ground level concentration, the more rapid the deposition (Figure 5.4). Efficiency of deposition, which is also called *deposition velocity*, is defined as:

V(deposition velocity) = deposition rate / air concentration

Deposition (adsorption) velocity has been measured experimentally for SO_2 and ranges from $5 * 10^{-3}$ m/s. A value $1 * 10^{-2}$ m/s is generally assumed.

Dry deposition is a series of processes where gas molecules and small particles are entrained from the air stream by turbulent eddies erected by the friction of air mass movement over the forest canopy. Gases/particles that move through the boundary layer surrounding a leaf will either adsorb to the surface of the leaf or enter the leaf through

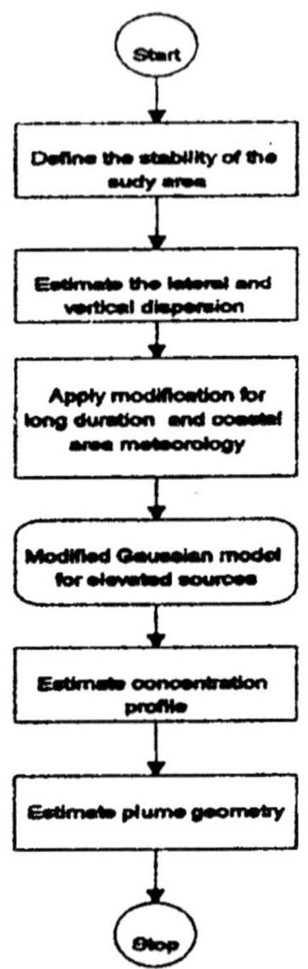

Fig. 5.3: Step involve in estimation of dispersion characteristics

stomatal opening. The dry deposition flux of gases and particles from the atmosphere to the receptor surface is governed by:

i. Concentration in the air and the transport through the boundary layer,
ii. The chemical and physical nature of depositing species, and
iii. The efficiency of surface to capture or absorb gases and particles.

5.4.2 Resistance analogy

$R_1(Z) = C(Z_1) - C(Z_2) / F$

Where, Z_1 and Z_2 are two heights, F is flux of pollutant

Dry deposition rate (mg/cm²/sec) = Deposition velocity (cm/sec) * Pollutant concentration (mg/cm³)

Deposition velocity = Rate of deposition/ conc. of pollutant in the boundary layer.

Deposition velocity depends on 16 micrometeorological variables, 14 potential characteristics, 4 gas characteristics, and 10 receptor variables. In general deposition velocity increases with

i. solubility of pollutant,
ii. particle diameter and density,
iii. wetness & roughness of surface, and
iv. turbulence and wind speed.

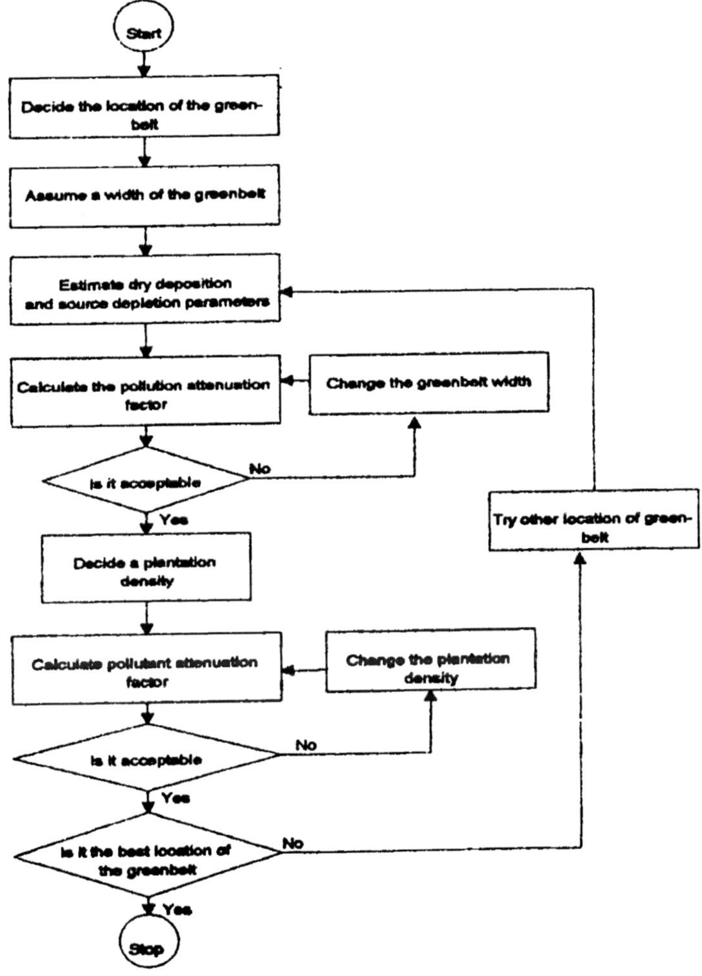

Fig. 5.4: Algorithm for the design of green-belt

Deposition velocity of a few gases determined under managed environmental conditions is as follows:

Species	*Deposition velocity*
O_3	0.2 to 0.7cm/s
NO	0.01 to 0.1 cm/s
NO_2	0.1 to 0.8 cm/s
MNO_3	0.5 to 5.0 cm/s
NH_3	0.2 to 0.6 cm/s
PAN	0.1 to 0.6 cm/s
SO_2	0.2 to 3.0 cm/s
H_2S	0.2 to 0.4 cm/s

Most of the gases have 0.1 cm/s deposition velocity under stable conditions and 10 in unstable conditions. It is not uncommon to assume a deposition velocity of 1 cm/s for general purpose.

5.5 MATHEMATICAL MODEL FOR THE REMOVAL OF POLLUTANT BY VEGETATION

The concentration of pollutant degausses exponentially in the forest or canopy of greenbelt (Kapoor and Gupta, 1984; 1992, Gupta and Kapoor, 1990; Smith, 1990).

$$Q_x = Q_c \exp(-ll\ x)$$

Where, Q_c is mass flux enters the greenbelt

Q_x is mass flux at distance x in the greenbelt

λ is pollutant attn. Factor(m^{-1})

λ *is commonly defined as :*

$$\lambda = K \rho_t v_d / u_c$$

where, V_d = dry deposition velocity (ms^{-1})

U_c = average wind speed through greenbelt (ms^{-1})

ρ_t = foliage surface area density of a single tree (m^2 / m^3)

$K = \rho_c / \rho_{tl}$

Where, ρ_c – average foliage surface area density of the greenbelt (m^2 / m^3)

5.5.1 Estimation of pollutant attenuation factor

The pollutant attenuation factor is defined as

$A_f = Q_{WB} / Q_B$

where, Q_{WB} = pollutant flux without greenbelt

Q_B = pollutant flux with after passing through greenbelt

The model estimates the source of pollutant at the starting point of greenbelt using source depletion equation (dispersion with deposition Figure 5.5).

$Q_A = Q_o FD(x_1)$

$FD(x_1)$ is source depletion factor defined as

$FD = [\exp {}_0\int^x 1/\sigma_z \exp[-H^2 / 2\sigma_z^2]\, dx]^{-(2/\Pi)^{1/2}[vd/u]}$

$FD = (F\Delta D_{100})^{vd/u}$

Q_A is further divided in two parts, one passes through greenbelt, one goes above the greenbelt (see Figure 5.5).

$Q_c = {}_0\int^\infty {}_{-\infty}\int^\infty C\, U(he)\, dy\, dz$

Where, U(he) can be estimated using

${}_0\int^{he} U(z)\, dz = h * Uc$

$Uz = (z/10)^b\ U(10)$

Where, h is height of tree

Uc is wind velocity in the greenbelt canopy

$Q_{AA} = {}_\infty\int^\infty {}_{-\infty}\int^\infty C\, U\, dydz$

$Q_A = Q_{AA} + Q_c$

Flux of the pollutant coming out of the canopy:

$Q_{BC} = Q_C \exp[-ll\, x_2]$

Flux going above the canopy but depleted due to source depletion.

$Q_{BA} = Q_{AA} FD(x_2)$

Finally,

$Q_B = Q_{BA} + Q_{BC}$

Pollutant flux when greenbelt canopy is not present.

$Q_{WB} = Q_{AA} FD(x_1 + x_2)$

Finally,

$Af = Q_{WB} / Q_B$

On simplification this equation can be written as:

$Af = FD(x_1 + x_2)/FD(x_1)$ [erf $\{he/\sqrt{z}s_z(x_1)\}\, e^{-\lambda^{x2}}$ + erfe$\{he/\sqrt{z}\sigma_z(x_1)$ $FD(x_2)\}$]

Where U(he) can be calculated using

$$\int_0^{he} U_s\,(z)\,dz. = \int_0^{h} U_e\,(z)\,dz$$

$$U_e = [U_f\,(h) / a]\,[1-e^{-a}]$$

$$A = \rho_c\, h^3 / 2\, l_h^2$$

Where, l_h = k (h-d) and K = 0.41

5.5.2 Estimation of the parameters considering interfacial mass exchange

λ^i = $0.1/x_i$

λ^i = interfacial pollutant exchange

ξ_i - travel distance x_i where σ_z reaches h/1.625,

Interfacial mass exchange coefficient (ll^i) in open terrain is given as

Mass flux through the greenbelt canopy (I_0) and above the greenbelt canopy (O_0) is given as (Figure 5.5).

$$I_0 = \text{erf}\,\{he / ÖÖ2\sigma_z(x1)\}\ FD(x_1)$$

$$O_0 = \text{erfe}\,\{he / ÖÖ2\sigma_z(x1)\}\ FD(x_1)$$

Where $FD(DDx_2)$ can be estimated as:

$$FD(\tilde{D}Dx_2) = [FD(DDx_2)]^{1/n}$$

The complete greenbelt width is divided in n boxes. The flux in the first box is given as:

$$I_1 = I_0\, e^{-l^i D^{Dx2}}\, e^{-l^{li} D^{Dx2}} + O_0\, FD(DDx_2)\,(1-e^{-l^{li} D^{Dx2}})$$

$$O_1 = O_0\, FD(DDx_2)\, e^{-l^{li} D^{Dx2}} + I_0\, e^{-l^i D^{Dx2}}\,(1-e^{-l^{li} D^{Dx2}})$$

Similarly for n^{th} box

$$I_n = I_{n-1} e^{-l^i D^{Dx2}}\, e^{-l^{li} D^{Dx2}} + O_{n-1}\, FD(DDx_2)\,(1-e^{-l^{li} D^{Dx2}})$$

$$O_n = O_{n-1}\, FD(DDx_2)\, e^{-l^{li} D^{Dx2}} + I_{n-1}\, e^{-l^i D^{Dx2}}\,(1-e^{-l^{li} D^{Dx2}})$$

Using these equations finally the Af can be computed as:

$$Af = [FD(x_2 + x_1) / I_n + O_n]$$

Af = [Source depletion / pollution attenuated due to greenbelt, considering interfacial mass exchange]

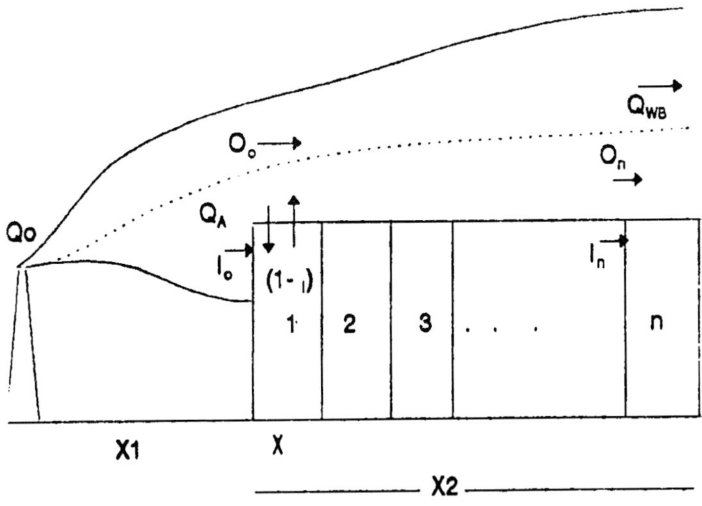

Fig. 5.5: The mechanism involved in the designing of greenbelt.

Chapter - 6

SOLUTION AND TESTING OF MODELS

In the preceding chapter we have presented a new mathematical model with which the pattern of dispersion of pollutant plume (to determine the location and geometry of the greenbelt) and the processes of pollution attenuation (to determine greenbelt species and sequence of their planting) can be ascertained.

The complete process of greenbelt design involves the following four pay steps (Figure 6.1):

i. stability characterization,
ii. pollutant concentration and plume geometry estimation,
iii. deciding the location of green belt, and
iv. estimation of greenbelt design parameters such as width of greenbelt, density and species of plantation.

The first step characterizes the atmospheric stability using synoptic meteorological data (which is generally available without much difficulty). The algorithm to characterize the atmospheric stability is shown in Figure 6.2. This step uses Mohn-Obukhov model to estimate the stability dependent parameter (Mohn-Obukhov length) which is subsequently used to characterize the atmospheric stability.

The main inputs to this sub-model are

i) atmospheric friction velocity
ii) intensity of solar radiation

iii) virtual atmospheric temperature, and
iv) physical properties of air.

We have incorporated coastal area effects in characterizing the atmospheric stability and estimating the dispersion co-efficients. This has been done using the model proposed by Skupniewiez and Schacher (1986). The complete model of atmospheric stability characterization has been solved for a wide range of data and the results are compared with the already reported results. A good agreement has been observed.

The second step - dispersion characteristic estimation - works out the concentration profile of pollutant and the geometry of the plume. The dispersion process has been modeled considering release of pollutant from an elevated with source. As here we are concerned with long duration release, we have used Pasquill-Gifford (Lees,1996) modifications to incorporate this effect (release for long duration). Similarly the effect of coastal area meteorology has also been accounted for pollutant dispersion. The algorithm of dispersion characterstic estimation is depicted in Figure 6.3. Finally, the complete model of pollutant dispersion as described in chapter-5, has been solved for predefined inputs and the results have been compared with already reported ones. A good agreement has been observed.

This third and the fourth steps *designing of green belt* use the information obtained in steps one and two. The third step leads to the location of greenbelt, considering:

i. The zone of occurrence of maximum pollutant concentration (plume touching the ground)
ii. Height of the planned greenbelt,
iii. Pollutant deposition and depletion rates,
iv. The surface available for the attenuation of pollutants (foliage area of one tree as well as the complete green belt).

The fourth step estimates the design parameters of greenbelt such as greenbelt width, pollutant attenuation factor, plantation density, etc.

The models for these steps (third and fourth) include a set of non-linear algebric equations, definite integrals, error functions, etc. These have been solved using numerical algorithms for non-linear function as well as numerical integral (siphons 1/3 method).

The algorithm to solve the third and fourth steps is depicted in Figure 6.4.

TESTING

The complete model of greenbelt design has been solved for a set of inputs (Table 6.1), and the results have been compared with the ones obtained using the model of Gupta and Kapoor (1986). Figure 6.5. depicts comparison of concentration profile as predicted by the present model and the one reported by Gupta and Kapoor. It is evident from the figure that a good agreement of predicted and reported profiles has been observed. It is particularly so up to a distance of 900 m. Thereafter the deviation between these two values increases. The little deviation that exist between the reported and the predicted values is due to following reasons:

i. The present model has incorporated coastal area effects, while the reported one (Gupta and Kapoor 1996) is an essentially inland-terrain model.
ii. The present model has incorporated the effect of longer duration of release.
iii. The present model has accounted for the elevated release sources while in the reported model the height of release has been restricted to 7 m.

Table 6.1. Typical input data used in the solution of the model

Parameters	*Values*
Pollutant release rate, kg/s	45
Wind speed (m/s) at 10 m height	3.5
Downwind distance, m	1100
Cross wind distance	150
Vertical distance, m	170
Height of pollutant release, m	25
Atmospheric temperature, K	300.15
Density of air, kg/m^3	2.1
In coming solar radiation (W/m^2)	135
Friction velocity, m/s	0.35
Pollutant deposition velocity (ms^{-1})	0.025
Height of tree (m)	25
Proposed greenbelt width, m	200

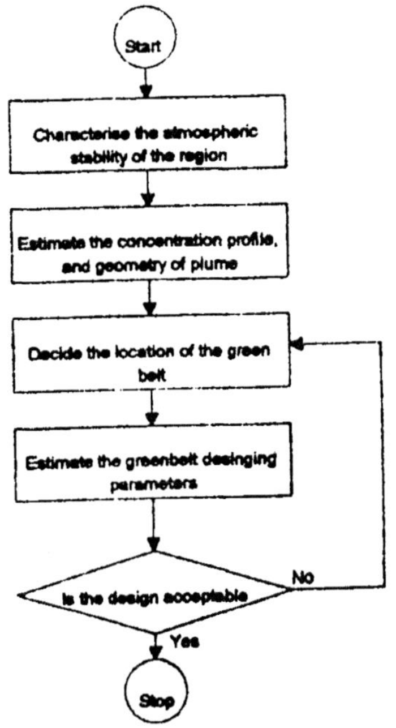

Fig. 6.1: Complete process of the greenbelt design

The results of model solution, for a set of inputs given in Table 6.1, is presented in Table 6.2. For a source of 45 kg/s in neutral atmospheric conditions at a distance of 1100 m downwind, the green belt width is estimated as 200 m. This width of greenbelt reduces the sources strength from 43.33 kg/s (at a distance of 1300 m downwind when greenbelt is not present) to 14.06 (at the same distance). This signifies more than 65% removal of pollutant, and a pollutant attenuation factor of 3.1.

We have compared the profile of pollutant attenuation factor (AF) as predicted by present model with the one reported by Gupta and Kapoor (1986). Figure 6.6 presents comparison of profiles of AF as function of greenbelt width. It is also evident that a very good agreement (more than ~ 95%) exists between the profile predicted by present model and the one reported by Gupta and Kapoor (1986). It is also observed from the profile that initially up to a width of 500m, AF increases non-linearly, Later, upto a distance of 800 it increase linearly (with a slope of more

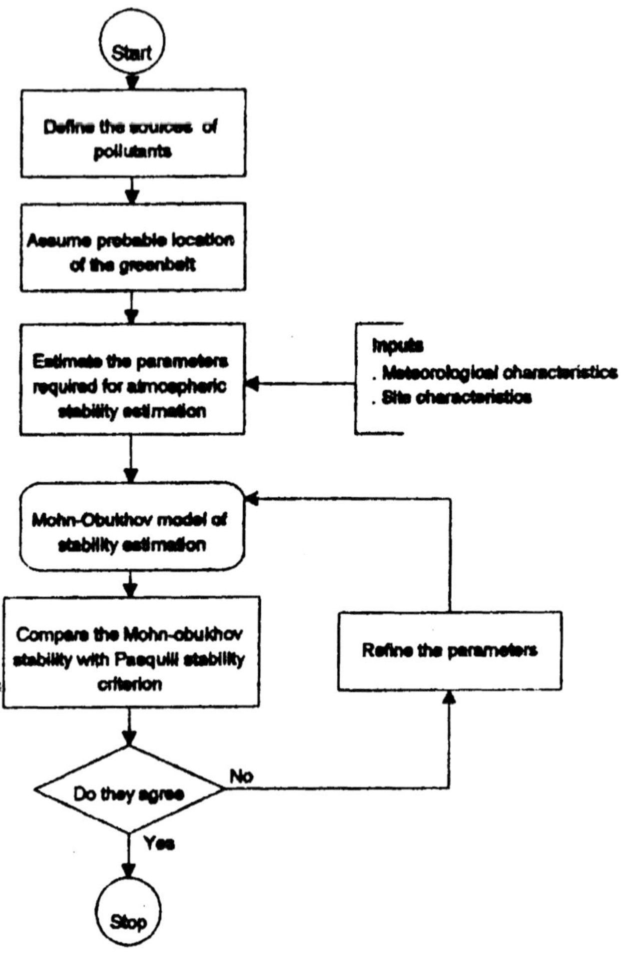

Fig. 6.2: Steps involve in Characterising Atmospheric Stability

than one). Thereafter the rate of increase of AF decreases sharply. Thus, a greenbelt width of less than 800 m is recommended. The values of AF as a function of distance from the source to greenbelt edge (X) has been plotted in Figure 6.7. As X increases the value of AF decreases. The rate of decrease in AF is steep upto a distance of 1000m, followed with slays decline. Similar profile (Figure 6.7) has been observed with the model of Gupta and Kapoor (1986).

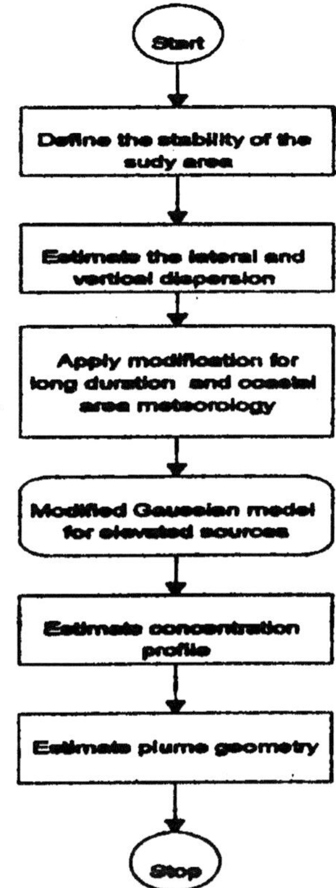

Fig. 6.3: Steps involve in estimation of dispersion characterstics

Table 6.2. ***Typical results from the model for an input set presented in Table 6.1***

Parameters	*Values*
Stability class	D, Neutral
The concentration at x=1100.0,y=150.0,z=170.0, Kg/cum	= $1.232490e^{-04}$
The concentration at cloud axis, Kg/cum	= $6.487372e^{-04}$
The maximum ground level concentration at cloud axis, Kg/cum	= $1.095529e^{-03}$
The maximum ground level concentration at cloud axis, Kg/cum	= $1.112611e^{-04}$
Distance at which maximum ground level concentration occurs, m	= 770.000000
Width of greenbelt, m	= 200.000000
The height of tree as, m	= 25.000000
The value of k (plantation density parameter)	= 1.000000
The source strength without passing through green, Kg/s	= $4.332890e^{+01}$
The source depletion when passing through green belt (interaction), Kg/s	= $1.406573e^{+01}$
The value of attenuation factor considering interaction	= 3.091461

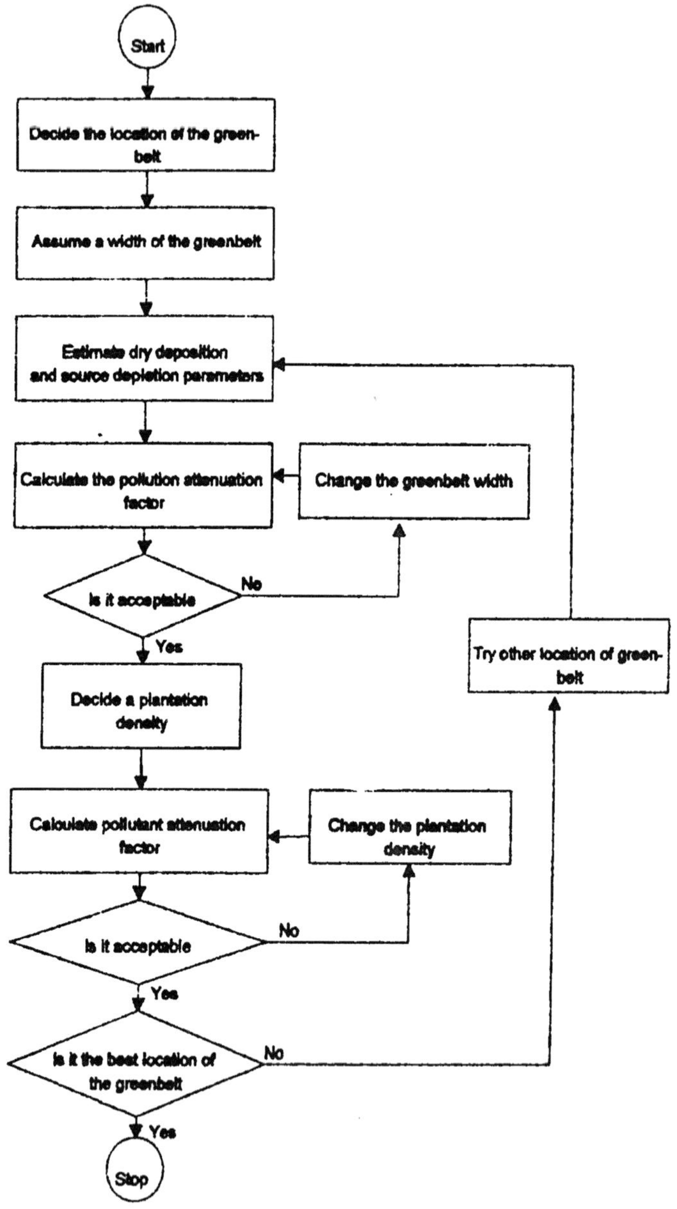

Fig. 6.4: Algorithm for the design of green-belt

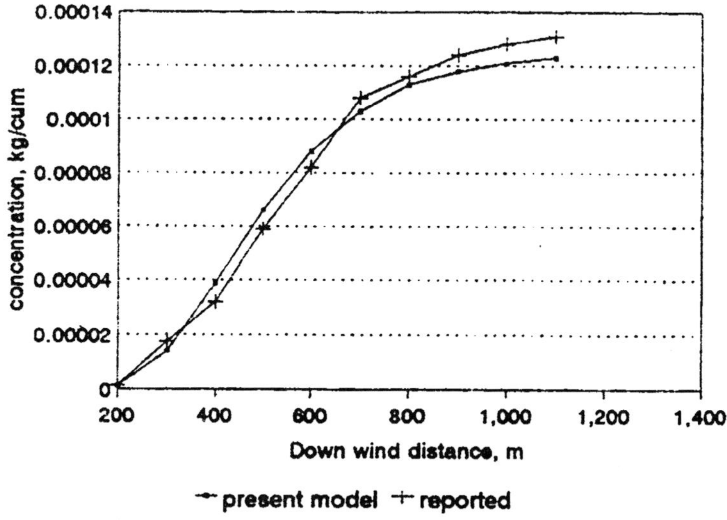

Fig. 6.5: Comparison of pollutant concentration (SO2)estimated by present model with that of the model reported by Gupta and Kapoor for stability class D, source strength 45 kg/s, and source of release at height of 25m.

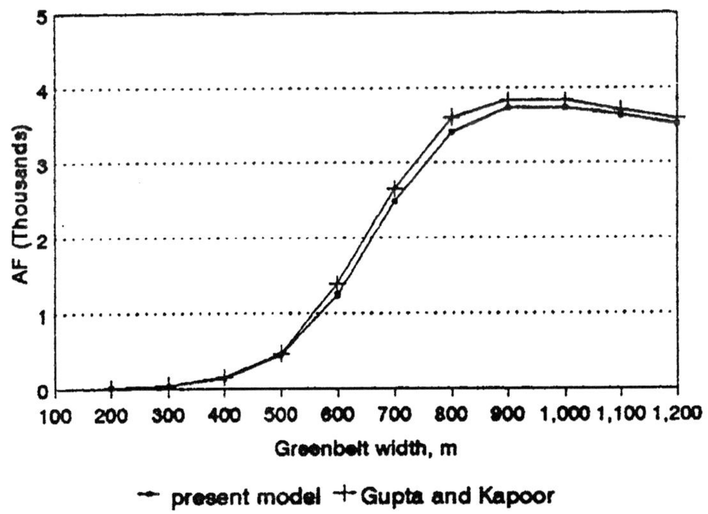

Fig. 6.6: Comparison of pollutant concentration factor (AF) estimated by the present model with that of the model reported by Gupta and Kapoor (1986) for stability class D, and at a distance of 1100 m from the source of pollutant release.

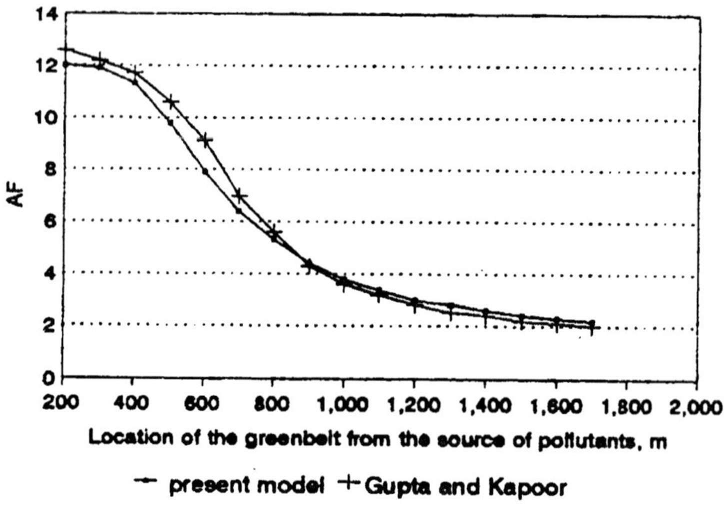

Fig. 6.7: Comparison of pollutant attenuation factor estimated by the present model with that of the model reported by Gupta and Kapoor (1986) for stability class D, and greenbelt width of 200 m.

Chapter 7

SOME USEFUL GUIDELINES EMERGING FROM OUR GREEN BELT DESIGN MODEL

In Chapter 5 we have described a new model developed by us for greenbelt design. In Chapter 6 the testing ad validation of the model has been described. We now present the significance of the various important variables and the guidelines that emerge from the use of our model.

We have modelled two different pollution attenuation factors: one considering interfacial mass interaction between greenbelt and the open space above greenbelt, and the other neglecting this effect. A detailed comparative study of these two attenuation factors under different conditions is now presented.

In general, it has been observed that AF1 (pollution attenuation factor neglecting interfacial mass interaction) predicts lower values compared to AF2 (pollution attenuation factor with interfacial mass interaction). It is because of the interfacial mass interaction concept that here two pollutant mass fluxes have been considered: one from greenbelt to open space and another from open space to greenbelt. The second type of flux would always be denser, as while going downwind more and more pollutant mass (from open space above greenbelt) would interact with the greenbelt. This would cause high pollution attenuation compared to the assumption of no mass interaction. Further, the values of AF2 are more realistic compared to AF1, as it models more realistic process.

We have conducted simulations to assess the impact of various parameters of the values of AF1 and AF2. The results are summarised in the following pages.

7.1 Impact of the distance of greenbelt form the pollution source, and greenbelt width on attenuation (values of AF1, and AF2)

We have explained in section 5.1 (chapter 5), that after a gaseous plume containing a pollutant has been released from a tall stack into the atmosphere, it would travel some distance before it would come close to the ground level. During this travel the plume shall get diluted by air to some extent, and its shape would also go through alterations (Abbasi 1998, Chapter 5). A large number of variables influence this phonemena, mainly the atmospheric conditions and the physical, chemical, and physico-chemical properties of the plume. This being the situation, the maximum ground level concentration of an air pollutant exiting form a stack in a byoyant plume would occur some distance from the stack. This distance, for a plume of given characteristics, would be dependant on atmospheric conditions. A typical situation is illustrated in Figure 7.1.

One major component of mathematical modelling for greenbelt design is to work out this important variable i, e the distance from the stack at which the air pollutant(s) shall reach maximum ground level concentrations because the front edge of the greenbelt should ideally begin at that point.

We have simulated the effect on attenuation of pollutants by the greenbelt if this edge is located farther and farther away from the point of occurrence of maximum ground level pollutant concentration. The studies, expectedly, reveal that father is the greenbelt edge from the point mentioned above, lesser shall be the attenuation. In other words the values of AF1 and AF2 decline sharply as the distance of the greenbelt edge increases with reference to the point of occurrence of maximum ground level pollutant concentration.

Vis-à-vis the relationship of Afs with the belt width, Figure 7.2 indicates increase in the values of AFs with increase in the width of the greenbelt. The rate of increase in the AF values is high upto a distance of 700m, while later it becomes almost constant. Another notewerthy feature of Figure 7.2 is that upto a distance of 600m the values of AF2 are higher than to AF1, on proceeding further the trends reverses. It is because the incoming (open space to greenbelt) and outgoing (greenbelt to open space) pollutant fluxes would increase which going along the downwind direction, but after a certain distance the incoming flux would become almost constant. This results in the decrease in the value of AF2 after a certain distance when compared to the value of AF1. Thus, it is not advisable to have a width of more than 700m at any region of the greenbelt.

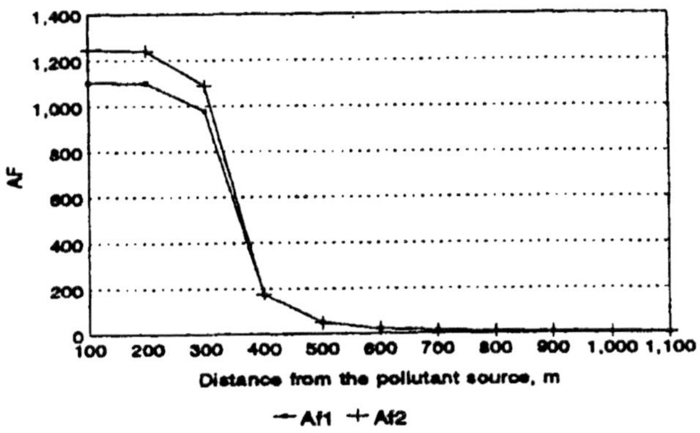

Fig. 7.1: Comparison of af1 with af2 for a range of distance from the pollutant source (width of geen belt 600m. height of trees 25m, stability class D)

Figure 7.3 depicts the values of AFs under different atmospheric stability conditions. It is evident that during unstable conditions (Pasquill stability class, A,B and C) the values of AFs are very low (far less than 10), while the same are quite high for neutral and stable conditions (Pasquill stability class D and E). This indicates that the greenbelts are more effective during neutral and stable atmospheric conditions than when the atmosphere is unstable. This fact hardly weighs against the effectiveness of greenbelts because it is during neutral and stable conditions that the dispersion of pollutants by air is not efficient and the greenbelts are needed. When the atmosphere is unstable, the air movements are after sufficient to attenuates the pollutants by rapid dispersion and dilution.

7.2 Parameteric Effect of Greenbelt Width on AF2 Under Different Atmospheric conditions

Figure 7.4 depicts the profiles of AF2 for various greenbelt width under different conditions of atmospheric stability. Following conclusions are drawn.

i. The values of AF2 decrease as the instability in the atmosphere increases.
ii. AF2 values increases with the increase in the greenbelt width.
iii. The impact of greenbelt width is pronounced only upto a distance of 400m thereafter the values of AF2 become constant.
iv. The rate of increase in the value of AF2 decrease as the atmosphere becomes more and more unstable.

Figure 7.5 also reveals similar profiles for neutral and stable atmospheric conditions. It is seen that:

i. The values of AF2 increase exponentially during stable atmospheric conditions while the rate of increase is slower in neutral conditions.
ii. The effect of greenbelt width is more pronounced upto a distance of 400m while later the value of AF2 remains almost constant.

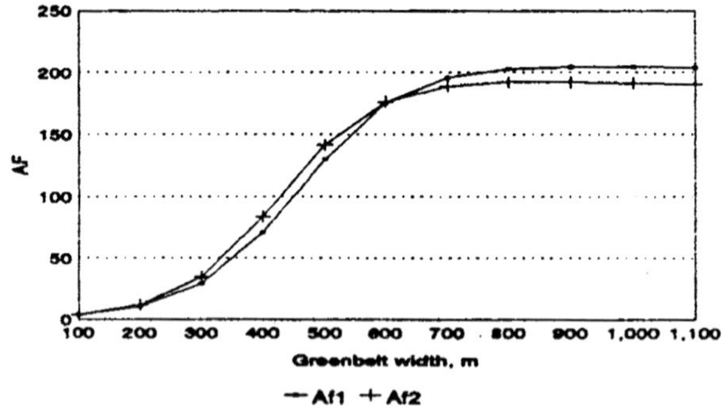

Fig. 7.2: Variation of AF with geenbelt width (distance from pollutant source 400, height of trees 25m, stability class D)

In summary greenbelt width strongly helps in pollutant attenuation upto a limit; thereafter the impact of increase in greenbelt width does not cause significant attenuation. Further, for a given greenbelt width, the degree of attenation increases as the atmospheric stability increases.

7.3 Impact of Distance Between Greenbelt and Pollutant Release Source on AF Under Different Atmospheric Stability Conditions

A simulation study has been conducted to analyse the role of separation distance between greenbelt and source under different atmospheric stability conditions.

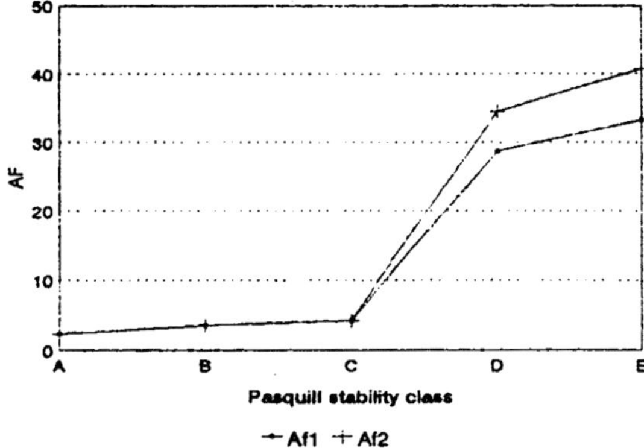

Fig. 7.3: Attenuation as a function of atmospheric stability (distance from pollutant source 400m, greenbelt width 200, height of trees 25m)

The results are plotted in Figures 7.6 and 7.7. Figure 7.6 reveals that with the increase in the turbulence in atmosphere (moving towards unstable condition) the value of AF2 decreases. Moreover, with the increase in the separation distance between greenbelt and pollutant release source, the AF2 values decrease. The rate of decrease is very sharp upto a distance of 300m while proceeding further it remains constant.

Similar to Figure 7.6, Figure 7.7 also depicts similar trend for stability classes D and E (neutral and stable). Here, the values of AF2 are higher for stable atmospheric as compared to conditions the neutral ques. Further, the trend of decrease in the value of AF2 is noticeable only upto a distance of 500m. From the above discussion it is concluded that

i. Values of AF2 are higher for stable atmospheric conditions and decrease sharply as turbulence increases in atmosphere.
ii. Increase in the separation distance between greenbelt and source decreases the value of AF2. This effect is more pronounced till a distance of 300 m during stability classes A, B and C and 500m for stability classes D and E.
iii. In the existing situations (referred in the present study) a value of 300 m would be the optimal.

7.4 Effect of Height of Trees on AF2 Under Different Atmospheric Stability Conditions

The results of simulation are plotted in Figures 7.8-7.12. Following observations are made:

i. Values of AF2 increase with the increase in tree height.

ii. The rate of increase in the value of AF2 as above is very slow for stability class A (highly unstable) and linear for stability class B (moderately unstable).

iii. For the stability class C initially the value of AF2 increases linearly (upto a height of 20 m) while later it becomes almost constant.

iv. Similar trends, as observed for stability class C, have been observed for stability classes D and E. However, in these situations (classes D and E) the rate of increase in the value of AF2 is higher compared to class C.

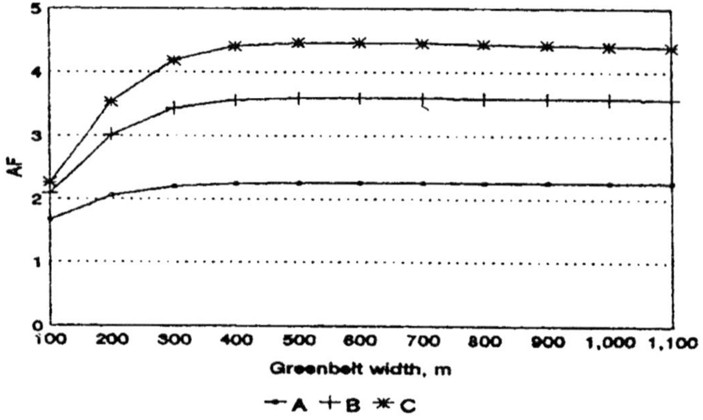

Fig. 7.4: Variation of attenuation with geenbelt width under atmospheric stability A,B,C (distance from pollutant source 600m, height of trees 25m)

In summary, increase in the tree height, increases the pollution attenuation. This effect diminishes as atmospheric conditions move towards greater instability. Under neutral or stable conditions, a tree height of 20 m appears optimal.

7.5 Effect of Plantation Density on AF2 Under Different Atmospheric Conditions.

Simulations were done to assess the impact of plantation density under different atmospheric stability conditions on AF2. The plantation density in present context is defined as the ratio of foliage area of one tree to the foliage area of the total greenbelt.

The simulation results are plotted in Figures 7.13 and 7.14. It is inferred from Figure 7.13 that an increase in the value of plantation density increases the values of AF2. For all the three stability classes

(A, B, and C) illustrated in Figure 7.13 the increasing trend is almost linear. The slope for stability class C is the highest, while it is the lowest for class A. Unlike stability classes A through C, the trend of increase in the value of AF2 is non-linear for stability classes D and E (Figure 7. 14).

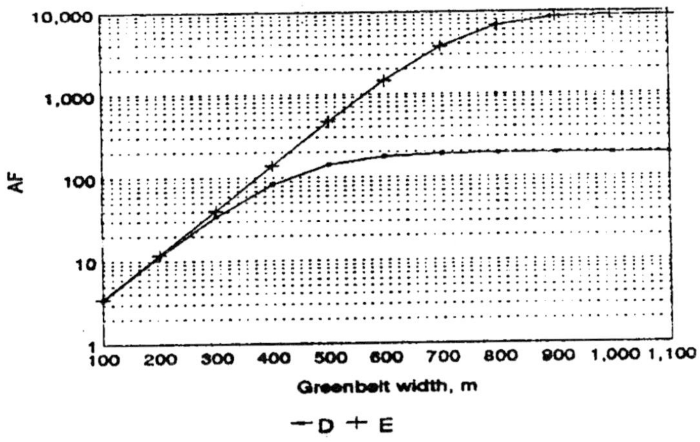

Fig. 7.5: Variation of attenuation with greenbelt width under atmospheric stability class D, E (distance from pollutant source 600m, height of trees 25m)

In is interesting to note that atmospheric stability does not play as important role in the relationship of plantation density with AF as it does in the four other simulations, discussed earlier.

In summary, an increase in plantation density increases the value of AF2. However trees can't be planted denser than a maximum *viable* value. A density of 0.01 (as per abovementional definition) appears optimal.

In conclusion it must be emphasised that several variables, have to be considered and balanced for an optimal design of greenbelt. As there factors are strongly dependent on the site characteristics (meteorology, land availability, soil type, water availability, horticultural factors etc) as also the characteristics of the pollutant source (stack dimensions, source strength and source characteristics), no single recipe can be given for all greenbelts. We do hope that the model developed by us covers most of the variables that influence greenbelt design. It should, therefore, be possible to design cost effective and useful greenbelts under widely different situations using this model.

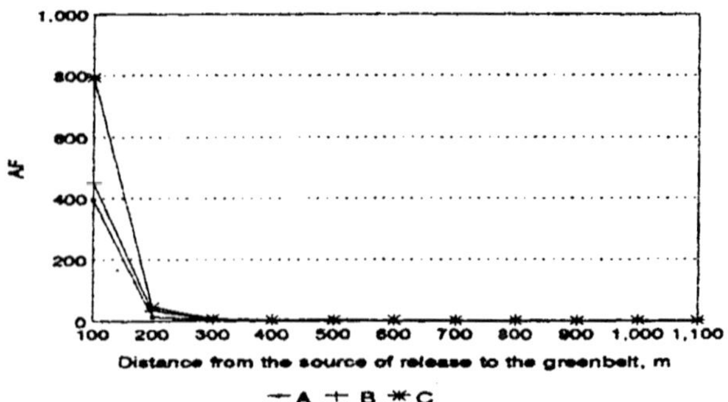

Fig. 7.6: Variation of attenuation with greenbelt width under atmospheric stability class A, B, C, (greenbelt width 400m, height of trees 25m)

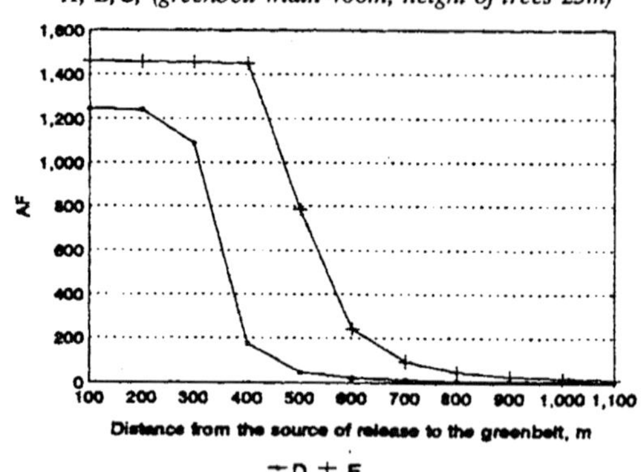

Fig. 7.7: Variation of attenuation with greenbelt width under atmospheric stability class D, E (greenbelt width 400m, height of trees 25m)

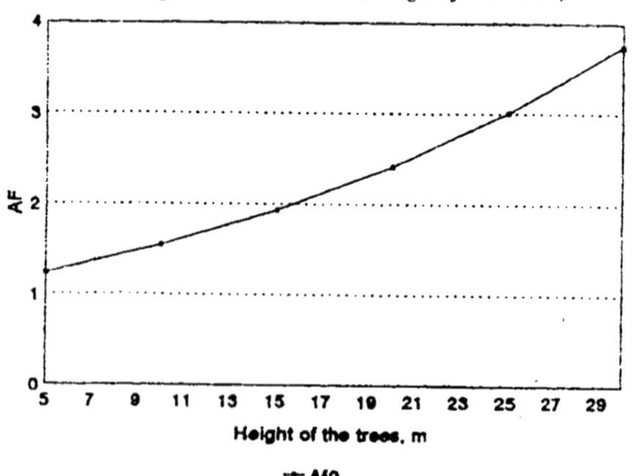

Fig. 7.8: Variation of AF with tree height (distance from pollutant source 400m, greenbelt width 200m, stability class A)

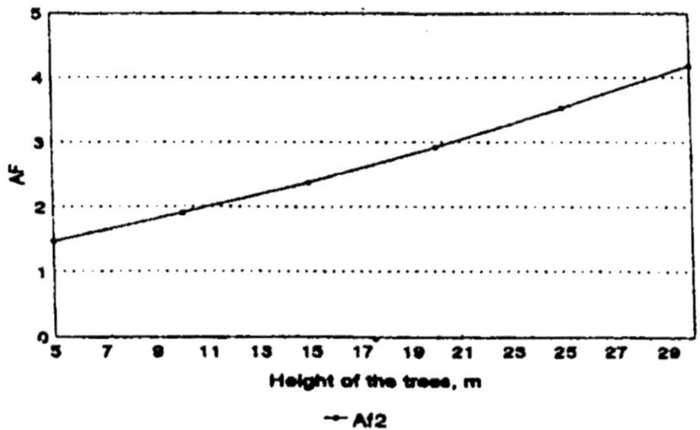

Fig. 7.9: Variation of AF with tree height (distance from pollutant source 400m, greenbelt width 200m, stability class B)

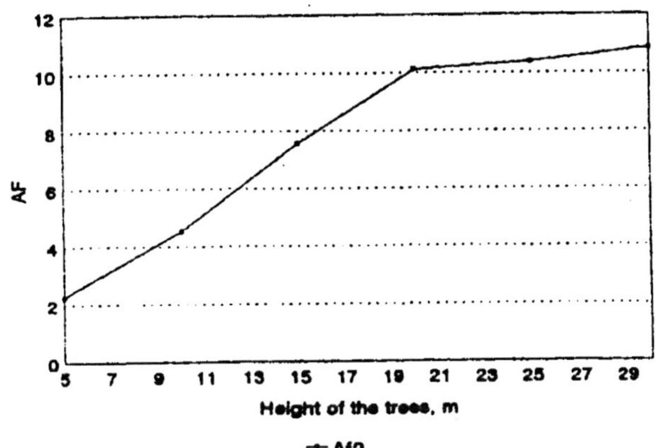

Fig. 7.10: Variation of AF with tree height (distance from pollutant source 400m, greenbelt width 200m, stability class C)

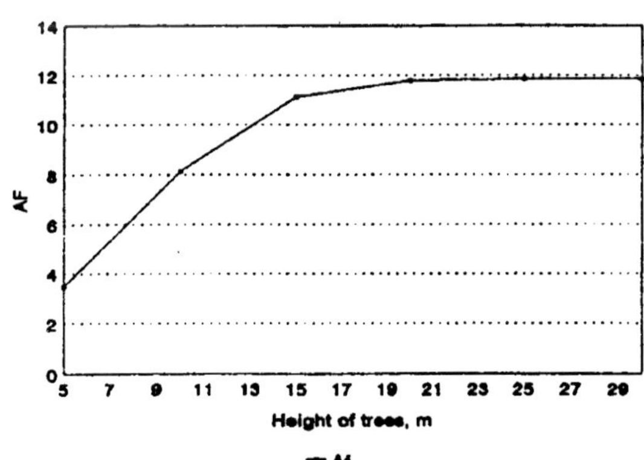

Fig. 7.11: Variation of AF with tree height (distance from pollutant source 400m, greenbelt width 200m, stability class D)

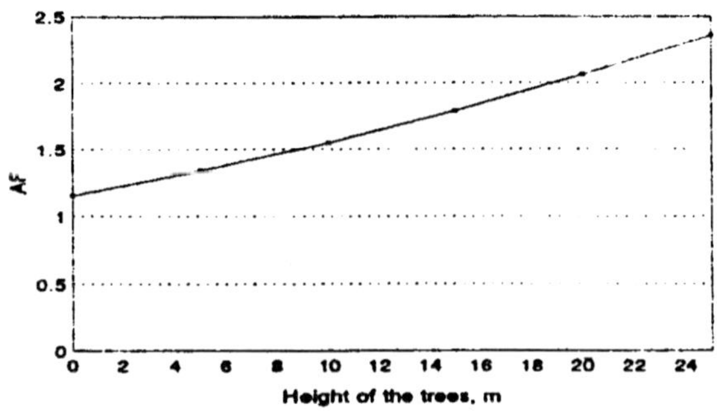

Fig. 7.12: Variation of AF with tree height (distance from pollutant source 400m, greenbelt width 200m, stability class E)

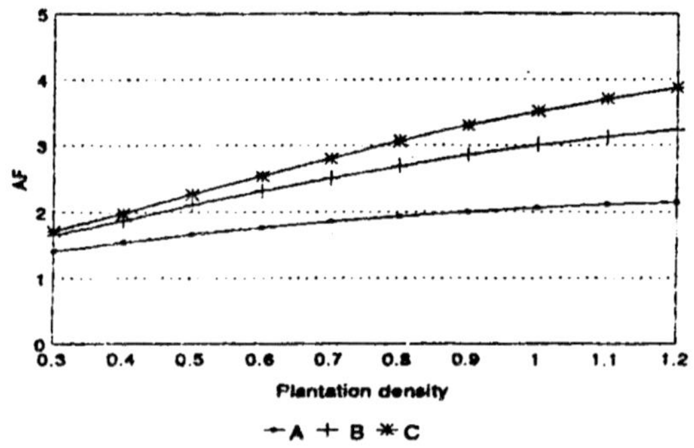

Fig. 7.13: Variation of AF with plantation density (distance from pollutant source 600m, height of trees 25m, width of geen belt 400m, stability class A,B,C)

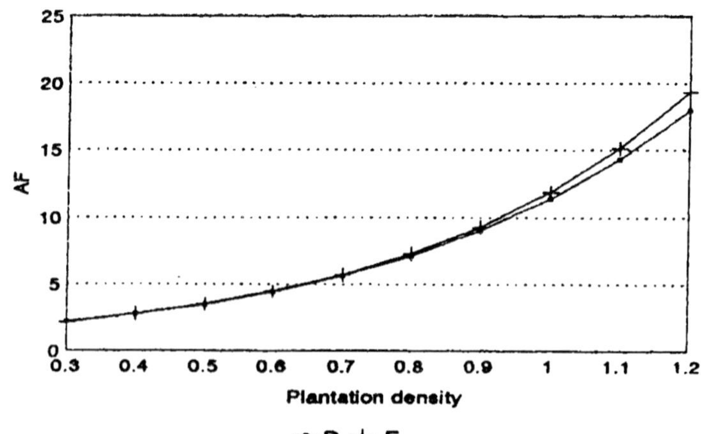

Fig. 7.14: Variation of AF with plantation density (distance from pollutant source 600m, height of trees 25m, width of green belt 400m, stability class D and E)

Chapter - 8

DESIGN OF GREENBELTS FOR THE INDUSTRIAL COMPLEXES OF PONDICHERRY

8.1 INTRODUCTION

Pondicherry region consists of four industrial estates with a total of some 5600 (small, medium and large scale) industries (Government of Pondicherry, 1997). These four estates are:

i. Sedarapet Industrial Estate located west of downtown Pondicherry.
ii. Mettupalayam Industrial Estate located west of downtown Pondicherry.
iii. Thattanchavady Industrial Estate located near downtown Pondicherry.
iv. Kirumambakkam (Kattukuppam) Industrial Estate located south of downtown Pondicherry.

These four estates are situated within 15 Km of each other, and have very similar macroclimatic setting. Of the four, the industrial estates situated at Kirumambakkam and Setharapet are bigger and are farther away from densely populated urban neighborhoods than the other two, smaller, estates of Mettupalayam and Thattanchavdy. The two smaller states are located so close to each other that we have treated them as a single industrial complex.

8.2 GREENBELT FOR KIRUMAMBAKKAM INDUSTRIAL ESTATE

In Kirumambakkam industrial estate the main pollutants emitted from the various sources are SO_2, NO_x, SPM, H_2S, Cl_2 and H_2SO_4 mist. The concentrations of these pollutants in and around the area is presented in Tables A-18 to A.21, Appendix. It is evident from the data that the area is highly polluted, necessitating control measures including a greenbelt. For the purpose of greenbelt design we have taken the dominant pollutant, So_x, as a reference and a value of 45 kg/s has been assumed to be its source strength. This value is higher than the present strength of release source; because we have also taken future expansion into consideration.

8.2.1 Meteorology and Atmospheric Stability

The wind roses for different seasons (three seasons namely winter, summer and rain) have been plotted in Figures 8.1 to 8.3. Figure 8.1 reveals that during winter the most frequent wind direction is the north-west (more than 50% of the time, with an average wind speed of 2.5 m/s) and the next most frequent is South-West(45%) with an average wind speed of 1.36 m/s. During summer, the wind blows equally in all directions, while during rains south-west is the most frequently observed direction of the wind.

The monthly variation of temperature is presented in Figure 8.4. It indicates that May to July are the hottest months, while December, January and February are the cooler ones.

Using synoptic meteorological data, atmospheric turbulence has been estimated for each month. This has than been scaled down to a 0-1 scale and plotted in Figure 8.5. It is seen that the turbulence intensity is lower during January and February, and maximum during May and June. Based on the turbulence intensity and Mohn Obkov length, the atmospheric stability has been characterized for each month. For the sake of making the calculations easier to handle, we have divided the year into three different seasons and the stability has been averaged for these seasons (Figure 8.5).

As all the four industrial estates are governed by the same meteorological conditions, the stability classes worked out by us shall be applicable throughout the Pondicherry city .

8.2.2 Dispersion of Pollutants

Using the model detailed in Chapters 5-7, dispersion of pollutant (SO_2) has been assessed for various seasons as a function of downwind distance. The resulting concentration profiles are presented in Figures 8.6-8.8. It is evident that during summer the dispersion is fastest (Figure 8.7) while it is slowest during winter. The values of maximum ground-level concentrations are seen to occur during winter, that too at larger distances from the release source (Figure 8.8) than in other seasons. It is expected to be so because if the rate of pollutant dispersion is low, the maximum ground-level concentration shall occur at larger distance from the source than when the dispersion is swifter.

The maximum ground level concentrations and the distances at which they would occur, are plotted in Figure 8.9.

8.2.3 Design of Greenbelt

Various greenbelt design parameters have been estimated using the model detailed in chapters 5 -7. Design calculations have been carried out for the three different seasons and the design parameters have been identified.

Pollution attenuation factor, is the most important parameter in deciding the location of the greenbelt, the greenbelt width, the plantation density, and the height of trees. Figures 8.10 to 8.13 depict profiles of AF as a function of distance between greenbelt and source, and plume width for the three different seasons. Figure 8.10 indicates that for the rainy season and north-west wind direction, a greenbelt of 200m would be optimal (AF value of 7.25). In the south-west direction, a width of 150mwould to required. Thus, a greenbelt of 200 m width would be required to optimally attenuate the air pollutants in the rainy season.

Figures 8.12 and 8.13 reveal that greenbelt widths of 200m and 500m would be optimal for summer and winter seasons.

An analysis to decide the plantation density reveals that K (ratio of foliage area) value of 0.9 would give most favorable results. The final values of these design parameters are presented in Table 8.1, while a simple layout of proposed greenbelt is depicted in Figure 8.14.

8.2.4 Canopy and Selection of Trees Species

A study has been conducted to decide the canopy of the tree plantation and the spacing between the trees. It is suggested that a triangular pitch canopy should be developed and the spacing of 25-30 ft. should be maintained between trees of middle height and the tall ones.

We recommend that a combination of tall trees, trees of middle height, and shrubs be planted to capture maximum pollutants. Four rows of tall trees, six rows of trees of middle height and eight rows of shrubs are recommended. Five tree species in each category, suitable for the given macroclimatic setting, are given in Table 8.2.

8.3 GREENBELT FOR SEDARAPET INDUSTRIAL ESTATE

Sedarapet is the next most important industrial area in Pondicherry. The main pollutants released from the area are SO_x, NO_x, H_2SO_4, mist and H_2S. The concentration of these pollutants in and around the area is presented in Tables A.18-A.21 in the Appendix. This study has been conducted taking a pollutant release source strength of 36 kg/s (cumulative of all release sources).

8.3.1 Meteorology and Atmospheric Stability

The meteorology, and the atmospheric stability classifications used in Kirumambbakkam area, are applicable to the present study because observations made at both places reveal that the meteorology of the two areas is identical; therefore the atmospheric stability conditions estimated for Kirumambbakkam area are applicable in Sedarapet as well.

8.3.2 Dispersion of Pollutants

A plot of maximum ground level concentration and the distance where it would occur in the three different seasons is depicted in Figure 8.15. The maximum concentrations would occur during winter.

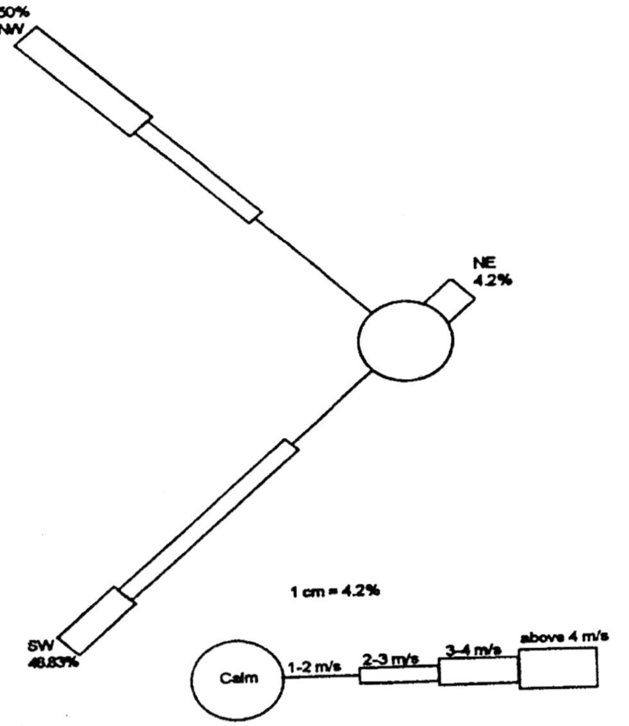

Fig. 8.1: Windrose for winter season (November to February)

8.3.3 Designing of Greenbelt

The values of pollution attenuation factors, AF, have been computed for various sets of parameters (Figures 8.16-9.19). Figure 8.16 & 8.17 illustrate the profile of AF during rainy seasons (for two different wind directions). They reveal that a width of 125 m would be optimal for the south-west direction, and 150 m for the north-west direction. Figure 8.18 indicates that 150m width of greenbelt would be sufficient to achieve desired pollution attenuation during summer, while the same could be achieved by a width of 100m during winter (Figure 8.19). Thus, all things considered, a greenbelt of 150m width would serve the purpose of desired level (AF 3.0) pollution attenuation.

Table 8.1 Values of greenbelt design parameters for Kirumambakkam industrial estate

Parameters	*Values*
Distance from pollutant source to greenbelt	100m
Greenbelt width	200m
Value of K(se/st)	0.9
Pitch	Triangular
Inter tree spacing for tall tree	25-30 ft.
Inter tree spacing for middle height tree	30-40 ft.
Inter tree spacing for shrub	-25 ft.
Pollution attenuation factor	3.0
Tree species	as given in table

Table 8.2 Tree species recommended for greenbelt plantation for the present study area.

TREES :
1. Tall trees
2. Azadirachta indica (Neem)
3. Tamarindus indica(Tamarind)
4. Ficus religiosa (Peepal)
5. Mangifera indica (Mango)
6. Tectona grandis (Teak)

Trees of medium height
1. Butea monosperma
2. Poinciana regia (Gulmohar)
3. Parkinsonia aculeta
4. Thevetia nerifolia
5. Acaccia arabica (Kateria Babul)

SHRUBS :
1. Bougainvillea (Baganvillas)
2. Calotropis Procera (Madar)
3. Ipomoea fistula (Behaya)
4. Nerium odorum (Lal kaner)
5. Thevetia nerifolia (Peela kaner)

HERBS :
1. Vinca rosea 2.
   Cynodon dactylon
3. Ipomaea cornea
4. Achyranthes aspera (Latjira)
5. Solanum xanthocarpum (Bhatkatauja)

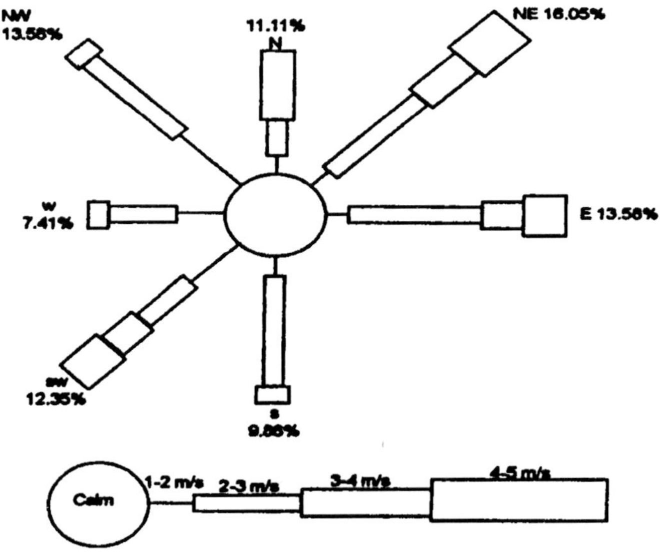

Fig. 8.2: Windrose for summer season (March-June)

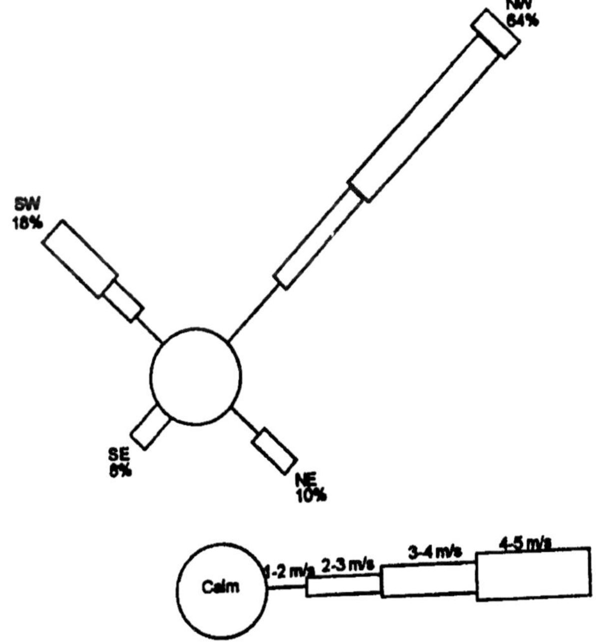

Fig. 8.3: Windrose for rainy season (July to October)

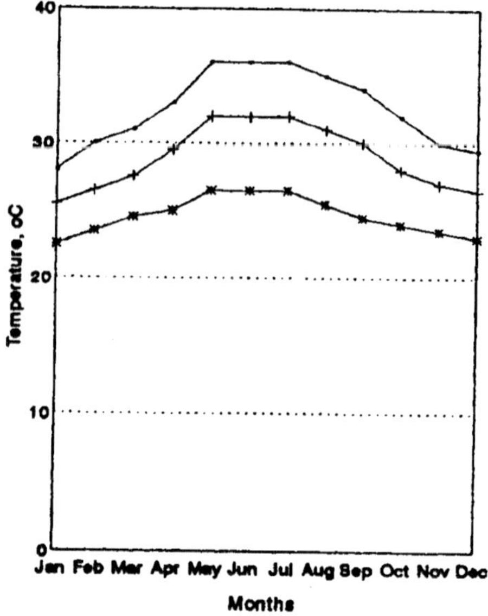

Fig. 8.4: Pattern of minimum, maximum and average temperature at the project site.

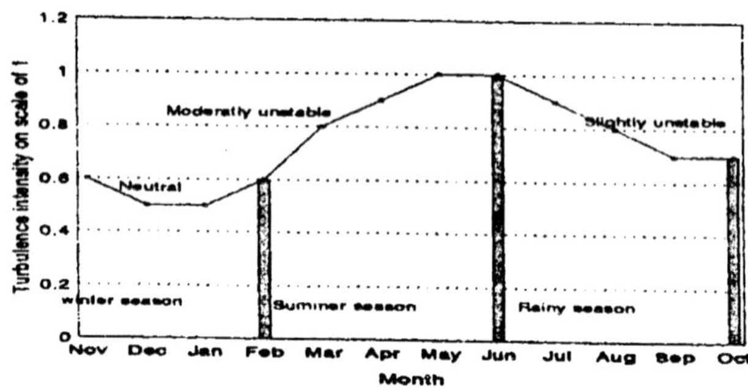

Fig. 8.5 Varition of turbulence intensity (on scale of 1.0) with months

The full set of design parameters is presented in Table 8.3. The proposed layout of the greenbelt is depicted in Figure 8.20.

8.3.4 Canopy and Selection of Trees

Triangular pitch canopy has been recommended for plantation. A distance of 25-30 ft should be maintained between the trees. The shrubs can be planted with a spacing of 5-10ft intermittently between the trees.

A list of trees suitable for the plantation with respect to macroclimatic conditions and capacity to tolerate the given pollutants, is presented in Table 8.2.

8.4 METTUPALAYAM INDUSTRIAL ESTATE

Mettupalayam industrial area is basically a combination of Mettupalayam and Thattanchavady industrial estates. The main pollutants of the area are SO_x, NO_x,H_2S and H_2SO_4. The release strength of the source is approximately 26 kg/s.

8.4.1 Meteorology and Atmospheric Stability

The atmospheric stability conditions are the same as have been described in the preceding sections.

8.4.2 Dispersion of Pollutants

The study reveals that during summer, the dispersion is faster and comparatively lower pollutant concentrations are observed than during winter.

Figure 8.25 reveals that maximum ground level concentration would occur during winter season at a distance of 190m form the focal point, while the maximum concentration during summer would occur at about 80m.

8.4.3 Designing of Greenbelt

As before, pollution attenuation factors have been estimated as functions of distance between the edge of the greenbelt and the starting point of occurrence of maximum ground level pollutant concentration, and greenbelt width for three seasons (Figures 8.21 to 8.26), Table 8.4. Figures 8.21 and 8.22 present the profiles of AF during rainy season (for two different wind directions). It is evident from these figures that greenbelt width of 125m (during SW wind direction) and 175m (during NW wind direction) would achieve the desired pollution attenuation during the rainy season. During summer and winter season greenbelts of 130m and 100m respectively would serve the purpose. All in all, a greenbelt

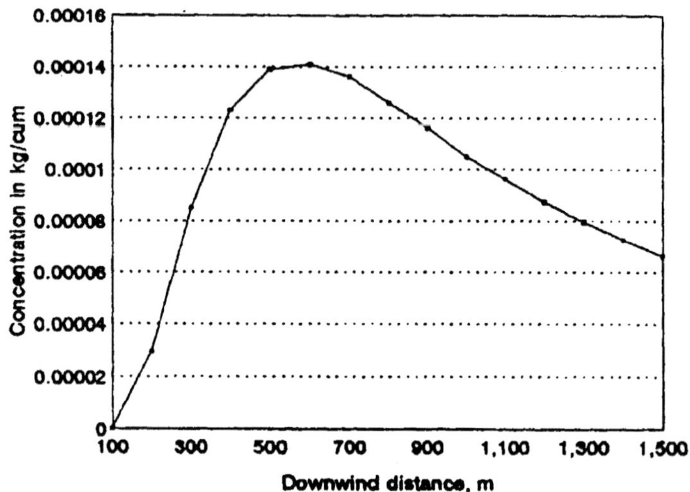

Fig. 8.6:Plot showing variation of concentration along the downwind distance for slightly unstable atmospheric condition during rainy season

125m wide would be sufficient to attenuate the pollution to a accepted level.

Table 8.3 Values of greenbelt design parameters for Sedarapet industrial estate

Parameter	*Values*
Distance form Pollutant source to greenbelt	75-100m
Greenbelt width	125-150m
Value of K(Se/St)	0.9
Pitch	Triangular
Inter tree spacing for tall tree	25-30 ft.
Inter tree spacing for middle height tree	30-40 ft.
Inter tree spacing for shrub	15-25 ft.
Pollution atteunation factor	3.0
Tree species	as given in Table

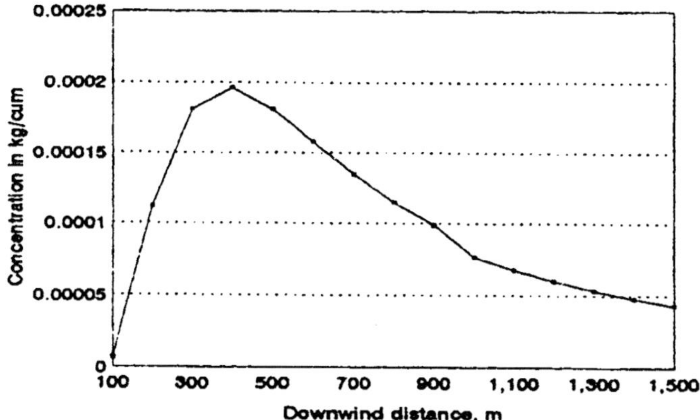

Fig. 8.7: Plot showing variation of concentration along the downwind distance for slightly unstable atmospheric condition during rainy season

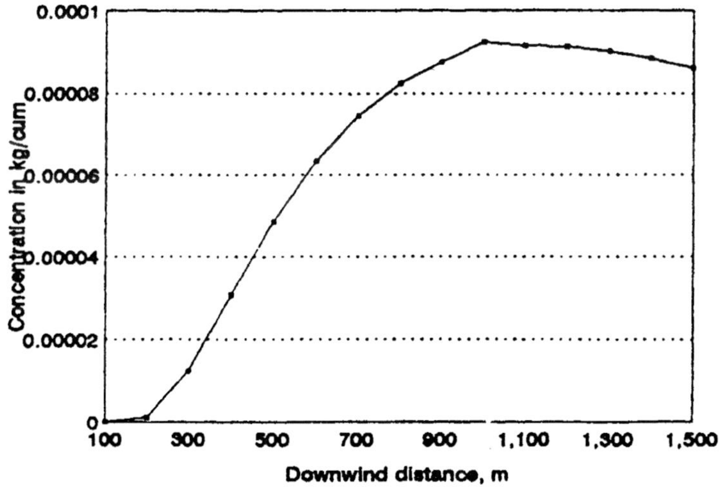

Fig. 8.8: Plot showing variation of concentration along the downwind distance for slightly unstable atmospheric condition during rainy season

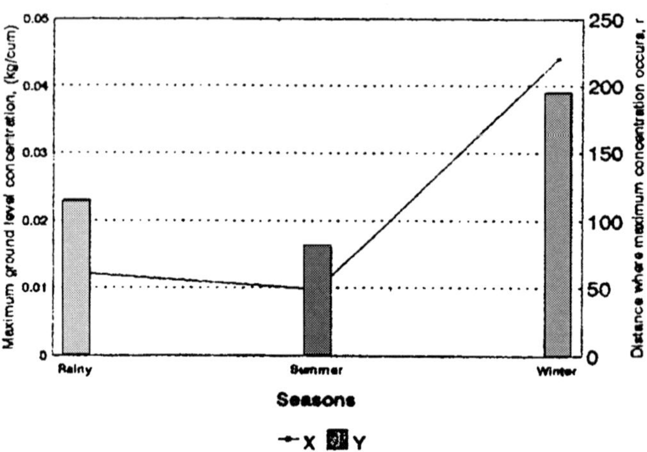

Fig. 8.9: Variation of maximum ground level concentration (x) and distance where this concentration (Y) occurs with seasons for kirmambakkam industrial area.

Table 8.4 Values of greenbelt design parameters for Mettupalayam industrial estate

Parameters	*Values*
Distance from pollutant source to greenbelt	50-75m
Greenbelt width	100-125m
Value of K(Se/St)	0.9
Pitch	Triangular
Inter tree spacing for tall tree	25-30 ft.
Inter tree spacing for middle height tree	30-40 ft.
Inter tree spacing for shrub	15-25 ft.
Pollution atteunation factor	3.0
Tree species	as given in Table

8.4.4 Canopy and Selection of Trees.

It is recommended to have the same triangular pitch arrangement as suggested for other industrial estates. The selection of trees can be made using the list presented in Table 8.2. The trees should be planted in the order of increasing height as depicted in Figure 8.27.

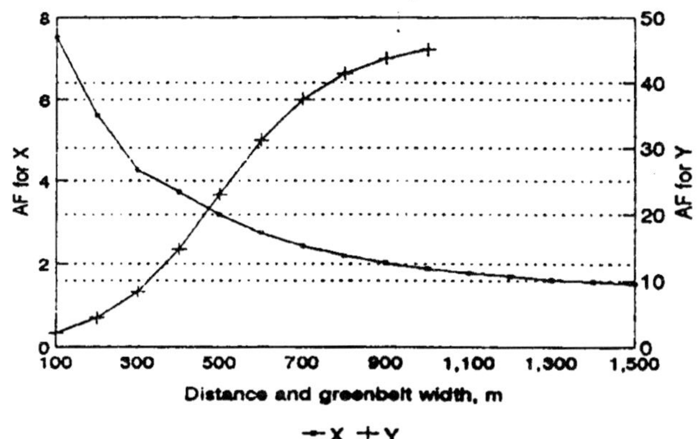

Fig. 8.10: The variation of AF as a function of distance between greenbelt and pollutant source (X), and greenbelt width (Y) for winter season in Kirmambakkam industrial estate.

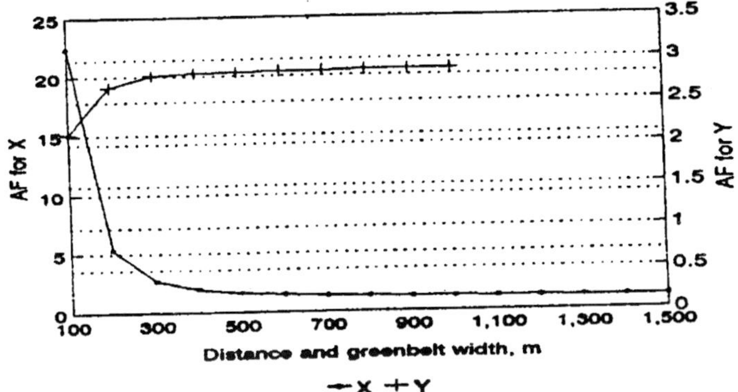

Fig. 8.11: The variation of AF as a function of distance between greenbelt and pollutant source (X), and greenbelt width (Y) for summer season Kirumambakkam industrial area.

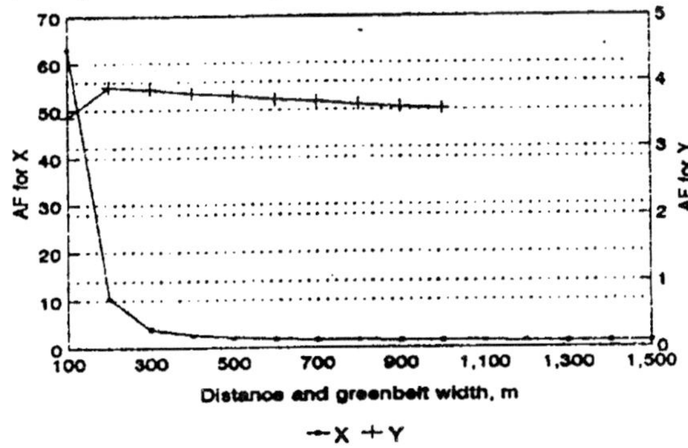

Fig. 8.12: The variation of AF as a function of distance between greenbelt and pollutant source (X) and greenbelt width (Y) for rainy season (II) in Mettupalayam industrial estate.

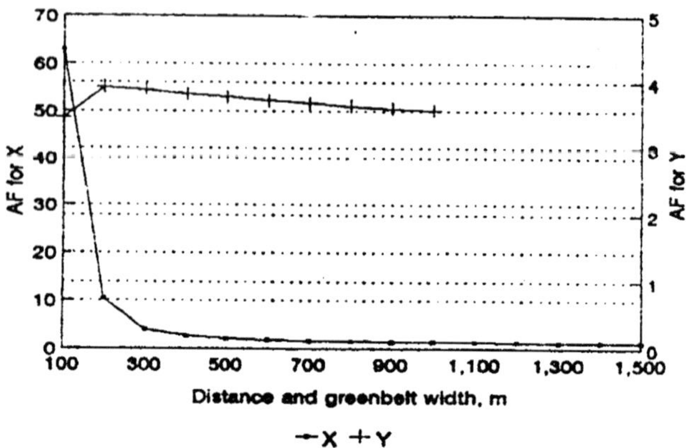

Fig. 8.13: The variation of AF as a function of distance between greenbelt and pollutant source (X), and greenbelt width (Y) for rainy season (II) Kirumambakkam industrial area.

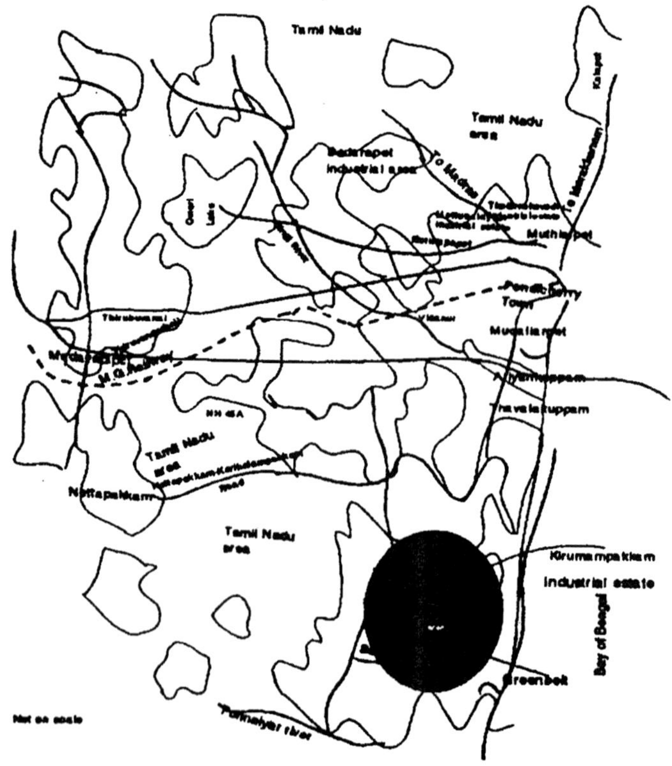

Fig. 8.14: Proposed greenbelt around the Kirumambakkam industrial estate

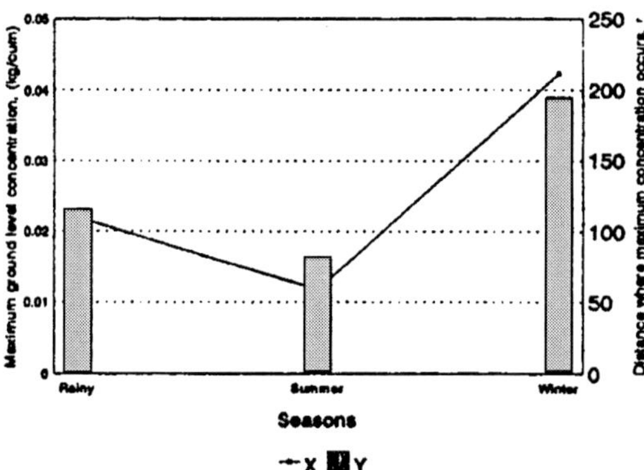

Fig. 8.15: Variation of maximum ground level concentration (X) and distance where this concentration (Y) occurs with seasons for Sedarapet industrial estate.

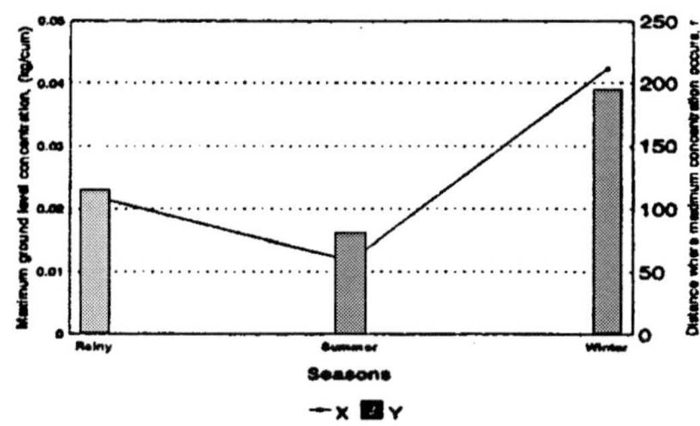

Fig. 8.16: The variation of AF as a function of distance between greenbelt and pollutant source (X), and greenbelt width (Y) for rainy season (II) in Sedarapet industrial estate.

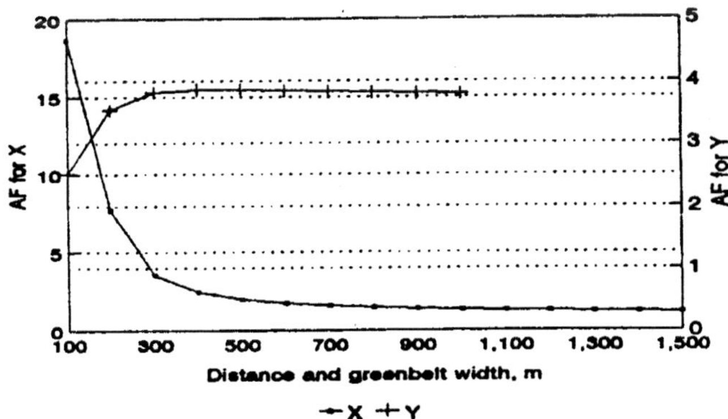

Fig. 8.17: The variation of AF as a function of distance between greenbelt and pollutant source (X) and greenbelt width (Y) for rainy season (II) in Mettupalayam industrial estate.

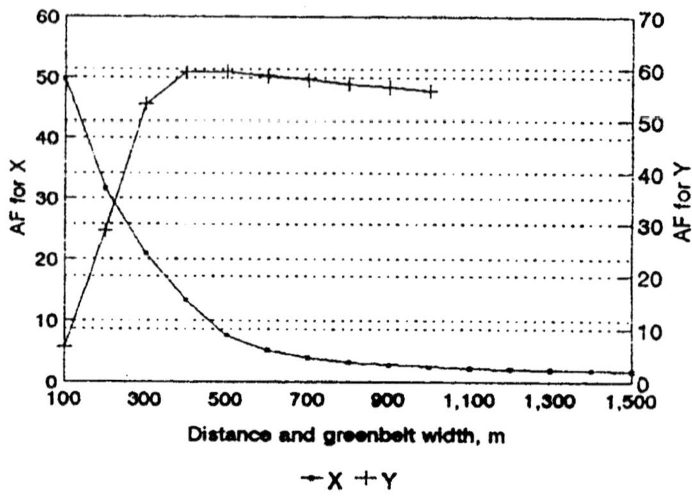

Fig. 8.18: The Variation of AF as a function of distance between greenbelt and pollutant source (X), and greenbelt width (Y) for winter season in Sedarapet industrial estate.

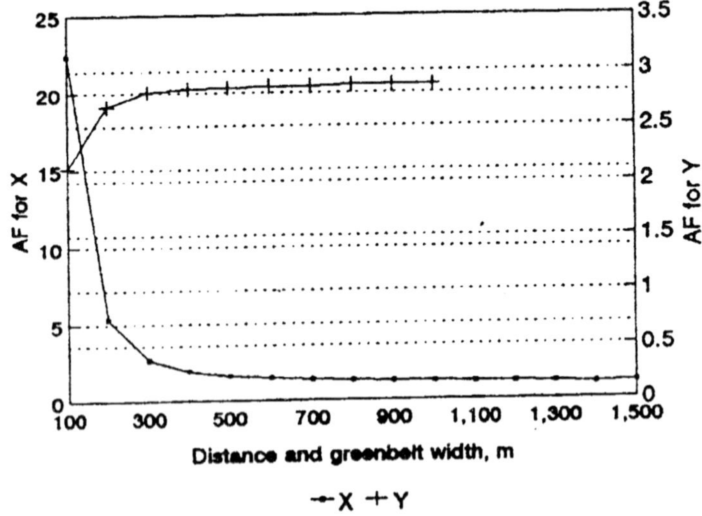

Fig. 8.19: The variation of AF as a function of distance between greenbelt and pollutant source (X), and greenbelt width (Y) for rainy season (II) in Sedarapet industrial estate.

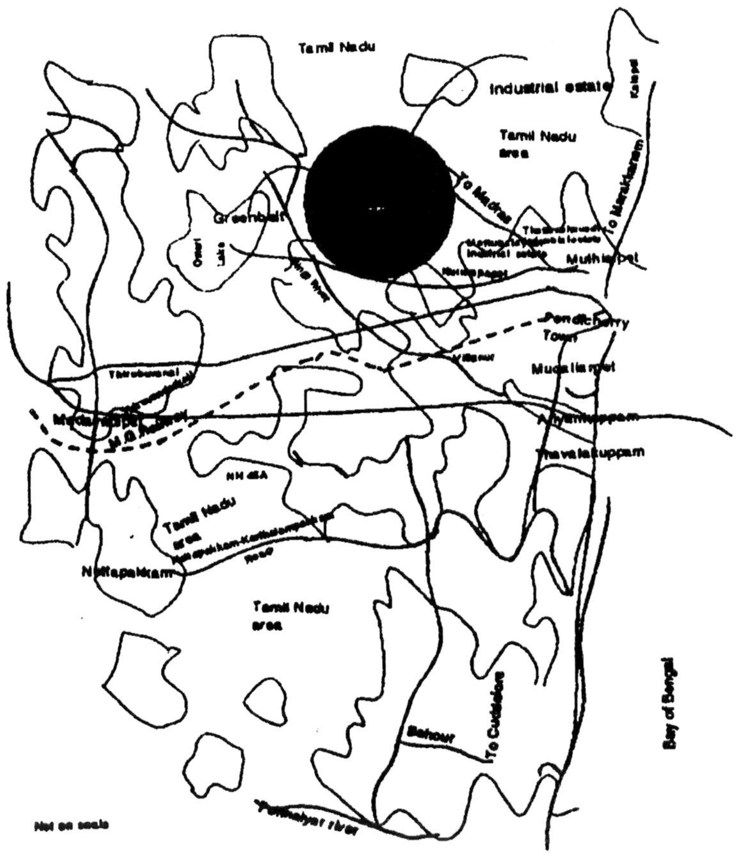

Fig. 8.20: Proposed greenbelt around the Sedarapet industrial estate.

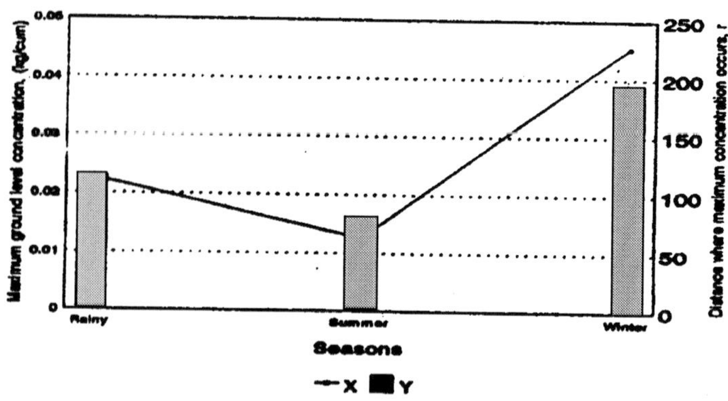

Fig. 8.21: Variation of maximum ground level concentration (X) and distance where this concentration (Y) occurs with seasons for mettupalayam industrial estate.

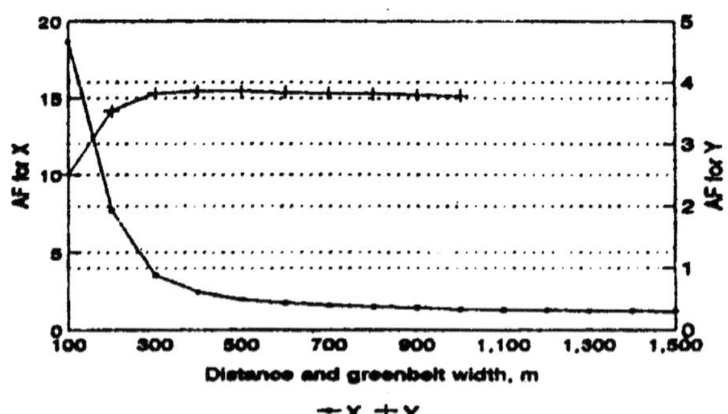

Fig. 8.22: The variation of AF as a function of distance between greenbelt and pollutant source (X), and greenbelt width (Y) for rainy season (I) in Mettupalayam industrial estate.

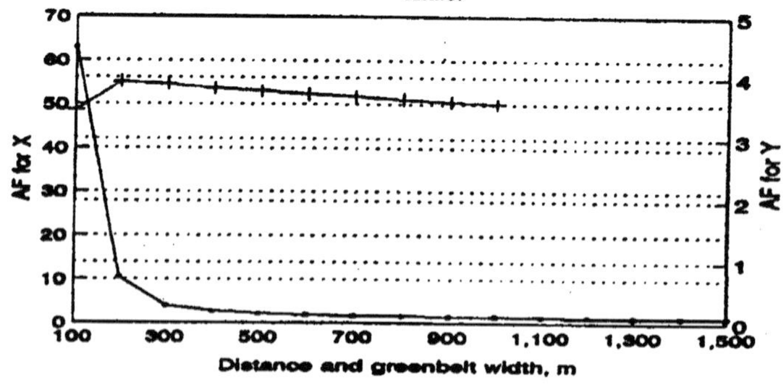

Fig. 8.23: The variation of AF as a function of distance between greenbelt and pollutant source (X) and greenbelt width (Y) for rainy season (II) in Mettupalayam industrial estate.

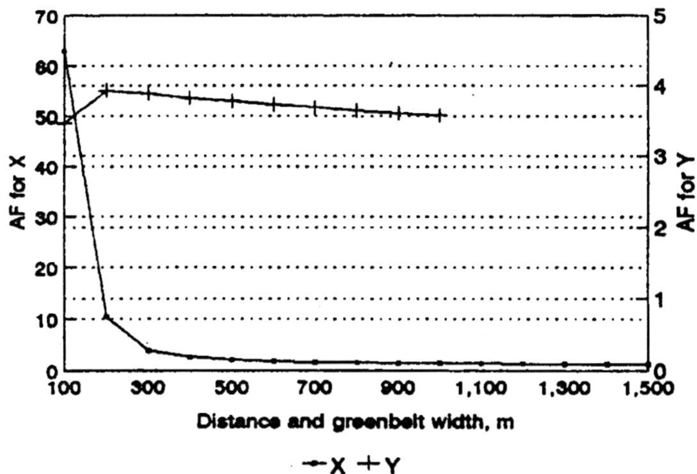

Fig. 8.24: The Variation of AF as a function of distance between greenbelt and pollutant source (X), and greenbelt width (Y) for summer season in Mettupalayam industrial estate.

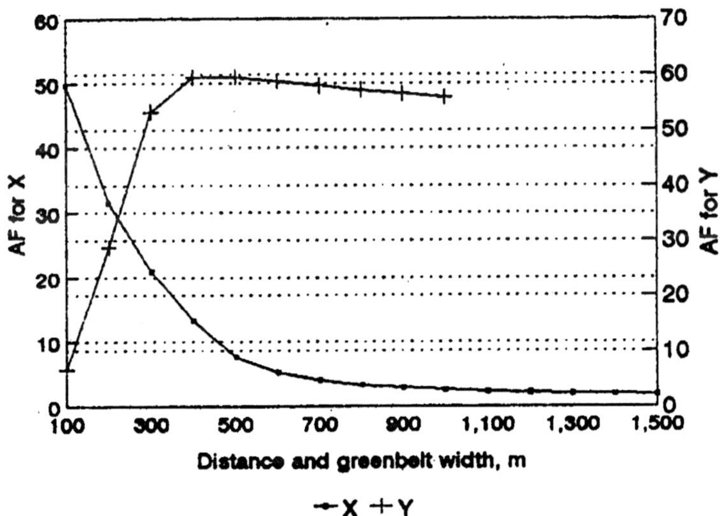

Fig. 8.25: The variation of AF as a function of distance between greenbelt and pollutant source (X), and greenbelt width (Y) for winter season in Mettupalayam industrial estate.

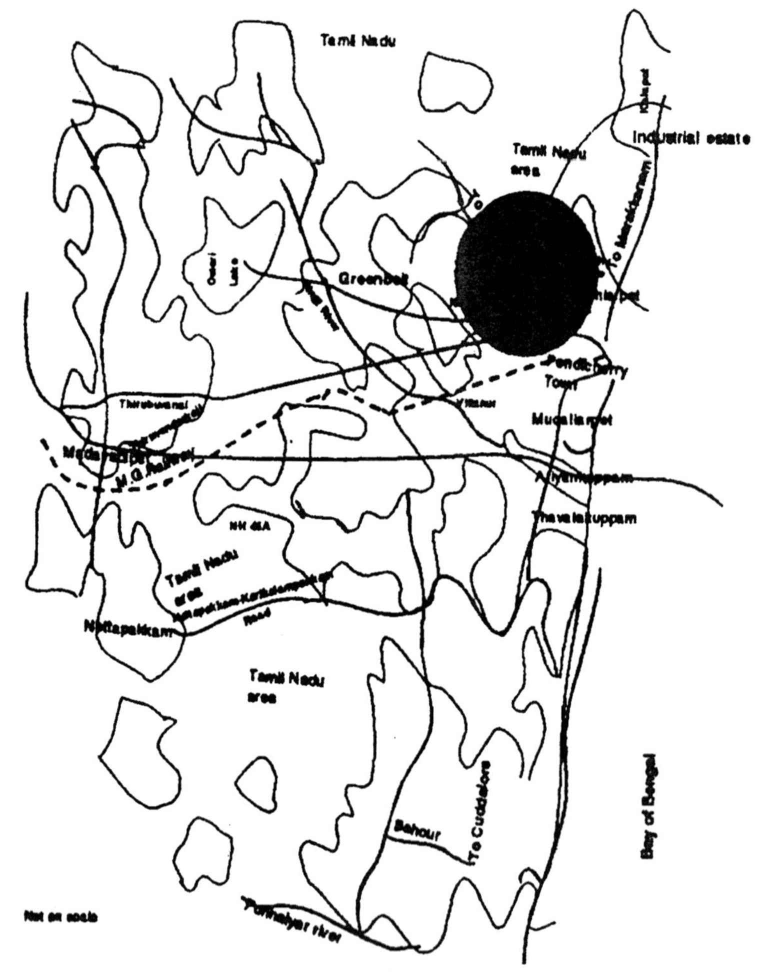

Fig. 8.26: Proposed greenbelt around the Mettupalayam industrial estate.

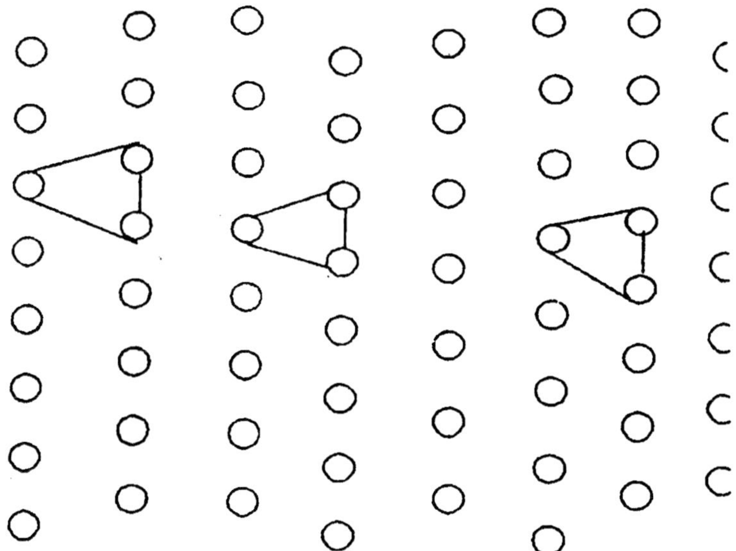

a) proposed plan of the tree plantation

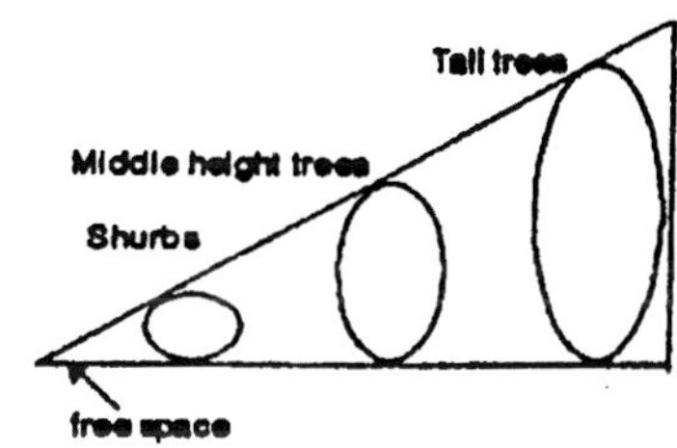

b) canopy of trees

Fig. 8.27:The plan and canopy of the proposed greenbelt

Appendix

PONDICHERRY REGION : AN INTRODUCTION

A.1 GENERAL INTRODUCTION

A.1.1 Location and extent

Pondicherry is one of the union territories (quasi-status) of India. It comprises of your domains situated geographically apart from each other.

These domains are:-

i) Yanam, situated as an enclave in the state of Andhra Pradesh, about 400 km west of Vishakhapatnam.
ii) Mahe, an enclave, situated in the state of Kerala, about 100 km east of Kottayam.
iii) Karaikal, located as an enclave in the state of Tamil Nadu, about 200 km west of Pondicherry.
iv) Pondicherry town is located at the centre of the area, about 162 kms east south of Madras and 22 kms northeast of Cuddalore. The Town occupies an area of about 15 sq.kms. the three sides of the town is bordered by the Tamil Nadu state and on side .i.e. in the east, is bordered by the Bay of Bengal.

Pondicherry region is an enclave in Tamil Nadu situated on the coromandel coast (East) between 11°45' and 12°3' North latitude and 79°37' and 79°53' East longitude (Figure A.1) is about 160 kms South of Madras and the region is bounded on three sides by the lands of South Arcot District of Tamil Nadu and the eastern side is bounded by the blue waters of Bay of Bengal. The region covers an area of 293 sq.kms. (29,377 hectares) and consists of 179 villages. The Pondicherry region is divided into seven regions/communes viz. Pondicherry, Ariyankuppam, Ozhukarai,Mannadipet, Villianur,Bahour and Nettapakkam.

A.1.2 Access (Communication)

All the enclaves of the Pondicherry region are connected by a network of all weather motorable roads. The Madras-Cuddalore State Highway which bifurcates the National Highway No.45 at Tindivanam passes through Pondicherry town. It is also linked with Madras-Trichirapalli of Southern Railway from Villupuram junction. Pondicherry also have a port located on coast of the Bay of Bengal. It is also connected by air through vayudoot services from Madras Airport.

Pondicherry town is accessible by rail and road from neighbouring town. The town is highly transversed by network of roads. Pondicherry town is well connected with pucca road with neighbouring town (belonging to Tamil Nadu) such as Cuddalore (a district headquarters) Villupuram (another district headquarters) and Tindivanam (a big town situated on National High ways as shown in Figure A.2). Pondicherry town is well connected by road with all its seven communes where each commune has more than twenty villages which in turn facilitate people to move from rural to town for various socio-economic purpose.

A.1.3 History

Pondicherry entered modern history when the French East India company established their foothold in 1673, Karaikal was obtained from the king of Thanjavur in 1738. Mahe was handed over to the French by the ruler of Badagara in 1721. Yanam came into their possession in 1731. (Source : Manorama Year book 1998, Malayala Manorama, Kottayam).

The French converted this obscure little village into a flourishing trading centre. The French were the last European power to come to India for trade. The Dutch and the English had already established

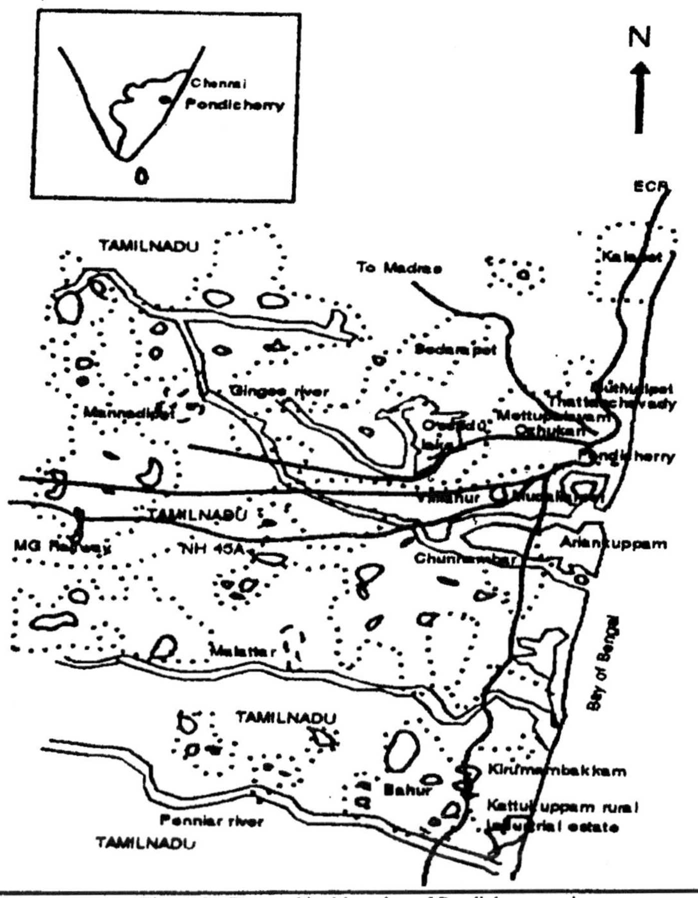

Fig. A.1: Geographical location of Pondicherry region

themselves at various centres in India. The Dutch were the first to cross words with the French. They captured Pondicherry in 1693 but returned it to France under the treaty of Ryswick in 1699. Pondicherry regained its prosperity in a few years. In 1706 Pondicherry had a population of 40,000 while the English town of Calcutta had barely 22,000.

In the meantime, the french East India company had run into financial difficulties and the company was forced to abandon their trading in Bantum, Surat and Masulipatnam. In 1720 the company was reconstituted as the "Perpetual Company of the Indies" and new French establishments sprang up in the East. Mauritius was occupied in 1721, Mahe on the

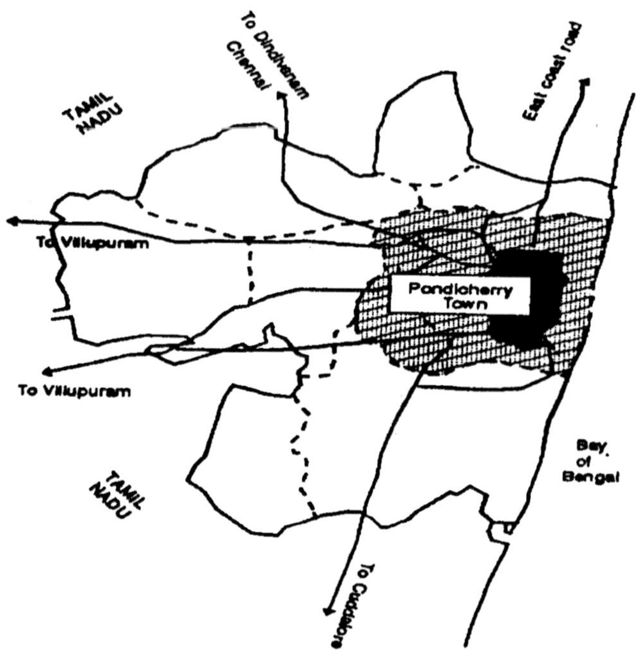

Fig. A.2: Location of downtown Pondicherry

Malabar Coast soon after, Yanam in 1731 and the Karaikal in 1738. With the appointment of Dupleix as Governor of Pondicherry in 1742 France become involved in Indian politics. Dupleix harboured ambitions of establishing a French Empire in India. When at last British paramountcy was established in India, Pondicherry ceased to be of any political importance and the British let the french continue in their possessions in India. The French Government handed over the administration of their territories in India in November, 1954. The territory thus handed over were constituted into the Union Territory of Pondicherry. Pondicherry is a living monument of french culture in India. There are over 14,000 French nationals in Pondicherry.

Now Pondicherry is administered by the President through a Lt. Governor who is advised by a council of Ministers which is responsible to the Legislative Assembly, consisting 33 members. Normally the council of Ministers under a Chief Minister carries on the Administration.

A.2 GENERAL DESCRIPTION OF THE AREA :

A.2.1 Demographic features

The population of Union Territory of Pondicherry is 7,89,416 (1991 census) with an urban population of 64.00%. The number of males are 3,98,324 and females are 3,91,092. The population density in 1,605 per sq.km. with the growth rate of 30.60% Sex ratio (Females per 1000 males) is 982. Literacy is 74.91% with males contributing 83.91% and females 65.79%.

The population of Pondicherry region as per 1991 census data is 6,07,600 and the annual growth rate is around 2% of which the rural population is 2,06,263 (33.95%) and urban population is 4,01,337(66.05%). The growth rate of town population is 2.9%. The density of population is 2073 per sq.km. The number of males are 3,09,300 (50.91%) and females are 2,98,300 (49.09%). (Source : State land use board, Pondicherry).

Population density (persons/sq.km)

Region	Headquarters	AreaSq.kms	Population 1991	Density census 1961	1971	1981	1991
Pondicherry	Pondicherry	293	6,08,338	892	1173	1517	2076
Karaikal	Karaikal	160	1,45,703	522	621	7501	911
Mahe	Mahe	9	33,447	2165	2570	3157	3716
Yanam	Yanam	30	20,297	352	415	388	677
Union Territory	Pondicherry	429	8,07,785	769	983	1229	1642

Source : State land use board, Pondicherry

A.2.2 Climate

The Pondicherry region experiences hot and tropical retarded monsoonic climate characterised by small daily range of temperature, humid weather and moderate rainfall. There is no such demarcation of seasons and the months from March to June is considered as summer and December to February as cooler months.

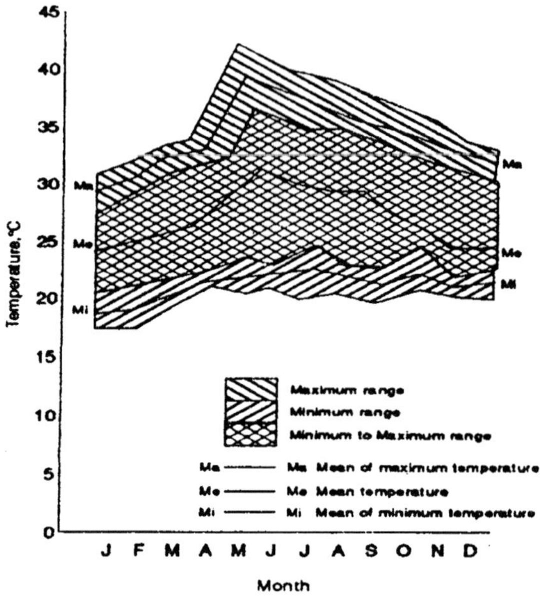

Fig. A.3: Monthly variation in temperature during 1974-1980

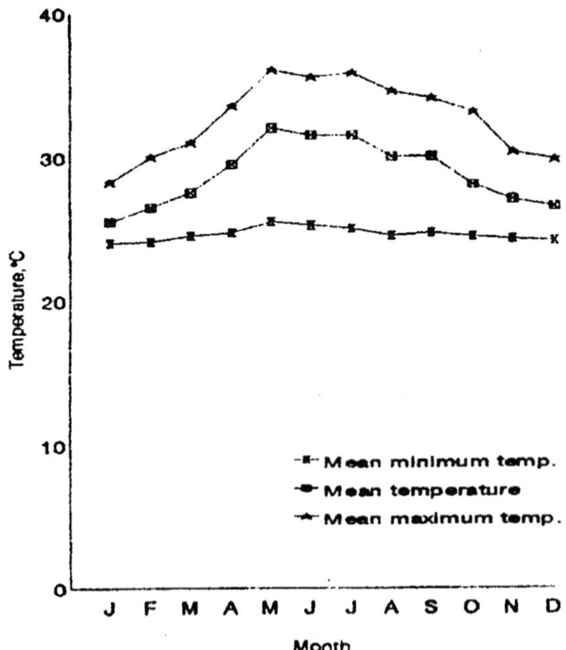

Fig. A.4: Pattern of minimum, maximum average temperature at the project site

A.2.3 Meteorology (Meteorological Conditions)

i. Temperature and Humidity : The winter and summer months are not very severe. The temperature ranges from a minimum of 16.5°C to a maximum of 41°C. The maximum temperature of Pondicherry region varies from 35°C to 41°C and minimum temperature varies from 17°C to 22°C. Figure A.3 and A.4 show monthly variation in temperature, and also indicates the range of maximum and minimum-temperature values for the period 1974-80. For the same months of different years a difference of 2°C to 10°C is observed in the maximum recorded temperature. Temperature High variation is observed in the lower limit of minimum temperature during the months of June and October. The humidity is comparatively high ranging from 60 to 80.5 in general and becoming as high as 85% or more at times. Month wise temperature data for 10 years (1975-1984) is furnished in Table A.1. The variation of temperature 16.5°C to 41°C and the existed variation in the relative humidity (1960-1988) is shown in Table A.2.

ii. Rainfall : The union territory of Pondicherry benefits from rain by both south west monsoon and northeast monsoon. The Northeast monsoon which normally sets in October and lasts up to December brings heavy rain to Pondicherry and Karaikal region which are located in the east coast.

There is only one rainguage station (at Pondicherry) in the Pondicherry region. The average annual rainfall at Pondicherry is 1254.4 mm. The region receives rainfall from both the monsoons, west-south monsoon occurring from June to September and eastnorth monsoon occurring during October to December. Figure A.4 with annual rainfall spread over a period of eight months.

Table A.1 Temperature data of Pondicherry region – (1975-84) (in centigrade)

Months		1975	1976	1977	1978	1979	1980	1981	1982	1983	1984
JAN	Max.	29.0	28.0	29.0	29.1	30.0	31.0	30.0	28.9	29.2	28.9
	Min.	18.5	19.1	20.0	18.0	21.0	20.5	19.0	22.0	22.4	22.6
FEB	Max.	30.4	30.0	30.0	31.5	31.6	31.0	30.0	29.9	30.6	28.9
	Min.	18.6	18.0	21.0	21.7	22.0	21.0	20.0	22.0	22.9	23.4
MAR	Max.	32.0	31.5	32.0	32.5	33.0	32.0	33.5	31.1	31.5	30.6
	Min.	21.3	20.0	23.0	22.0	22.5	21.0	22.0	23.5	23.8	24.0
APR	Max.	32.9	38.3	33.0	34.5	34.2	35.0	35.2	32.5	32.3	32.8
	Min.	23.5	23.5	24.0	24.0	24.0	24.0	23.0	23.6	24.0	25.9
MAY	Max.	40.0	41.1	37.6	41.0	37.0	43.0	41.5	33.5	34.8	34.6
	Min.	25.0	26.0	23.8	24.0	24.0	22.5	22.6	27.1	26.8	26.7
JUN	Max.	40.0	36.5	38.0	39.5	39.0	39.0	39.1	37.3	37.3	37.5
	Min.	22.6	23.5	24.0	25.5	23.9	24.0	24.9	26.1	26.8	26.4
JUL	Max.	35.5	37.5	38.0	37.0	38.5	39.0	37.5	34.6	35.2	33.8
	Min.	21.0	22.5	24.0	23.5	24.6	28.0	22.6	25.1	26.1	24.5
AUG	Max.	36.8	36.5	36.0	37.0	38.0	36.0	37.5	35.5	33.9	35.0
	Min.	22.0	21.0	22.0	24.0	24.0	24.0	21.6	25.3	25.0	25.0
SEP	Max.	34.5	36.5	36.0	36.0	35.0	37.0	32.6	34.3	32.4	32.9
	Min.	23.0	22.0	23.6	20.5	23.0	23.5	24.9	23.8	24.8	24.3
OCT	Max.	34.5	33.0	33.6	34.5	36.0	34.0	31.9	31.5	31.5	31.8
	Min.	22.5	21.5	22.8	23.0	23.0	28.0	24.7	23.9	24.1	23.8
NOV	Max.	31.5	32.0	31.5	31.0	31.0	33.0	30.5	30.1	30.5	29.8
	Min.	20.5	22.0	22.5	22.0	20.5	20.5	24.1	23.7	23.1	22.9
DEC	Max.	29.5	29.5	30.0	30.0	30.2	31.0	29.0	37.3	28.4	29.5
	Min.	19.2	21.5	20.0	21.5	21.0	24.0	22.6	26.1	22.8	22.4

Source : Soil survey report, state land use board, Pondicherry

Table A.2 Temperature and relative humidity at Pondicherry

	Temperature			Relative Humidity (Percent)	
Years	Maximum (°C)	Minimum (°C)	Mean (°C)	07.30 hrs	17.30 hrs.
1960	36.5	21.0	28.7	88.7	87.5
1961	34.5	21.0	27.8	89.9	89.4
1962	35.0	20.0	27.5	88.2	88.3
1963	35.5	20.0	27.8	88.2	88.9
1964	36.5	21.5	29.0	88.7	89.2
1965	36.5	21.5	29.0	89.8	90.9
1966	38.0	20.5	29.0	90.8	89.3
1967	38.0	20.4	29.2	84.3	83.5
1968	40.0	18.1	29.4	76.6	75.1
1969	40.8	17.1	29.0	77.3	77.8
1970	38.9	17.4	28.2	79.3	80.5
1971	39.8	19.9	29.4	78.8	76.3
1972	38.8	17.0	27.5	77.8	76.9
1973	41.0	19.5	30.3	75.9	71.6
1974	38.8	16.5	27.7	75.9	72.6
1975	33.8	21.5	32.6	72.6	73.4
1976	34.2	21.7	27.9	78.7	76.6
1977	33.7	22.6	28.1	79.5	76.9
1978	34.5	22.5	28.5	79.5	76.4
1979	34.5	22.8	28.6	80.3	78.1
1980	35.1	23.4	29.2	77.2	77.0
1981	34.0	22.5	28.4	76.9	79.7
1982	33.0	24.4	28.7	73.3	72.9
1983	32.3	24.4	28.4	76.3	73.4
1984	32.2	24.3	28.3	79.1	75.3
1985	32.4	24.3	28.4	80.8	77.1
1986	32.6	24.8	28.7	79.2	77.8
1987	33.3	25.0	29.2	78.3	87.4
1988	32.8	25.0	29.0	80.3	76.9

Source : Soil survey report, state land use board, Pondicherry.

The average annual rainfall for the period 1911-1961 is 1233 mm and for the period 1881 to 1910 is 1234 mm. The quantum of rainfall received for the period 1975-97 (Table A.3) and the no. of rain days (1975-84) are furnished month wise in Table A.4. Study of the rainfall data for the period of 1977 to 1985 points that the rainfall was normal for 4 years; more than normal for three years and below normal for two years.

However, the quantum of normal rainfall is very fluctuating. The average rainfall received during the four monsoon periods were computed for the years 1967-68 to 1987-88 and furnished in Table A.5. It was found that out of the average annual rainfall, the average rainfall received during east-north monsoon period was 63.35% followed by south-west monsoon 27.19%. Rainfall received during other two periods was only 9.46% of average annual rainfall. It was also observed that the twin adverse behaviours of inadequacy and erratic were prevalent in the union territory. The co-efficient of variation (C.V) computed for the years 1967-68 to 1987-88 revealed that there existed uneven distribution of rainfall. Dr. V.M. Meher-Homji (Renowned ecologist of the French Institute, Pondicherry) while analysing the climate of Pondicherry has pointed, that based on the data for the period 1911-61 the mean of the precipitation for the period October-January is 808 mm as opposed to 330 mm received during June-September. About 50% of the total rain is concentrated over the two months October-November. However, in spite of such high differences in the quantity of the rain between the two monsoons, the difference in the number of rainy days during the two periods is considerably less; 21 during June-September as against 28 for October-January. Thus the difference in the number of rainy days is just a meagre 7 days. Thus it may be inferred that though the rainfall received during southwest monsoon is less yet it is well distributed enabling proper utilization of the rain-fall. Mehr-Homji has observed for the period 1911-61 that the frequency of the precipitation class of 900-1000 and 1100-1200 and 1200-1300 is more than other precipitation range class.

A study of the distribution of rainfall (Figure A.5) reveals that there is a decrease in the rainfall from east to west (i.e) from about 1300 mm near coast to 1100 mm near the western and northern border. The precipitation increases from west to east during south-west monsoon whereas the reverse occurs during the northeast monsoon.

The variability of rainfall is fairly large and that of seasonal/monthly rainfall still larger. The variation in rainfall from year to year are very significant to agriculture operations and ground water recharge. The seasonal rainfall and ombrothermic diagram is furnished in Figure A.6 and A.7.

iii. Wind Pattern : The data for Pondicherry region as obtained from Cuddalore station (situated 18 kms from Pondicherry) is furnished in Table A.6.

A.3 PHYSIOGRAPHY, RELIEF AND DRAINAGE

The topography of Pondicherry region in general is a flat plain and alluvial coastal region with an average elevation of about 15 mts above mean sea level (MSL). The terrain becomes a little undulatory with prominent high grounds varying from 30 to 40 m above city. These high grounds are mostly covered by red laterite soil and are intersected by a number of gullies and ravines as seen near Gorimedu, Kalapet, Idaiyanchavadi, Lawspet, etc. However, 3 major physiographic units are observed in the region viz. The coastal plain, alluvial plain and the elevated lands (Uplands) on the north-east and north-west portion of Pondicherry region.

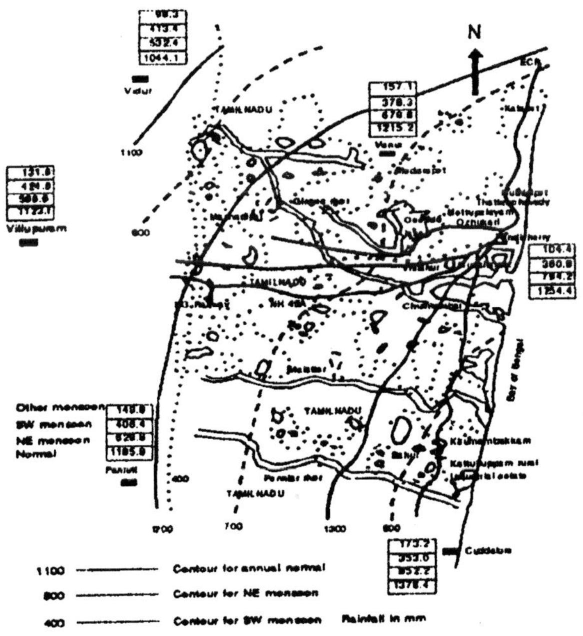

Fig. A.5: Rainfall distribution in Pondicherry region

Table A.3 The quantum of rainfall received for the period 1975 – 1997

Year	Jan	Feb	Mar	Apr	May	June	July	Aug	Sep	Oct	Nov	Dec
1975	2	-	19	-	26	50	190	197	110	163	428	53
1976	-	-	-	4	-	9	60	123	55	216	500	175
1977	16	6	-	2	63	38	25	199	92	570	561	31
1978	3	-	-	2	9	18	106	78	343	249	578	470
1979	-	31	15	-	77	16	2	34	237	355	544	142
1980	-	-	-	0.5	7	13	124	72	91	137	281	69
1981	4	-	-	-	120	8	114	77	119	332	132	188
1982	5	-	-	5	7	82	101	30	75	91	292	154
1983	-	-	-	-	17	6	72	176	118	299	320	531
1984	42	272	36	28	-	18	198	78	117	64	321	107
1985	187	-	-	-	30	261	81	167	216	313	655	117
1986	104	25	43	-	2	30	5	107	27	117	210	133
1987	6	-	45	-	-	64	-	35	165	252	208	378
1988	32	-	6	21	58	6	54	215	84	6	464	NA
1989	15	-	-	-	80	-	94	20	77	88	517	NA
1990	54	30	4	-	12	94	55	237	193	546	211	24
1991	57	7	-	-	-	131	26	103	161	400	299	20
1992	5	-	-	-	20	46	46	45	169	99	449	75
1993	-	8	31	-	46	100	59	90	165	336	458	384
1994	-	65	-	-	5	27	92	142	32	249	376	235
1995	41	-	-	5	174	18	113	144	113	192	150	16
1996	-	-	-	-	83	229	25	253	326	202	301	736
1997	12	-	-	-	19	51	142	265	97	112	711	-

Source : Soil survey report, state land use board, Pondicherry

Table A.4 Rain days in Pondicherry 1975-84

Year	Jan	Feb	Mar	Apr	May	Jun	Jul	Aug	Sep	Oct	Nov	Dec
1975	1	-	2	-	2	6	15	12	8	15	11	4
1976	-	-	-	1	-	4	6	15	4	8	24	10
1977	3	3	-	2	5	6	9	8	8	22	23	6
1978	1	-	-	2	3	5	12	11	17	13	10	21
1979	-	3	1	-	2	2	1	3	8	11	20	7
1980	-	-	-	-	2	1	8	5	3	6	11	3
1981	1	-	-	-	2	1	5	4	6	10	9	8
1982	1	-	-	1	1	6	6	3	4	7	11	5
1983	-	-	-	-	2	1	9	9	7	9	5	14
1984	4	8	4	2	-	2	9	2	6	6	14	5

Source : Directorate of Statistics and Economics, Pondicherry

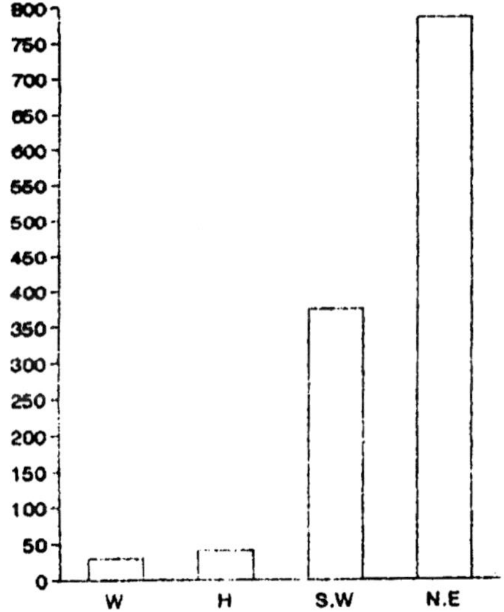

Fig. A.6: Seasonal rainfall in mm (From 10 years data 1975

Table A.5 Seasonwise rainfall in Pondicherry region (mm)

Year	South West monsoon (June to Sep)	North East monsoon (Oct to Dec)	Winter period (Jan & Feb)	Hot weather period (Mar to May)	Total Rainfall
1967-68	163	748	3	91	1005
1968-69	118	354	7	22	501
1969-70	151	1362	1	22	1536
1970-71	182	951	56	334	1523
1971-72	289	885	19	113	1306
1972-73	184	1036	7	-	1227
1973-74	459	573	-	61	1093
1974-75	333	270	2	45	650
1975-76	549	646	-	5	1200
1976-77	249	893	23	65	1230
1977-78	356	1163	3	12	1534
1978-79	546	1299	31	23	1899
1979-80	291	1042	-	8	1341
1980-81	302	489	5	120	916
1981-82	319	653	5	13	990
1982-83	289	538	-	18	845
1983-84	372	1152	314	64	1902
1984-85	472	493	187	30	1182
1985-86	728	1086	129	43	1986
1986-87	172	461	6	45	684
1987-88	266	839	32	86	1223
Normal Rainfall	328.00	764.00	33.00	81.00	1206.00
		(27.19)	(63.35)	(2.74)	(6.72)
(100.00)					
Mean Rainfall	323.33	806.33	39.52	58.09	1227.29
Std. Deviation	155.05	317.00	78.62	72.32	396.63
C.V.	47.95	39.31	198.94	124.49	32.32

Source : Department of Agriculture, Government of Pondicherry

A.3.1 The coastal plain:

The coastal plain is straight and narrow stretches along the Bay of Bengal for about 22 km with a breadth ranging from four to six hundred metres. The sea coast has a narrow flat beach with sea water almost touching the main land at some places. The major portion of the coastal plain comprises of gently sloping lands with a chain of sand dunes almost extending all along the coastal region of Pondicherry region. Other characteristic coastal physiographic units such as spit bars, mud flats, lagoons, tidal inlets, sand bars are also observed in the coastal plain.

Table A.6 Mean monthly wind speed in Pondicherry region (Unit: Km./Hr.)

Year	Jan	Feb	Mar	Apr	May	Jun	Jul	Aug	Sep	Oct	Nov	Dec
1979	7.13	5.65	7.04	8.98	8.43	9.82	7.87	8.06	5.74	5.65	6.48	8.53
1980	8.15	5.56	6.76	8.06	9.72	6.05	10.46	9.07	8.70	7.13	11.95	10.46
1981	10.19	6.33	7.13	8.98	10.19	11.90	9.17	8.32	6.48	6.76	7.32	7.32
1982	6.57	6.39	9.26	12.69	9.72	10.83	8.70	7.87	6.57	7.13	8.33	10.09
1983	6.57	7.32	7.36	11.11	11.85	10.46	5.28	6.1	7.32	6.95	8.89	10.00

Source : Department of Agriculture, Government of Pondicherry

A.3.2 Alluvial plain:

This unit occupies a major portion of the Pondicherry region. Two major rivers flows across the alluvial plain and drains into the Bay of Bengal. The alluvial plain are generally flat monotonous plain with slope ranging from 1 to 3%. Micro depression topography are very common in the alluvial plains. The lands are partitioned into small plots for cultivation purpose. The alluvial plains are intensively cultivated with crops all along the year. Besides the rivers and major canals there are depression storage tanks spread all along the terrain which serve as water reservoirs.

A.3.3 Uplands (elevated lands) :

In the west, north-western and north-east parts of the region the elevation is about 30 to 45 meters above MSL. The land is undulating with small hillocks with slope gradient range, 8 to 12 m/km covering northern part of Mannadipet, Villiayanur and Ozhukarai communes. These uplands are intersected by a number of gullies and deep ravines giving rise to badland topography. These high grounds with small hillocks are popularly known as "Les Montagnes Rouges" or the "Red Hills" of Pondicherry. Also in the north-west portion of the region there is a patch of gently sloping fossiliferous limestone terrain.

Thus inspite of the limited extent of the region the physiograph exhibits a varied diversification and is of great academic interest. Meher-Homji while conducting the phytosociological studies in Pondicherry and its environ has classified the area into 4 well defined geographical zones viz; the coastal zone comprising newer and older dunes, the second zone is made up of the two plateau called the Pondicherry plateau and the Tiruvakkarai plateau composed of sand stones and thirdly the Valudavur plateau between the two plateau and lastly the alluvial zone which occupies a major portion of Pondicherry.

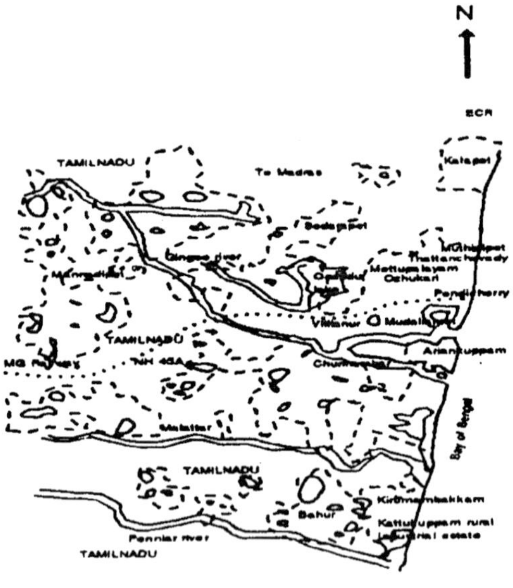

Fig. A.8: Rivers of Pondicherry region

A.3.4 Drainage: There are two major rivers draining the Pondicherry region namely the Gingee river in the north and Penniar river in the south with their tributaries into the Bay of Bengal (Figure A.8). The alluvial plain formed due to two rivers that pass through the area occupies major portion of Pondicherry region covering the Bahour, Nettapakkam, Ariyankuppam, southern half of Mannadipet and Villianur and parts of Ozhukarai communes.

i. River Gingee: The River Gingee flows across diagonally from north-west to south-east. This river is also known as the Varahanadsi or Sankaraparani. The River Gingee originates from Melmalayanur hills in the South Arcot district of Tamil Nadu. Though the river has a total length of 78.89 km, it has a run of only about 34 km in this region. At about 7 km from the sea the river splits off into two branches namely; Ariankuppam river in the north and Chunnambar in the south. The Vikravandi, the Pambaiyar and the Kuduvaiyar are the tributaries of the Gingee river. The Pambaiyar traverses for about 13 Km in the Pondicherry region before merging with the Gingee river while the

Kuduvaiyar flows for 12 km before joining the Chunnambar near Thirukanji. The river Gingee is not a perennial river and it flows only during rainy seasons and floods.

ii. River Penniar: The river Penniar originates from the hills of Karanataka and enters Pondicherry region after flowing through Dharmapuri district, Salem district, North Arcot district and South Arcot district. The river forms the southern border of the region. The Malattar river, a branch of the Penniar touches southern part of Nettapakkam, Pondasozhanur, Nadunayapuram, Sambadapet, Vadukuppam, Manakuppam, Karikalampakkam and Thirumarayakkampalayam and finally discharges into the sea near Pannithittu and Alidimedu.

The region is also having about 140 small and two big tanks viz, Usteri and Bahour lakes. These tanks are linked and act as water storage for cultivation purpose and also for recharge of ground water considerably.

A.4 ENVIRONMENTAL STATUS

A.4.1. Water resources

a. Surface water:

i. River Source : Looking at the local scenario, Pondicherry region on the river basins of Sankaraparani and Pennaiyar and other streams. The river Sankaraparani is also known as Gingee river. The tributaries of the Gingee river are Pambaiyar North and Pambaiyar South. The Pennaiyar river branches off into a number of spill channels(Kuduvaiyar & Malatar).

There are 3 anicuts across Gingee and Pennaiyar rivers, viz Suthukeny anicut and Pilliyarkuppam anicut across river Gingee and the

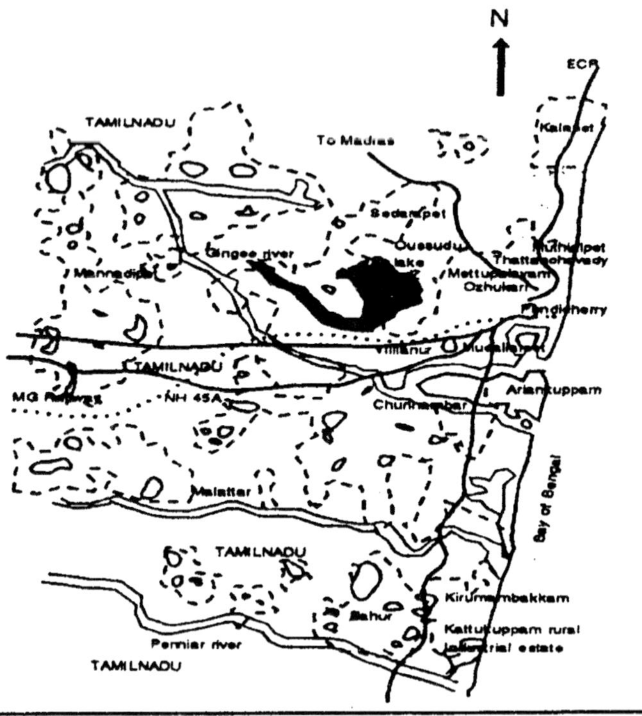

Fig. A.9: Map showing location of Oussudu lake

Sornavur anicut across Pennaiyar. These three bed dams divert the river water and feed 55 irrigation(System) tanks in the region which includes the Major system tanks like Oussudu and Bahour. (Source : Centre ground water board, Pondicherry).

ii. Direct run off : The average rainfall in this region is 1254.4 mm. The storage capacity of 31 rainfed tanks (Non-system Tanks), which receives water from local catchment area is 7.24 million cubic metre (Mm^3). A considerable portion of the run-off is stored in the System-Tanks also. Being located at the tail end of rivers, the region is prone to flood and major portion of both rural and urban area are inundated.

iii. Tanks and Ponds : There are 86 surface water storage tanks and 140 small tanks for harvesting surface water. During the Ex-French Regime there were 87 surface water storage tanks, out of which one tank has now been lost due to urbanisation. Two tanks viz, Kanaganeri and Olandai tank have lost their anicuts and irrigation importance. However, the storage of surplus water is effectively made in all 86 tanks. The 55 nos. of System Tanks and 31 Nos. of Non-system Tanks put together have an original aggregate storage capacity of 45.84 Mm^3. But now the same is estimated to have been reduced to 41.34 Mm^3 (ie. nearly 10% reduction). The largest tank namely Ossudu Tank (Figure A.9) is the main source of sustenance of drinking water supply to Pondicherry town due to recharging capacity of its acquifers in the vicinity of Muthirapalayam water works.

GROUND WATER

The Pondicherry is blessed with a rich resource of groundwater which is exploited well enough to meet the water requirement for Agriculture, Industries, Drinking water and Domestic purpose. Irrigation is covered by tube wells which constitute 99% of the net area irrigated. The quality of ground water ranges from excellent to good for irrigation except the water drawn from ottai clay stone.

The entire area of Pondicherry region is covered by alluvial and sedimentary formation. Ground water occurs both under confined and unconfined conditions in the sedimentary formation. The shallow alluvial aquifers, the deep Cuddalore sandstone aquifers and Vanur-Ramanathapuram aquifers constitute the three major potential aquifer systems of this region. Ground water from the above aquifer systems is developed by means of shallow and deep tube wells. The major source of recharge to these aquifers are the precipitation, water flow from agricultural lands and seepage from existing tanks and canals.

c. Water Resources Assessment

As a part of comprehensive programme, the Public Works Department (Pondicherry) in consultation with Water and Power Consultancy Services Ltd., New Delhi has assessed the availability and utilisation of water for the present and the foreseeable future upto 2006 A.D. as follows:-

i. Present Situation

	Surface water	Ground water	Total
Water Availability	35.00 mm^3	150.00 mm^3	185.00 mm^3
Water required	0.00 mm^3	151.50 mm^3	186.50 mm^3
Water balance	35.00 mm^3	(-) 1.50 mm^3	(-)1.50 mm^3

ii. Future Situation (2006 AD)

	Surface water	Ground water	Total
Water availability	75.00 mm^3	150.50 mm^3	225.50 mm^3
Water required	0.00 mm^3	167.00 mm^3	242.00 mm^3
Water balance	75.00 mm^3	(-)16.50 mm^3	(-) 16.50 mm^3

A.4.2 Land resources

i. Soils : The soil of the Union Territory of Pondicherry can be broadly classified into three categories, viz. Clay, Alluvial and Sand. In Pondicherry region, the soil is either ferralitic (or) black clay (or) coastal alluvial. Coastal and dunes are seen in the saline tracts of the region. (Source: State soil survey organization, Pondicherry).

The soil survey wing of the Agricultural Department, Government of Pondicherry had carried out detailed soil surveys in the region during the year 1984-85. Based on the surveys carried out, 19 types of soils were identified in the region. The occurrence of different type of soils in the region and the extent of the different soil series in the region along with the percentages to total geographical area is furnished in Table A.7.

In spite of the limited land in Pondicherry region, it provides an exhibition of soils ranging from sandy soil to heavy clay soil, red soil to black soil, very deep to shallow soil, fertile soil to unfertile soil, calcareous soil to non-calcareous soil (Figure A.10). The reason for the wide variation in the type of soils may be due to non-contiguous location of enclaves which are interspread with parts of South Arcot district of Tamil Nadu and also because of the different kinds of geological formation found in Northern Pondicherry and the change of topography in the North-eastern and North-western parts of Pondicherry region.

Table A.7 Soil series and its extent in Pondicherry region

Sl. No. (1)	Soil Series (2)	Extent in HA (3)	% (4)
1.	Gorimedu	905	3.6
2.	Kalapet	812	3.1
3.	Ayyankuttipalayam	186	0.8
4.	Sedarapet	464	1.8
5.	Tuhipet	328	1.3
6.	Karasoor	186	0.8
7.	Kuppam	2550	10.1
8.	Mannadipet	2362	9.3
9.	Kattery	66	0.01
10.	Gingee	310	1.2
11.	Pennaiyar	180	0.6
12.	Pondicherry	3460	14.6
13.	Nettapakkam	1682	6.6
14.	Villianur	1440	5.6
15.	Bahour	5820	22.8
16.	Palayam	2650	9.1
17.	Ariankuppam	1880	7.4
18.	Manapattu	65	0.3
19.	Mer	225	0.9
20.	Swamps & Marshes	35	

Source:State Soil survey organisation, Pondicherry

Alluvial soils are the dominant soils in this region, because the variation in deposition of sediments by the rivers and land topography exhibits a wide range of variation in texture, colour and other morphological and physico-chemical properties. The soils formed over various geological formations exhibit different features each being a characteristic of the formation (Figure A.11a and b).

The soils based on the land capability and irrigability and productivity potential are classified into different classes. For efficient land use management and to prevent misuse of precious agricultural lands only those lands classified under land capability class – IV and above may be converted for non-agricultural purposes. The total extent of the land under this category in the region is 2,460 ha out of which, about 75 percent can be used for other developmental sectors. Lands under Thuthipet, Karasur, Sedarapet and Ariyankuppam series may be converted into industrial sector. The areas under problem soils can be contemplated for non-agricultural purposes. A map showing the area recommended by Government of Pondicherry by considering the above factors for location of Industries in Pondicherry region is presented as plate-IV (Figure A.12).

ii. Geology : The geology is varied and complex considering the limited extent of the region. There are a very few rock out crops in Pondicherry region thereby making geological study and mapping difficult. However with the help of bore holes drilled by O.N.G.C and C.G.W.B. the stratigraph and other characteristics of various formation have been studied. Details of stratigraphy is given as follows with geological map (Figure A.13).

A.4.3 TERRESTRIAL ECOLOGY (FLORA, FAUNA, FOREST & WILD LIFE)

There are no forests in Pondicherry region. However, the flora of Pondicherry has an appreciable diversity which may be attributed to the diverse soil type and the physiography. Meher-Homji and Marlange have studied the flora of Pondicherry and have brought out the phytosociological patterns in the Pondicherry region and have classified the flora (Table A.8) into fixed plant communities and associations, each typical to their habitation. Some of the flora observed in different soils type are also furnished below. No information is available about fauna but the available list for Avian fauna of Pondicherry is furnished in Table A.9.

A.4.4 SOCIAL INFRASTRUCTURE:

Nearly 45% of the population is engaged in agriculture and allied pursuits. In the town, occupational structure is heterogenous, i.e. as the town does not possess agricultural land, people are engaged in Official (State & Central Government) jobs, manufacturing and trading (Private sectors). All the government offices, commercial complexes, trading centres, educational institutions are located almost in the town. The town is highly transversed by network of roads from nearly and far off places. Facilities such as education, commercial, healthcare, and recreation are easily assessible to public.

A.4.5 AGRICULTURE:

Agriculture in terms of output and employment is the most important enterprise in this region. Agriculture in Pondicherry region is well diversified and almost all the crops with different types of cropping pattern are cultivated here. The lands are with crops all through the year and are rarely kept fallow. Due to increased use of land [for non agricultural purposes like industrialization urbanization and lease] agricultural lands for brick making etc. there is a declining trend in net area sown and net area irrigated.

Out of the total geographical area of 29,377 ha the net area sown is 16,589 (56.47%) during the year 1991-92. The cropping intensity of the Pondicherry Region is 174.68 percent. The major food crop raised is paddy and the minor crops are ragi, cumbu and cholam. The cash crops raised are groundnut and sugarcane. The extent of important crops raised in Pondicherry region during the year 1991-92 are presented in Table A.10.

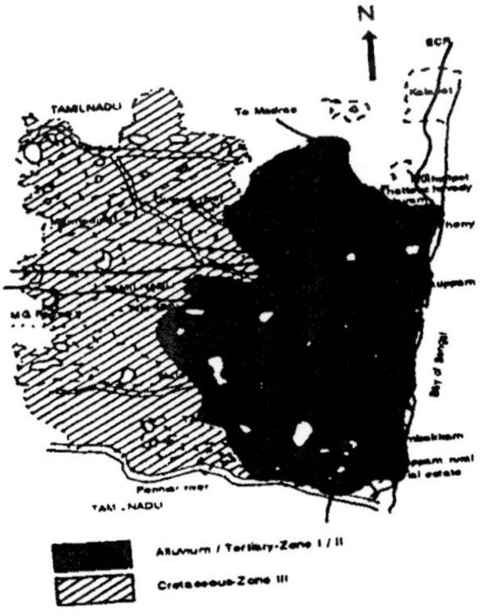

Fig. A.10: Soil status of Pondicherry region

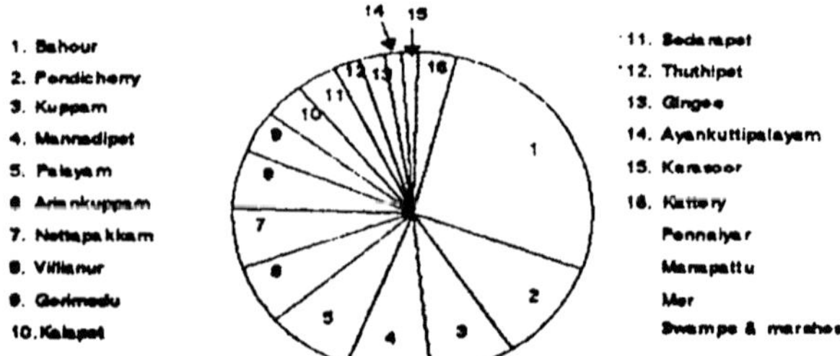

Fig. A.11a. Soil series distribution-Pondicherry region

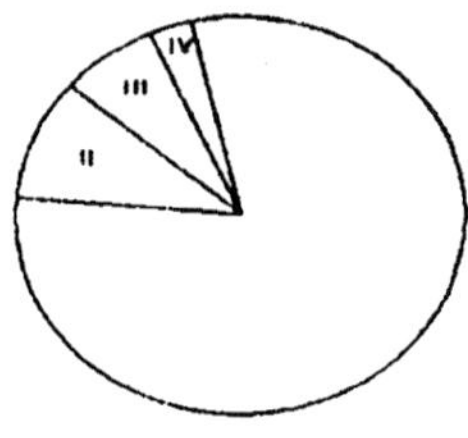

Fig. A.11b. Soil series distribution-Landform wise

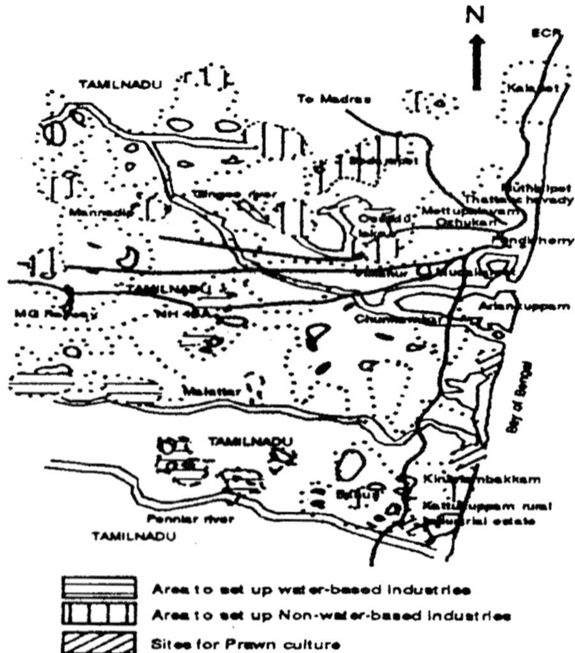

Fig. A.12. Location of areas for setting up of industries in pondicherry region

Table A.8 Flora of Pondicherry region

Plants of Saline Soils :

1. Fimbristylis spathacea Roth.
2. Cyperus monocephala Rottb.
3. Cyperus arenarius Retz.
4. Aeluropus lagopoides (L) Trim.
5. Portulaca pilosa (Linn.)
6. Pedalium murex L.
7. Cressa cretica L.
8. Heliotropium curassavicum L.
9. Launaea sarmentosa (Willd.) Alston
10. Geniosporum prostratum Benth

Plants of Coastal sandy soils and dunes :

1. Catharanthus roseus (L.) G. Don
2. Spinifex littoreus
3. Cyperus arenarius Retz.
4. Launaea sarmentosa (Wild.) Alston
5. Canscora diffusa R. Br.
6. Allimania nodiflora R. Br. var. procumbents
7. Waltheria indica (L.)
8. Perotis indica O.kty.
9. Tephrosia purpurea Pers.
10. Mollugo disticha ser
11. Turnera ulmifolia L.
12. Cleome aspera Koen. ex DC.
13. Desmodium rottleri Baker'
14. Justicia prostrata Gamb.
15. Tridax procumbens L.
16. *Ipomaea pes-caprae Sweet*

Plants of ferralitic soils :

1. Borassus flabellifer L.
2. Phoenix sylvestris (L.) Roxb
3. Phoenix humilis Royle var. pedunculata
4. Anacardium occidentale
5. Dodonaea viscosa L.
6. Cassia auriculata L.
7. Heteropogon contortus Beauv
8. Dichrostachys cinerea W. et A.
9. Securinega leucopyrus (Willd.) M. Arg.
10. Randia dumetorum Lam.
11. Ixora arborea Roxb
12. Linociera zeylanica Gamb.
13. Aristida hystrix L.
14. Desmodium rottleri Baker
15. Tephrosia purpurea Pers

Plants on alluvial soils :

1. Boerhaavia verticillata
2. Amaranthus gracilis Desf.
3. Ipomoea pes-tigridis L.
4. Commelina benghalensis L.
5. Portulaca quadrifolia L.
6. Chloris barbata
7. Tridax procumbens L.
8. Corchorus aestuans L.
9. Eragrostis cilianensis
10. Centella asiatica (L.) Urb.
11. Euphorbia hypericifilia L.
12. Cleome gynandra L.
13. Trianthema portulacastrum L.
14. Arundo donax L.
15. *Xanthium strumarium L.*

On black clayey soils :

16. Curculigo orchioides Gaertn.
17. Biophytum sensitivum D.C.
18. Jatropha glandulifera Roxb.
19. Brachiaria sp.
20. Vetiveria zizanioides Nash.

Aquatic plants :

1. Nepuntia oleracea Lam.
2. Nympnaea Stellata Willd
3. Lemna spp.
4. Aponogeton natans Engl. and Kr.
5. Eichhornia crassipes Solmns.

Common Avenue trees :

1. Azadirachta indica Juss
2. Ficus benghalensis L.
3. Ficus religiosa L.
4. Madhuca longifolia (L) Macbride
5. Parkinsonia aculeata L.
6. Samanea saman (Jacq.) Merr .
7. Syzygium cumini (L) Skeel
8. Tamarindus indica L.
9. Thespesia populnea Cav.
10. Berrya cordifolia
11. Mimusops elengi L.
12. Lannea coromandelica (Houtt.) Merr.

Source : State soil survey report, state land use board, Pondicherry

Table A.9 List of birds of Pondicherry region

Common Name	Scientific Name
1. Dabchick	*Podiceps ruficollis*
2. Grey or Spottedbilled Pelican	*Pelecanus philippensis*
3. Large Cormorant	*Phalacrocorax carbo*
4. Little Cormorant	*Phalacrocorax niger*
5. Grey Heron	*Ardea cinerea*
6. Purple Heron	*Ardea purpurea*
7. Darter or Snake Bird	*Anhinga rufa*
8. Large Egret	*Ardea alba*
9. Little Green Heron	*Ardeola striatus*
10. Pond Heron	*Ardeola grayii*
11. Cattle Egret	*Bubulcus Ibis*
12. Smaller or Median Egret	*Egretta intermedia*
13. Little Egret	*Egretta garzetta*
14. Indian Reef Heron	*Egretta gularis*
15. Night Heron	*Nycticorax nycticorax*
16. Little Bittern	*Ixobrychus minutus*
17. Chestnut Bittern	*Ixobrychus cinnamomeus*
18. Yellow Bittern	*Ixobrychus sinensis*
19. Black Bittern	*Ixobrychus flavicollis*
20. Painted stork	*Mycteria leucocephala*
21. Openbill stork	*Anastomus oscitans*
22. Whitenecked Stork	*Ciconia episcopus*
23. Spoonbill	*Platalea leucorodia*
24. Barheaded Goose	*Anser indicus*
25. Pintail	*Anas acuta*
26. Common Teal	*Anas crecca*
27. Spotbill Duck	*Anas poecilorhyncha*
28. Wigeon	*Anas penelope*
29. Garganey	*Anas querquedula*
30. Common Pochard	*Aythya ferina*
31. Tufted Pochard	*Aytha fuligula*
32. Redcrested Pochard	*Netta rufina*
33. Garganey	*Anas querquedula*
34. Shoveller	*Anas clypeata*
35. Cotton Teal	*Nettapus coromandelianus*
36. Indian Moorhen	*Gallinula chloropus*
37. Purple Moorhen	*Porphyrio porphyrio*
38. Coot	*Fulica atra*
39. Pheasant-tailed Jacana	*Hydrophasianus chirurgus*
40. Bronzewinged Jacana	*Metopidius indicus*
41. Blackwinged Kite	*Elanus caeruleus*
42. Pariah Kite	*Milvus migrans*

43.	Brahminy Kite	*Haliastru indus*
44.	Shikra	*Accipiter badius*
45.	White-eyed Buzzard Eagle	*Butastur teesa*
46.	Montagu's Harrier	*Circus pygargus*
47.	Pied Harrier	*Circus melanoleucos*
48.	Marsh Harrier	*Circus aeruginosus*
49.	Short-toed Eagle	*Circaetus gallicus*
50.	Osprey	*Pandion haliaetus*
51.	Kestrel	*Falco tinuunculus*
52.	Grey Partridge	*Francolinus pondicerianus*
53.	Whitebreasted Waterhen	*Amaurornis phoenicurus*
54.	Blackwinged stilt	*Himantopus himantopus*
55.	Oystercatcher	*Haemotopus haemotopus*
56.	Redwattled Lapwing	*Vanellus indicus*
57.	Yellow-wattled Lapwing	*Vanellus malabaricus*
58.	Grey Plover	*Pluvialis squatarola*
59.	Little Ringed Plover	*Charadrius dubius*
60.	Ntish Plover	*Chardrius alexandrinus*
61.	Lesser Sand Plover	*Charadrius mongolus*
62.	Spotted Redshank	*Tringa erythropus*
63.	Common Redshank	*Tringa totanus*
64.	Marsh Sandpiper	*Tringa stagnatilis*
65.	Greenshank	*Tringa nebularia*
66.	Green Sandpiper	*Tringa ochropus*
67.	Wood or Spotted Sandpiper	*Tringa glareola*
68.	Terek Sandpiper	*Tringa terek*
69.	Common Sandpiper	*Tringa hypoleucos*
70.	Pintail Snipe	*Gallinago stenura*
71.	Common or Fantail Snipe	*Gallinago gallinago*
72.	Little Stint	*Calidris minuta*
73.	Temminck's Stint	*Calidris temminckii*
74.	Curlew-Sandpiper	*Calidris ferruginea*
75.	Herring Gull	*Larus argentatus*
76.	Brownheaded Gull	*Larus brunnicephalus*
77.	Whiskered Tern	*Chlidonias hybrida*
78.	Blackbellied Tern	*Sterna acuticauda*
79.	Common tern	*Sterna hirundo*
80.	Little Tern	*Sterna albifrons*
81.	Blue Rock Pigeon	*Columba livia*
82.	Indian Ring Dove	*Streptopelia decaocto*
83.	Indian Spotted Dove	*Streptopelia chinensis*
84.	Roseringed Parakeet	*Psittacula krameri*
85.	Pied Crested Cuckoo	*Clamator jacobinus*
86.	Common Hawk Cuckoo or Brain fever Bird	*Cuculus varius*
87.	Indian Plaintive Cuckoo	*Cacomantis merulinus*
88.	Koel	*Eudynamys scolopacea*
89.	Small Greenbilled Malkoha	*Rhopodytes viridirostris*
90.	Crow pheasant	*Centropus sinensis*
91.	Spotted Owlet	*Athene brama*
92.	Common Nightjar	*Caprimulgus asiaticus*

93. Palm Swift — *Cypsiurus parvus*
94. Lesser Pied Kingfisher — *Ceryil rudis*
95. Common Kingfisher — *Alcedo atthis*
96. Whitebreasted Kingfisher — *Halcyon smyrnensis*
97. Bluetailed Bee-eater — *Merops philippinus*
98. Green Bee-eater — *Merops orientalis*
99. Indian Roller or Blue Jay — *Coracias benghalensis*
100. Hoopoe — *Upupa epops*
101. Lesser Goldenbacked Woodpecker — *Dinopium benghalense*
102. Redwinged Bush Lark — *Mirafra erythroptera*
103. Ashycrown Finch-Lark — *Eremopterix grisea*
104. Eastern skylark — *Alauda gulgula*
105. Swallow — *Hirundo rustica*
106. Baybacked Shrike — *Lanius vittatus*
107. Brown shrike — *Lanius cristatus*
108. Golden Oriole — *Oriolus oriolus*
109. Black Drongo — *Dicrurus oriolus*
110. Grey Drongo — *Dicrurus adsimilis*
111. Ashy Swallow-shrike — *Artamus fuscus*
112. Greyheaded Myna — *Sturnus malabaricus*
113. Brahminy Myna — *Sturnus pagadorum*
114. Rosy Pastor — *Sturnus roseus*
115. Common Myna — *Acridotheres tristis*
116. Indian tree Pie — *Dendrocitta vagabunda*
117. House Crow — *Corvus splendens*
118. Jungle crow — *Corvus macrorhynchos*
119. Common wood shrike — *Tephrodornis pondicerianus*
120. Blackheaded Cuckoo-Shrike — *Coracina melanoptera*
121. Common Iora — *Aegithina tiphia*
122. Redvented Bulbul — *Pycnonotus cafer*
123. Whiteheaded Babbler — *Turdoides affinis*
124. Brown Flycatcher — *Muscicapa latirostris*
125. Brownbreasted Flycatcher — *Muscicapa muttui*
126. Paradise Flycatcher — *Terpsiphon paradisi*
127. Ashy Wren Warbler — *Prinia socialis*
128. Tailor Bird — *Orthotomus sutorius*
129. Thickbilled Warbler — *Phragamaticola acdon*
130. Great Reed Warbler — *Acrocephalus stentoreus*
131. Blyth's Reed Warbler — *Acrocephalus dumetorum*
132. Lesser whitethroat — *Sylvia curruca*
133. Largebilled Leaf Warbler — *Phylloscopus magnirostris*
134. Dull Green Leaf Warbler — *Phylloscopus trochiloides*
135. Magpie-Robin — *Copsychus saularis*
136. Paddyfield Pipit — *Anthus novaeseelandiae*
137. Forest Wagtail — *Motacilla indica*
138. Yellow Wagtail — *Motacilla flava*
139. Yellowheaded Wagtail — *Motacilla citreola*
140. Grey Wagtail — *Motacilla caspica*
141. Large Pied Wagtail — *Motacilla maderaspatensis*
142. Tickell's Flowerpecker — *Dicaeum erythrorhynchos*

143.	Purplerumped Sunbird	*Nectarinia zeylonica*
144.	Purple Sunbird	*Nectarinia asiatica*
145.	House Sparrow	*Passer domesticus*
146.	Weaver Bird	*Ploceus bengalensis*
147.	Whitethroated munia	*Lonchura malabarica*
148.	Whitebacked munia	*Lonchura striata*
149.	Spotted munia	*Lonchura punctulata*
150.	Blackheaded munia	*Lonchura malacca*

Source : Department of Forest and Wild life, Pondicherry

A.4.6 LAND USE

The total geographical area of the Pondicherry region is 29,377 Ha. The Pondicherry region is devoid of any forest. Land put to non-agricultural use is 30.14 percent of the total geographical area. The net area sown is 56.47 percent and the area sown more than once is 42.17 percent. From the land use classification furnished in Table A.11 it may be observed that there has been a steady decrease in net area sown and a steady corresponding increase in land put to non-agricultural use and cultural waste land. The reason may be attributed to the sudden spurt in Urbanisation, Industrialisation and leasing of agricultural lands for brick making.

The particulars of land use of the Pondicherry for the year 1991-92 are presented in Table A.12 and Figure A.14.

A.4.7 INDUSTRIAL DEVELOPMENT

Pandit Jawaharlal Nehru had envisioned a special status for Pondicherry to preserve "The Window to the French Culture in India". While Nehru was laying strong foundations for a modern industrialised nation, Pondicherry had joined the Union of India in 1954 with limited industrial inheritance. There were only 3 large textile mills and some 5 odd small industrial institutions. The territory has since come a long way. Pondicherry has achieved rapid industrial progress in all these years and is poised for spectacular growth. By February 1997, we have an impressive establishment of 25 large scale industries, 88 medium and 5,492 small scale units. Over the years, there has been massive growth of industries in Pondicherry. Figure A.15 and A.16 represent Pondicherry region with its industrial estates and its access. (Source : Industrial Policy 1997, Industries Department Government of Pondicherry).

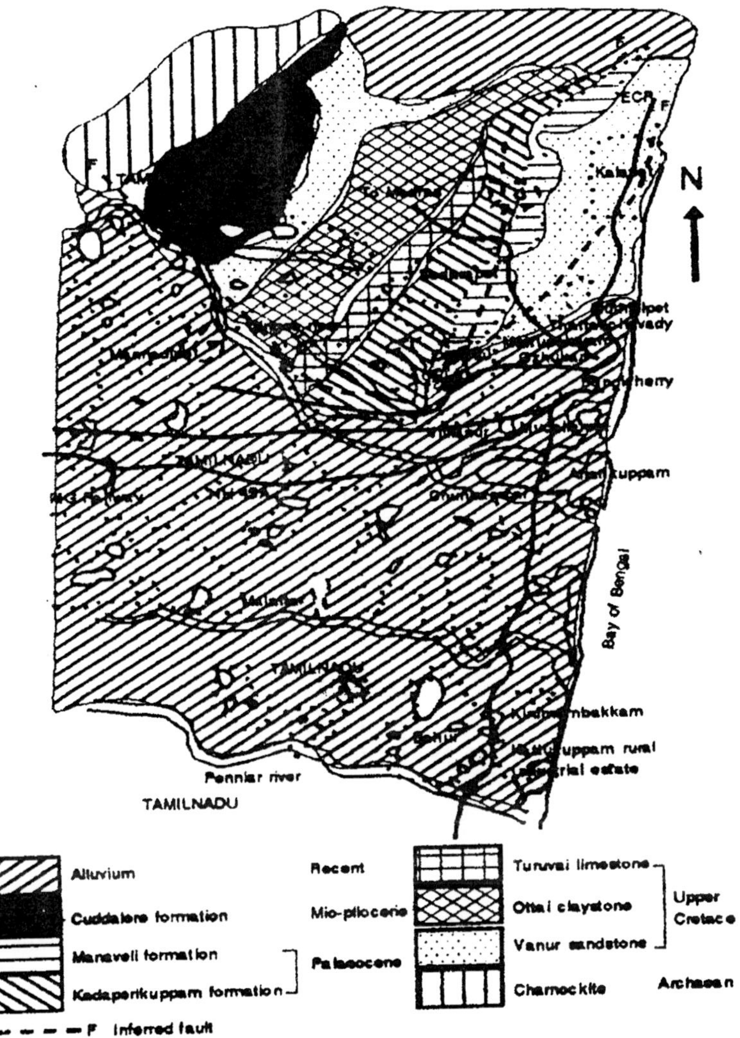

Fig. A.13. Geological map of Pondicherry region

The industrial sector employed just about 8,000 persons in the early fifties. Now, with investment of over Rs.883 crores, industries are the life-blood of economy providing livelihood to over 64,323 people. 187 investment proposals are currently in the pipeline promising a total outlay of about Rs.2,042 crores, having potential to employ over 19,894 persons. More than 40% of these projects are under various stages of execution. Pondicherry has deservedly magnetised many large industrial houses of national repute and several renowned multinational corporations. List of medium and large scale industries are given in Table A.13 and A.14.

The present status of industries in Pondicherry can be summarised as below:

As in Feb. 1997	No. of Units	Investment in Rs. (Crores)	Employment in Number
Large Scale	25	547	14,096
Medium scale	88	197	6,014
Small Scale	5,492	139	44,213
Total	5,605	883	64,323

Source : Industries Department, Government of Pondicherry

A. SMALL SCALE INDUSTRIES (SSI UNITS)

The "Directory of Industrial Units" published by the Directorate of Industries, Pondicherry, in the year 1988 and 1995, were utilized for identifying the catalogue of registered SSI Units.

Table A.10 Details of crops raised and its extent (1991-92)

Food Crops	(Area in hectares)
I Crop	3602
II Crop	6763
III Crop	5558
Raggi	273
Cumbu	460
Other cereals	24
Pulses	
Blackgram	236
Greengra	58
Other millets	47
Oil Seeds	
Ground nut	2428
Coconut	870
Sesamum	336
Other Oil Seeds	15
Sugar Crops	
Sugar cane	3301
Fruits	
Plantain	177
Mango	174
Other Fruits	13
Other Crops	
Cotton	686
Tappioca	705
Chillies	24

Source : State land Use Board, Pondicherry

Table A.11 Classification of the area in Pondicherry region (in hectares)

Classification	1974-75	1975-76	1976-77	1977-78	1978-79	1979-80	1980-81	1981-82	1982-83	1983-84
Total geographical area to survey of India	129100	29100	29100	29100	29100	29100	29100	29100	29100	29100
Total geographical area to village propose	29377	29377	29377	29377	29377	29377	29377	29377	29377	29377
Forest	-	-	-	-	-	-	-	-	-	-
Land put to Non-Agricultural use	7852	7872	7926	7919	7886	7962	8013	8018	8076	8187
Barren and unculti-vable lands	35	34	34	7668	65	81	82	77	77	
Permanent pastures and other grazing lands	7	7	7	5	-	-	-	-	- -	

Land under misc. Tree crops and groves not included in net area sown	1424	1225	973	1107	1334	1517	1885	2276	2231	1765
Cultural wastes	677	656	629	662	722	742	709	719	716	701
Other fallow land	64	42	29	103	189	215	248	258	13050	588
Current Fallows	1213	1084	1294	946	1091	1272	1167	913	11620	1355
Net area sown	18105	18457	18485	18559	18087	17604	17274	17111	16352	16744
Area sown than once	12667	13379	13007	14137	13285	12199	14314	13953	1494	12319
Total cropped Area	30772	31836	31492	32696	31372	29803	31588	31064	27846	26063

Source : State land use board, Pondicherry

Table A.12 Particulars of land use in Pondicherry region (1991-92)

1. Land Use	Area (in ha)	Percentageto
Geographical Area		
1. Geographical Area	29377	—
2. Forests	——	——
3. Land put to Non-Agricultural Use	8854	30.14
4. Barren and Uncultivable Waste	80	0.27
5. Permanent pastures and other Grazing lands	Nil	——
6. Land under Misc. Tree Crops and groves not included in net Area sown	179	0.61
7. Cultivable waste	917	3.12
8. Current Fallow land	1160	3.95
9. Other Fallow land	1598	5.44
10. Net Area Sown	16589	56.47
11. Area Sown more than once	12388	42.17
12. Total cropped Area	28977	98.64

Source : State land use board, Pondicherry

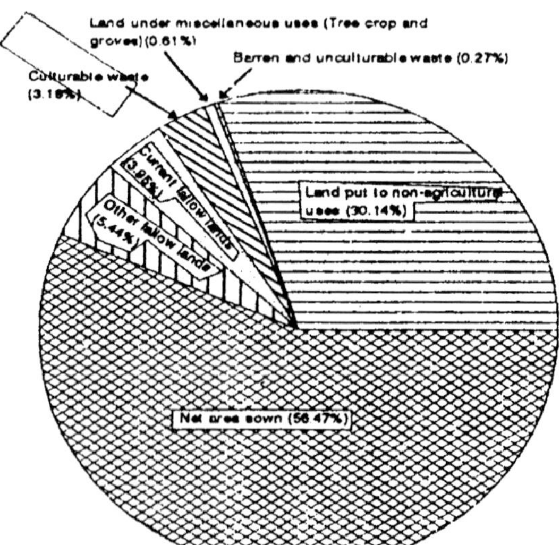

Fig. A.14. Land use particulars of Pondicherry region

Table A.13 List of medium scale industrial units registered in the Pondicherry as on 31-03-1998 (Source : Industrial Department, Government of Pondicherry).

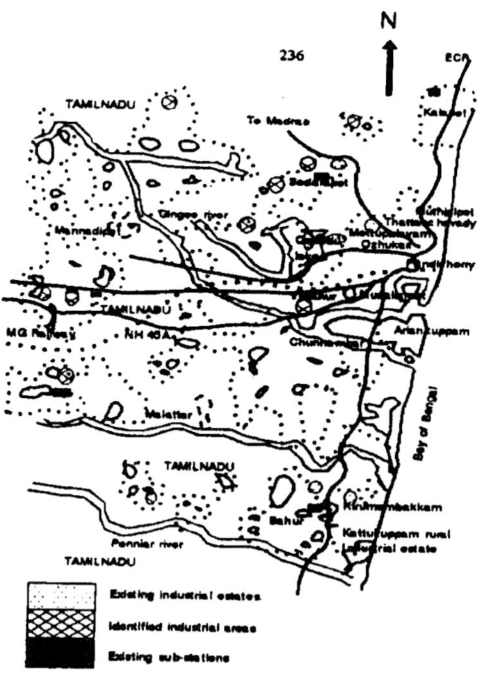

Fig. A.15. Identified industrial areas of Pondicherry region

S.No.	Name and address of the unit	Product Manufactured
1.	Alternative Energy Industries (P) Ltd., Kalitheerthalkuppam Madagadipet Pondicherry.	Solid fuel from agricultural waste.
2.	Amaravathi Chemicals Ltd., Abishekapakkam Post, Pondicherry.	Sorbitol liquid glucose
3.	Amman Woven Sackes Pvt. ltd., Sedarapet Industrial Estate, Pondicherry.	Woven sacks
4.	Associated Cylinders and Accessories Ltd.. Thirubuvanai, Pondicherry.	LPG Cylinders
5.	Chemfab Chlorates Thavalakuppam, Pondicherry.	Potassium Chlorates and Sodium Chlorates

6.	Coromandel Granite Co. (P) Ltd., Sedarapet Industrial Estate Pondicherry.	Cut and polished granite monuments blocks and slabs.
7.	Elgi Tyre and Trade Ltd., Korkadu Village Mangalam Post Via Villianur, Pondicherry.	Precured tread of tyre
8.	Gec Alsthom India Ltd., Industrial Estate,	Switch Gear Sedarapet Pondicherry.
9.	Ennaram Spinners, Pandacholanallur, Netapakkam Commune, Pondicherry.	Cotton and man made fibre yarn
10.	General Optics (Asia) Ltd., Thavalakuppam, Pondicherry.	Precision optical lenses.
11.	Golden Paper and Board Mills (P) Ltd., Sedarapet Industrial Estate, Pondicherry.	Paper boards
12.	Foseco India Ltd., Industrial Estate, Metupalayam, Pondicherry.	Foundry fluxes and chemicals
13.	Hindustan Lever Ltd., wear Division) Kurumbapet, Pondicherry.	Foot wear, shoe uppers and (Foot other components
14.	Hindustan Lever Limited (Personal Products Division) Industrial Estate, Metupalayam, Pondicherry.	Talcum powder
15.	Hydraulics Ltd., Mettupalayam Industrial Estate Pondicherry.	Automotive powder components
16.	India Cine Agencies Sedarapet Industrial Estate, Pondicherry.	Photographic papers, colour amateur, colour films.
17.	Elfotech Electrochemicals Ltd., Pannithittu road, Kirumampakkam, Pondicherry.	Tetro chloro ethane tricholoro ethylene and pencholoro ethylene and hexacholoro ethane
18.	Lakshmi PVC Products (P) Ltd., Villianur, Pondicherry.	PVC fittings
19.	Larsen and Tourbo Ltd., Mailam road, Saderapet., Pondicherry.	Transmission line towers

No.	Name and Address	Product
20.	Lebracs Rubber Linings (P) Ltd, Industrial Estate, Sedarapet, Pondicherry.	Industrial rubber linings, brake chamber diapharam and steel fabrication.
21.	Lichlor, Kalapet, Pondicherry.	Liquid chlorine
22.	Lotus Roofings (P) Ltd., Sedarapet, Pondicherry.	Corrugated plastic sheets
23.	Mailam Metallogen (P) Ltd., Sedarapet, Pondicherry.	Special purpose welding electrodes.
24.	Marine Filaments Corporation Villianur, Pondicherry.	Nylon mono filaments.
25.	Mittal Ispat (P) Ltd., Kirumampakkam, Pondicherry.	Steel Castings
26.	National Oxygen Ltd., Thiruvandar koil, Pondicherry.	Oxygen gas and nitrogen gas
27.	Pallava Granites Industries, Sedarapet, Pondicherry.	Cut and polished granites
28.	Pandian Extraction (P) Ltd., Manapet, Pondicherry.	Rice bran oil
29.	Ponds (India) Ltd., (Leather Division), Mettupalayam, Pondicherry.	Shoe Uppers
30.	Pond's (India) Ltd., (Soap Division) Vadamangalam, Pondicherry.	Toilet Soap
31.	Pondicherry Extraction (P) Ltd., Mettupalayam, Pondicherry.	Rice Bran Oil
32.	Pondicherry Flour Mills (P) Ltd., Thiruvandar Koil, Pondicherry.	Wheat Products (Maida, Suji, Atta)
33.	Pondicherry Oxy-Acetylane (P) Ltd., Thirubuvanai, Pondicherry.	Oxygen gas and dissolved acetylene
34.	Pondicherry Distilleries Ltd., Goubert Avenue, Pondicherry.	Alcohol
35.	Sri Ramiah Spinners (P) Ltd., Uruvaiyur village,	Cotton and manmade fibre yarn

	Villianur, Pondicherry.	
36.	Sharada Castings (P) Ltd, Kirumampakkam, Pondicherry.	Steel castings
37.	Sica Breweries Ltd. Kurumbapet, Pondicherry.	Beer
38.	Sumangala Steel (P) Ltd., Industrial Estate, Mettupalayam, Pondicherry.	Steel Ingots
39.	Supreme Industries Ltd., Industrial Estate, Sedarapet, Pondicherry.	Injection moulded plastic products
40.	Sri Sarbati Steel Tubes Ltd., Sedarapet Industrial Estate Pondicherry.	Steel pipes and tubes
41.	Triveni Metals and Alloys (P) Ltd., Pondicherry.	Cold rolled steel strips.
42.	Transplastics (I) Ltd., Sedarapet Industrial Estate, Pondicherry.	Disposable syringes
43.	Unicorn Bangalore (P) Ltd., Mettupalayam, Pondicherry.	Automobile components
44.	Venkatramana Food Specialities Ltd., Industrial Estate, Mettupalayam, Pondicherry - 9.	Macroni
45.	Vijay Industrial Alcohols Ltd., Lingareddipalayam, Pondicherry.	Industrial alcohol
46.	Vijay Marine Products (P) Ltd., Kattukuppam, Pondicherry.	Nylon Fishnets
47.	Balaji Detergents and Chemicals (P) Ltd., Industrial Estate, Mettupalayam, Pondicherry.	Detergent cakes
48.	Zenith Tine Ltd.,	Printed tin and metal container Industrial Estate, Mettupalayam, Pondicherry.
49.	AVM Cine Products	Cinematographic raw films A-32, Industrial Estate, Sedarapet, Pondicherry.
50.	Camphor and Allied Products	Fabricated filaments

		Ellapillaichavady, (polyethylene foam) Pondicherry.
51.	S&S Industries Ltd.,	Reinforced/Filled thermo plastic Industrial Estate, compounds sedarapet, Pondicherry.
52.	Bharath Starch Industries ltd.,	Modified starch Kalitheerthalkuppam Madagadipet, Pondicherry.
53.	TIL Limited, Kirumampakkam, Pondicherry.	Diesel generating sets
54.	Ucal Power Systems Ltd.,	Electric generating sets. Mettupalayam, Pondicherry.
55.	Hindustan Motors Ltd.,	Front and loaders Sedarapet, Pondicherry.
56.	Pondicherry Spinners Ltd., Madukkarai, Pondicherry.	Cotton yarn
57.	Himani Limited,	Ayurvedic Medicine Industrial Estate, Mettupalayam, Pondicherry.
58.	Godrej Hi-Care Ltd.,	Destroyer mosquito Industrial Estate, refills (mats) Sedarapet, Pondicherry.
59.	Ravishankar Films (P) Ltd.,	Cinema Print film Mettupalayam, Pondicherry.
60.	Godrej Hi-Care Ltd.,	Mosquito destroyer machine Industrial Estate, Thattanchavady, Pondicherry.
61.	Hindustan Lever Ltd.,	Perfumery blend Kurumbapet, Pondicherry.
62.	Raman Boards Limited Pondicherry.	Moulded components from Kodathur, electrical grade paper boards
63.	Battliboi & Co.,	Diesel generating sets EVR Street, Sedarapet, Pondicherry.
64.	Frontline Solutions (Madras) Ltd.,	Monitors and Key boards J.k. Towers, 100 ft. road,

		Ellapillaichavady, Pondicherry.
65.	Switzer instruments Ltd., C-16, industrial estate,	Flow measuring instrument, flow checking instrument Thattanchavady, pressure / measuring / checking Pondicherry. instruments.
66.	Lucas- TVS Limited,	Starters Eripakkam village, Nettapakkam commune, Pondicherry.
67.	Fal Industries Limited,	Electrical motors Industrial estate, Sedarapet, Pondicherry.
68	SSB Industries Ltd., Industrial estate, Sedarapet, Pondicherry.	Distribution tube surge arrestares
69.	Kamal Deep Synthetics Ltd., Uruvaiyur Village, Pondicherry.	Undyed texturised polyester yarn
70.	Sundaram Fastners Ltd., Korkadu Village, Pondicherry.	High tensile fastners
71.	Balaji Hotels and Enterprises Ltd., Industrial Estate, Sedarapet, Pondicherry.	Label printings
72.	Aurofood Ltd., Sannyasikuppam village, Thirubuvanai, Pondicherry.	Refined edible oil
73.	Swastik Filaments Corporation, A-180, 109, Industrial estate, Mettupalayam, Pondicherry.	Nylon mono filament
74.	Hydraulies Limited, (Shock Abserber Division) B-83 & 84, Industrial Estate, IIIrd main road, Mettupalayam, Pondicherry.	Automotive shock abserbers
75.	Pasumai Irrigation Ltd., Uruvaiyur road, Mangalam,	Drip irrigation system comprising pipes, drippers and accessaries Villianur Commune, and fitting LLD pipe, HDPE pipes Pondicherry.
76.	Alps Industries Ltd., B-160 & 161 Industrial Estate,	Awnings made out and other textile fabrics

	Mettupalayam, Pondicherry.	
77.	Rusch - AVT Medicals (P) Ltd., 23, Thirubuvanai, Pondicherry.	Foley balloon Catheter (which is a medical device used for removing urine from the bladder)
78.	Shriram Honda Plot No.B-16 & 30, Industrial Estate, Sedarapet, Pondicherry.	Portable electirc power generators
79.	S & S Power switch gear Ltd., Sedarapet & Post Pondicherry.	Fuse and fuse fitting above 100 volts
80.	Sahney Paris Rhone Ltd., Thondamanatham Road, Thuthipet Village, Pondicherry.	Auto electrical components
81.	Mac Agro Industries Ltd.,	Water treatment chemicals' cooling tower, Biocide, detergent, adhesive.
82.	J.R. Foods Ltd., J.K. Towers, 100 ft.Road, Pondy-13.	Rice Bran Oil
83.	Aravalli Pipes Ltd., 29/2 Thirubuvanai, Pondy.	PVC Pipes

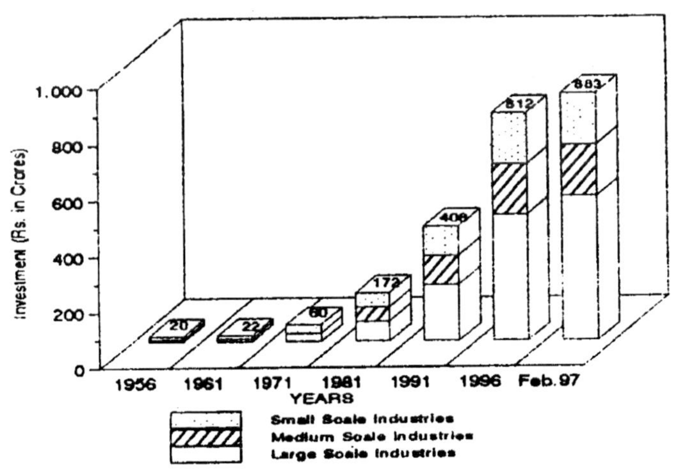

Fig. A.16: Growth of Industries in Pondicherry region

Table A.14 List of large scale industries as on 31-03-1998.

No.	Industry	Product
1.	Pondicherry Textile Corporation Ltd., Cuddalore road, Mudaliarpet, Pondicherry.	Cloth and yarn
2.	Owens Bilt Ltd., Thondamanatham village, Pondicherry.	Glass containers
3.	Brite Automotive and Plastics Ltd., Thirubuvanai, Pondicherry.	Injection moulded plastic goods.
4.	Chemfeb Alkalis Ltd., Kalapet, Pondicherry.	Caustic soda
5.	East Coast Steel Ltd., Pilliyarkuppam, Pondicherry.	Steel Ingots/Billets
6.	Hindustan Lever Ltd., (Bio-polymer Division) Kurumbapet Pondicherry.	Functionalised bio polymers
7.	Mohan Brewaries and Distilleries Ltd., Mettupalayam, Pondicherry.	Glass Containers
8.	Neycer India Ltd., Pilliyarkuppam, Pondicherry.	Ceramic tiles
9.	New Horizon Sugars Mills Ltd., Ariyur, Pondicherry.	Sugar
10.	The Pondicherry Papers Ltd., Pilliyarkuppam, Pondicherry.	Paper
11.	The Pondicherry Co-operative Spinning Mills Ltd., Thirubuvanai, Pondicherry.	Cotton yarn
12.	The Pondicherry Co-operative Sugar Mills Ltd., Lingareddipalayam, Pondicherry.	Sugar
13.	Protchem Industries (India) Ltd., Abishkapakkam, Pondicherry.	Amino acid
14.	Shibi Capsules Ltd., Pitchaiveerampet, Pondicherry.	Hard gelatine capsules

15.	Sri Bharathi Mills, Mudaliarpet, Pondicherry.	Textile Products
16.	Swadeshi Cotton Mills Ltd, Maraimalai Adigal Salai, Mudaliarpet, Pondicherry.	Textile products
17.	Whirlpool Washing Machines Ltd., Thirubuvanai, Pondicherry.	Launderette (Washing) Machine
18.	Chem Crown (India) Ltd., Sedarapet Pondicherry.	Thermoplastic shoe sole components
19.	Ucal Fuel Systems Ltd., A-98 & 100 Industrial Estate, Mettupalayam, Pondicherry.	Carburettors for four wheelers automobiles.
20.	H.C.L. Infosystems Ltd. R.S. No 34/4 to 34/7, Sedarapet, Pondicherry.	Computer systems

(*Source* : Industries Department, Government of Pondicherry)

Based on the two directories referred, contains 3501 SSI Units in Pondicherry regions. Of these, units with activities such as Baking, Repacking of food material, tailoring, wood carving, printing/binding, reselling readymade materials (footwear, furnitures, cosmetics, electronic goods, etc.), mat weaving, plumbing, vulcanizing, electronic data processing and repairing electrical/electronic appliances, form the major number of registered SSI Units.

Industries with activities related to food processing, textiles, rubber/ plastics, chemicals, metal/non-metal products, engineering, and automobile servicing formed the categories which could have an accountable impact on the surrounding environmental status. Thus industries falling under these categories were 813 in Pondicherry regions.

OPERATING SSI UNITS:

From the list of 766 industries in Pondicherry, only 281 units are presently under operation. Units Location Category: Only in the region of Pondicherry Proper SSI units establishment under the category of "Estates" is found significant (80.4%).

In the *region of proper Pondicherry* 80.4% of the operating SSI units falls under the perview of the four industrial estates, being 43.4% under Mettupalayam Industrial Estate, 18.5% under Sedarapet Industrial Estate, 15.3% under Thattanchavady Industrial estate, 3.2% under Kattukuppam Rural Industrial Estate while the remaining 19.6% of the units are as Isolated SSI units.

NATURE OF SSI UNITS:

The number of units operating in the Pondicherry region, have been further categorized according to the nature of process involved at the unit. In the *region of pondicherry proper,* the following industrial predominance is observed under each estates:

(i) Mettupalayam Industrial Estate (Total Units 122)

Engineering & Electrical > Plastics > others

(ii) Sedarapet Industrial Estate (Total Units 122)

Engineering & Electrical > Plastic > Packaging > Chemical > others.

(iii) Kattukuppam Rural Industrial Estate (Total Units 9)

Chemical > Food > Engg. & Electrical > others

(iv) Thattanchavady Industrial Estate (Total Units 43)

Engineering/Electrical > Food and Packaging > Others

Among the operating 55 "Isolated" SSI Units at Pondicherry proper, the following nature of industrial dominance is observed:

Food > Plastic > Chemical > Wood > Packaging > others.

Fuel Consumption Pattern:

In the region of Pondicherry the fuel consumption data for the four identified industrial estate have been compiled under Table A.15 which indicates that the fuel consumption by all the units at Mettupalayam Industrial estate is significantly high followed by Sedarapet, while at Kattakuppam and Thattanchavady the fuel consumption is insignificant.

RAW WATER CONSUMPTION :

Overall raw water consumption in the activities of the listed industries under Pondicherry Region reads in Table A.16.

Table A.15 Fuel consumption pattern for regions under Pondicherry

Region	Estate	Fuel Usage Pattern per Month			
		Coal	LSHS/LDO/HSD	Wood	LPG
Pondicherry					
	Mett. I.Est.	11.5	25.6	447	-
	That. I.Est.	-	-	20	-
	Katt. I. Est.	-	28	133	-
	Seda. I.Est.	-	15.2	85	-
	All Isolated Units		24	17	-
Overall Consumption for the region		11.5	92.8	702	-

Note : All Units in MT/M except LPG shown as Cu.m/M

Table A.16

(i) Raw water consumption

Region	Raw Water (KLD)
Pondicherry	321

(ii) Liquid effluent generation from the SSI units in the Pondicherry region is observed to be:

Region	Raw Water (KLD)
Pondicherry	99

Source : Department of Science, Technology and Environment, Pondicherry

B. Medium And Large Scale Industries:

83 Medium Scale Industries and 20 Large Scale Industries are registered in the Pondicherry region as on 31-03-1998 (Table A.13 and A.14).

A.4.8 ZONING OF INDUSTRIAL AREAS

Realising the limitations imposed by the restricted land area, nature of settlements, location of existing industries, soil characteristics, infrastructure, siting of power sub-stations, road networks, air and water quality in the areas and the limitations imposed by the Coastal Zone Regulations, 1991 (Under Environment Protection Act), zoning of industrial areas has been undertaken.

To check random and sporadic disbursement of industries, to earmark exclusive zones for systematic growth of industrial units, to protect agricultural operations and to safeguard peace of residential areas, it has become necessary to designate specific zones as "Industrial areas" with half a century vision of what Pondicherry should be like say, in the middle of 21st century. Accordingly, various zones have been identified and earmarked for development as "Industrial Areas". Such identified areas are summarized below and map of the identified "Industrial Areas" are appended in Figure A.12 and Table A.17.

A.4.9 AMBIENT AIR QUALITY, AMBIENT NOISE & HAZARDOUS MATERIAL

a. Ambient air quality

A comprehensive survey on the status of Industrial Estates & Small Scale Industries, in the region of Pondicherry had been carried out and the findings of the study is compiled here. The study was conducted by ENVIROCARE ENGINEERS AND CONSULTANTS, CHENNAI with the aid of their laboratory facilities located at Pondicherry. The information and data regarding ambient air quality is received from the Department of Science, Technology and Environment, Govt. of Pondicherry.

Ambient Air Quality Around Industrial and Rural Area :

Ambient air quality monitoring carried out at 12 locations in the region of Pondicherry. The ambient air quality reveals (refer Table A.18), that the SPM and SO_2 level at Kirumambakkam Area on the main Cuddalore-Pondicherry road significantly high as compared to other regions followed closely by Mettupalayam industrial area.

Presence of major category industries such as Mittal Ispat and East Coast Steels in the Kirumambakkam area and usage of wood to the tune of about 450 mt/m (18 mt/d) by the small scale industrial units in the Mettupalayam Industrial Area could be the factors attributing to higher SPM levels in ambient air (268 ug/cu.m and 186 ug/cu.m respectively) as observed in Table A.18. The level of SO_2 and NO_x at all monitoring stations in general indicated the safe level as compared to the prescribed standards applicable to the rural areas.

In the region of Pondicherry the air emissions data compilation have been done for each industrial estate and are presented in Table A.19. The overall emission scenario is as follows:

However all the SSI units utilizing wood as the source of fuel for the boilers were found to have not installed any special type of particulate arresting machanisms prior to discharge of emission through the stacks. WHO Emission factors for fuel is mentioned in Table A.20.

Air Quality Statistics :

The values of monthly and annual minimum, mean and maximum along with the number of monitored days for 16 or more hours of three monitored parameters viz, SO_2,

Table A.17 Identified industrial areas

Region (1)	Commune (2)	Revenue village (3)	Extent (4)	Survey No. (5)
			H.A. Ca	
Pondicherry	Mannadipet	1. Thirubuvanai	06-43-50	94,97 to 99
		2. Thiruvandarkoil	21-49-00	106,123,124,127,
160 to 163				
		3. Kalitheerthalkuppam	22-78-30	153 to 159, 166
		(Karamedu)		
		4. Lingareddipalayam	28-20-00	1,2,3,13,14,16 to 19
		5. Electronic Indl. Estate at -		
		(a) Thirubuvanai		6,7,8,11 pt
		(b)Thiruvandarkoil	18-24-00	1 pt., 2 pt
		(c) Sannyasikuppam		99 pt.
	Villianur	6. Sedarapet	215-09-85	2 to 19, 28, 29, 31 to 42, 98 to 101, 103 to 108, 110, 112 to 141
		7. Karasur	09-33-50	29, 35, 37
		8. (a) Thuthipet	93-04-25	5, 27, to 29, 34, 35, 37, 50 to 53, 55, 115 to 123, 135, 136
		(b) Thondamanatham	22-95-50	3 to 6, 9, 10
		9. Kurumbapet	27-47-50	1 to 6, 15 to 17
		10. Othiyampet	46-05-00	243, 244, 248, to 251, 253, 255, 258, 259
	Nettapakkam	11. Eripakkam	10-52-00	26, 27, 28, 32,35
	Bahour	12. Karayamputhur	10-26-00	72 to 77, 87
	Oulgaret	13. Sanjeevarayanpet and Alankuppam	32-81-50	2 to 4, 6, 25, 28, 29, 30, 32, 33, 38

Source : Industries Department, Government of Pondicherry

Table A.18 Ambient air quality levels in Pondicherry region

	Location - >			
Parameters	Mettupalayam	Sedarapet	Kattukuppam	
Thattanchavady				
Date	7/2/96	9/2/96	1/3/96	6/3/96
Sampling Duration	24 Hrs	24 Hrs	24 Hrs	24 Hrs
SO_2 (ug/cu.m)	26.5	14.6	9.4	18.8
NOx (ug/cu.m)	17.8	19.6	6.3	10.5
SPM (ug/cu.m)	186	60	48	124

Location - >				
Parameters	Town	Villianur	Nettapakkam	
Thattanchavady				
Date	9/3/96	18/3/96	24/3/96	4/3/96
Sampling Duration	24 Hrs	24 Hrs	24 Hrs	24 Hrs
SO_2 (ug/cu.m)	18.2	21.4	6.2	42.5
NOx (ug/cu.m)	7.2	10.8	5.6	26.2
SPM (ug/cu.m)	86	62	42	268

Location - >				
Parameters	Madagadipet	Muthialpet	Reddiyarpalayam	
Ariyankuppam				
Date	2/4/96	8/4/96	24/4/96	29/4/96
Sampling Duration	24 Hrs	24 Hrs	24 Hrs	24 Hrs
SO_2 (ug/cu.m)	18.6	22.6	12.6	24.2
NOx (ug/cu.m)	9.3	14.2	6.5	13.5
SPM (ug/cu.m)	78	106	40.2	69

Source : Department of Scinece, Technology and Environment, Pondicherry

Table A.19 Air emission status for different industrial estate of Pondicherry

Region	Indus. Estate	SO_2	NO_x (all values in Kg/d)	SPM
Pondicherry				
	Mettupalayam	36.9	307.6	190.4
	Sedarapet	26.9	37.8	14.6
	Kattukuppam	41.2	15.0	42.8
	Thattanchavady	-	6.8	5.9
	Isolated	36	12.6	4.4
Pondicherry (Overall Emis. Status)		141	380	258

Source : Department of Scinece, Technology and Environment, Pondicherry

Table A.20 Who emission factors for coal, lshs/fo and natural gas

Emission Factor	Particulates (SPM)	SO_2	NO_x
Kg/ton of Coal	8 (w/o Control Measures)	19 X (S)	9
Kg/ton of LSHS/FO	1.04	19.9 X (S)	13.2
Kg/ton of Nat.G.	negligible	nil	
11.2			

Source : Department of Scinece, Technology and Environment, Pondicherry

No_2 and SPM are presented in Table A.21 for locations sectional office, French Institute & Pipdic Industrial Estate (Mettupalayam).

b. Ambient Noise:

The study is based on the data related to 4 zones of Pondicherry town viz.

(a) Commercial zone
(b) Institutional zone (Educational),
(c) Silent Zone (Court, Hospitals, Government Secretariate) and
(d) Special zones (Central Bus-stand and Public Park).

In the commercial zone, the noise level ranged between 60-65 dß normally but at certain times when heavy vehicles used air horns, the noise level increased upto 70-75 dß. The frequency of such higher noise level depends on the frequency of passing of vehicles with air horn. The Government General Hospital area showed higher noise level due to the three wheelers; which is 20% higher than the permissible level. Traffic signal points are becoming noisy. It was found that the noise level is normally higher than 70 to 80 dß. In the special zone which includes the central bus stand and Public Parks, the noise levels are characteristically different. In the central bus stand the noise level was seemed to be maximum among all the four zones. The noise level ranged between 70-100 dß. In the Public-Park, the noise level is well below 45 dß.

Thus, in the Pondicherry town, the noise level in four selected zones are higher and in rural area it is in safe limit. Exposure to such a higher level of noise would cause significant negative impact on the psycho-behaviors of the individual causing headache, irritation and even impairment of hearing.

c. Hazardous Material :

Hazardous Material handling SSI Units and Perblic complains on SSI Units Operation in Pondicherry region is given in Table A.22 and A.23.

Table A.21 Ambient air quality statistics – 1993 & 1994 Pondicherry.

Month	SULPHUR DIOXIDE				NITROGEN DIOXIDE				SUSPENDED PARTICULATE MATTER			
	Min	Mean	Max	n	Min	Mean	Max	n	Min	Mean	Max	n
> LOCATION:	Sectional Office											
▶ Year :	1993											
January	2.5	7.0	18.8	6	7.1	15.7	31.7	6	96	138	160	6
February	2.3	5.5	7.0	8	7.2	17.8	44.1	8	115	137	156	8
March	6.3	8.8	12.1	7	23.7	31.4	41.7	7	84	104	118	7
April	2.3	14.5	32.2	9	4.3	26.8	68.2	9	90	131	182	9
May	4.7	7.6	11.2	9	23.0	26.5	34.2	9	96	137	170	9
June	6.8	10.8	16.1	7	22.3	27.7	32.8	7	127	177	269	7
July	3.5	21.5	49.2	9	29.6	39.4	51.4	9	202	236	271	9
August	6.3	15.5	43.2	9	262	37.7	83.5	9	127	206	299	9
September	6.6	19.3	45.6	8	172	47.0	10.19	8	142	206	305	8
October	4.9	7.8	12.4	7	15.3	33.0	47.9	7	75	159	217	7
November	14.3	24.6	36.4	8	25.3	44.4	67.2	8	99	162	264	8
December	3.6	13.1	20.2	6	23.5	33.6	46.8	6	94	109	121	6
Annual	2.3	13.3	49.2	93	4.3	32.2	104.9	93	75	101	305	93

Month	SULPHUR DIOXIDE				NITROGEN DIOXIDE				SUSPENDED PARTICULATE MATTER			
	Min	Mean	Max	n	Min	Mean	Max	n	Min	Mean	Max	n
> LOCATION:	Sectional Office											
▶ Year :	1994											
January	8.0	17.3	27.6	9	26.9	38.9	51.9	9	87	151	259	9
February	15.6	18.4	21.2	8	26.9	40.4	48.4	8	101	179	298	8
March	7.5	13.6	23.0	8	19.9	32.8	41.2	8	115	163	260	8
April	7.5	9.7	12.3	8	23.6	34.3	41.9	8	94	158	218	8
May	8.1	9.9	13.3	9	22.2	30.2	35.9	9	145	175	227	9
June	6.3	15.0	26.7	8	28.0	38.5	50.7	8	139	208	248	8
July	10.4	16.6	21.4	7	18.6	28.7	39.0	7	137	158	173	7
August	11.6	28.7	78.0	9	24.1	43.6	71.6	9	146	194	240	9
September	16.1	29.2	80.0	8	26.0	44.5	111.3	8	140	171	198	8
October	21.3	32.0	43.4	7	67.2	79.1	93.8	7	147	174	199	7
November	7.8	18.4	28.8	6	28.8	62.5	99.0	6	137	183	213	6
December	18.0	25.1	32.9	8	35.2	63.0	79.9	8	140	165	195	8
Annual	6.3	19.4	80.0	95	18.6	43.9	111.3	95	87	173	298	95

Note : N.A. – Data Not Available/Inadequate, Units in mmg/m^3, n – Number of > =16 hours monitored days

Month	SULPHUR DIOXIDE				NITROGEN DIOXIDE				SUSPENDED PARTICULATE MATTER			
	Min	Mean	Max	n	Min	Mean	Max	n	Min	Mean	Max	n
LOCATION:	French Institute, Pondicherry											
Year : 1993												
January	1.5	3.9	9.8	9	6.2	10.6	18.8	9	89	112	199	9
February	2.9	5.1	10.6	8	9.5	13.9	22.7	8	62	91	134	8
March	6.1	11.5	25.5	9	18.7	34.5	70.6	9	95	193	308	9
April	1.6	4.8	9.6	7	11.6	17.8	30.7	7	58	107	196	7
May	3.6	6.1	11.1	7	13.2	23.0	33.2	7	91	116	150	7
June	4.5	7.2	13.2	8	22.2	45.6	77.8	8	75	86	129	8
July	7.2	19.3	56.3	8	19.3	28.8	38.8	8	148	161	181	8
August	5.1	9.1	12.9	8	12.0	24.8	48.5	8	126	153	179	8
September	3.8	15.5	56.3	7	13.2	20.5	29.6	7	58	98	134	7
October	5.3	10.6	16.7	6	15.6	19.0	22.6	6	61	122	186	7
November	5.3	8.9	12.1	6	13.7	18.8	23.4	6	94	129	191	6
December	5.4	15.0	28.0	5	25.6	38.2	59.9	5	95	137	178	5
Annual	1.5	9.6	56.3	8.8	6.2	24.5	77.8	88	58	126	308	89

Month	SULPHUR DIOXIDE				NITROGEN DIOXIDE				SUSPENDED PARTICULATE MATTER			
	Min	Mean	Max	n	Min	Mean	Max	n	Min	Mean	Max	n
Year : 1994												
January	8.3	12.6	20.8	8	23.2	33.8	47.6	8	123	147	170	8
February	7.5	10.5	19.7	6	14.6	25.6	36.1	6	94	144	193	6
March	8.1	11.2	13.8	8	19.4	25.1	31.5	8	76	131	174	8
April	8.9	12.0	14.2	7	21.0	23.1	24.9	7	98	143	194	7
May	6.2	9.2	12.3	8	13.9	21.2	30.6	8	74	141	176	8
June	9.8	14.2	18.5	8	12.5	22.3	30.1	8	73	147	197	8
July	9.6	10.9	11.9	4	15.9	33.0	54.1	4	141	146	150	4
August	1.8	7.5	12.9	9	4.1	22.7	44.4	9	83	111	169	9
September	10.5	13.7	15.9	8	22.4	42.9	56.7	8	51	133	201	8
October	7.3	11.5	18.9	7	23.2	34.0	49.3	7	63	123	171	7
November	7.6	15.0	25.6	6	13.4	36.4	51.1	6	80	100	131	6
December	3.7	13.3	19.8	7	35.7	42.9	54.5	7	87	122	151	7
Annual	1.8	11.7	25.6	86	4.1	29.9	56.7	86	51	132	201	86

Note : N.A. Data Not Available/Inadequate, Units in ug/m3 n- Number of > =16 hours monitored days.

Month	SULPHUR DIOXIDE				NITROGEN DIOXIDE				SUSPENDED PARTICULATE MATTER			
	Min	Mean	Max	n	Min	Mean	Max	n	Min	Mean	Max	n
LOCATION: PIDIC Indl Estate, Mettupalayam												
Year : 1993												
January	10.8	20.8	29.3	6	15.4	23.9	36.6	6	106	162	220	6
February	5.0	17.1	41.9	8	12.9	28.7	54.0	8	157	206	242	8
March	8.9	25.7	85.6	9	22.6	33.9	45.0	9	71	197	300	9
April	3.6	17.9	39.3	8	12.2	25.7	58.5	8	78	164	283	8
May	14.2	27.8	38.9	8	27.0	57.3	144.4	8	199	259	318	8
June	11.6	33.0	48.9	7	24.2	54.0	86.5	7	130	182	264	7
July	16.0	48.4	194.	9	24.3	44.3	83.0	9	199	239	307	9
August	9.7	25.8	36.6	9	20.4	38.4	66.8	9	121	191	346	9
September	4.9	32.2	66.3	8	13.6	26.0	58.8	8	79	156	271	8
October	28.8	41.1	74.6	8	22.1	36.4	78.0	8	125	193	292	8
November	20.0	45.0	61.9	5	28.6	45.1	67.7	5	123	233	289	5
December	9.2	37.8	60.3	7	12.5	41.3	63.9	7	123	180	259	7
Annual	3.6	30.8	194.	92	12.2	37.8	144.4	92	71	197	346	92

Month	SULPHUR DIOXIDE				NITROGEN DIOXIDE				SUSPENDED PARTICULATE MATTER			
	Min	Mean	Max	n	Min	Mean	Max	n	Min	Mean	Max	n
Year : 1994												
January	16.4	36.9	46.9	8	21.8	43.6	58.9	8	162	240	283	8
February	21.2	31.3	45.5	7	22.4	30.0	35.4	7	99	222	331	7
March	26.4	37.4	15.5	9	36.1	50.0	58.9	9	149	260	326	9
April	20.4	26.1	30.9	8	32.8	42.0	52.1	8	90	189	267	8
May	35.3	69.9	93.0	9	40.1	68.7	95.4	9	198	284	381	9
June	42.2	65.3	80.9	8	57.3	79.1	108.9	8	173	257	407	8
July	32.9	64.8	111.2	8	31.7	64.7	116.5	8	176	226	343	8
August	11.3	77.6	183.8	8	39.8	62.2	107.8	8	142	198	254	8
September	40.6	62.6	97.8	9	49.4	82.7	113.4	9	81	215	291	9
October	51.8	111.9	175.7	6	56.4	80.6	130.6	6	153	256	395	6
November	26.1	49.5	62.9	6	46.8	64.5	91.2	6	223	285	373	6
December	23.1	47.7	74.5	9	47.4	79.8	107.9	9	129	234	341	9
Annual	11.3	55.9	183.8	95	21.8	62.6	130.6	95	81	238	407	95

Note : N.A.- Data Not Available/Inadequate, Units m mmg/m^3, n-Number of > = 16 hours monitored days.

Table A.22 Harzardous material handling SSI units in Pondicherry region.

Region/Estate	S.NO	Name of the Unit	Chemical
Pondicherry Met. Ind.Est.	01	Pearl Bond	Hexane
	02	Flourides & Chemicals	Sulphuric Acid
	03	Borax India Ltd	Sulphuric Acid
	04	Aaditya Chemicals Pvt. Ltd	Hydrochloric Acid
	05	Pondicherry Chemicals	Sulphuric Acid
	06	Carmel Industries	Xylene
	07	Ghuru Chemicals	Sulphuric Acid
Sed. Ind. Est.	08	New India Surfactants	Sulphuric Acid
	09	Anand Chemicals	Sulphuric Acid
	10	Prabhat Polyurethane Foam Pvt. Ltd.	Toulene Di-Isocyanate, Methylene Chloride
	11	D.P. Foam Pvt. Ltd.	Toulene Di-isocyanate Methylene Chloride
Isolated SSI	12	Arvind Chemical Products	Potassium Chloride Hydrochloric Acid
	13	Pondy Chlorates	Potassium Chloride Hydrochloric Acid
	14	Auro Foam Pvt. Ltd	Toulene Di-Isocyanate, Methylene Chloride

Table A.23 Public complaints on SSI units operations in Pondicherry region

Region/ Estate	S.No.	Name of the Unit and and Period of Complain	Nature of Complain	Rectification Work
Pondicherry	1	S.Kumaresan Bakery, June 1993	Heat Radiation & Smoke	Unit Closed
	2	Fluorides & Chemicals, August 1994	Solid waste Dumping on land	Solid Waste dump pit made
	3	Gee Pee Electro Plating & Engg. Dec 1993	Acid Fumes from HCL Boiling	Closed System Installed
	4	Mett. Ind. Estate Liquid Effluent disposal, Mar. 1995	Stagnation of effluent near Anna Nagar	Problem occurs at times till date
	5	Agra Leathers, Mar.1995	Dumping of leather cut wastes & Burning it in open	It does not occur presently after PPCC intervention
	6	Athiappa Chemical Works, Apr.1994	Air Pollution Problems in near by residential area	Stack of proper height installed

Reference : Pondicherry Pollution Control Board Office Records.

REFERENCES

Abbasi, S. A, Abbasi, N., and Soni, R., (1998) , Heavy Metals in Environment, Mittal Publications, New Delhi, Pages 314.

Abbasi, S. A., (1998) Environment Everyone, Discovery Publishing House, New Delhi; Pages 148.

Abbasi, S. A., (1998), Environmental Pollution and Energy Control, Cogent International, Pondicherry, Pages 442.

Abbasi, S.A., and Vinithan, S. (1997), Environmental Impact of Industries on Suburban Environments, Discovery Publishing House, New Delhi; pages 145.

Agnithotri, A K, and Sharma, J S, Review of Ecology of Micro-Organisma & Biodegradation of Oil Waste In S.K.Wahi, A.K.Agnihotri, J.S.Sharma pp.195-212, Environmental Management in Petroleum Industry

Agrawal, S, and Tiwari, S L, (1997) , Susceptibility Levels of a Few Plants on the Basis of Air Pollution Tolerance Index, The Indian Forester.123. pp. 319-322

Ahmad, S , Can we Afford to Ignore Corrosion in Pollution Control, In S.K.Wahi,A.K.Agnihotri,J.S.Sharma (Eds) , Environmental Management in Petroleum Industry, Wiley Eastern pp.85-89

Ahmed, K J, Mohd. Yunus, Singh, S N, Kanti Srivastava, Nandita Singh, Vivek Pandey and Jyoti Mishra .(1989) Study of Plants in Relation to Air Pollution, Report from NBRI, Lucknow, pages 11

Albritton, D F, Fehsenfeld, B, Hicks, J, Miller, S, Liu, J, Hales, J, Shannon, J, Durham, and Patruios, A, (1987)

Atmospheric process.*In Atmospheric Processes and Deposition. Interim Assessment.* III. National Acid Precipitation Assessment Program, Washington, DC, pp.37-59.

Altshuller, A P, (ed). (1984), The Acidic Deposition Phenomenon and Its Effects, In Atmospheric Sciences, Publ.No.EPA-600-8-83016AF, U.S.E.P.A., Washington,DC.

Anil Bhardwaj, *Effluent Standards & Testing Methods*, In S.K.Wahi, A.K.Agnihotri, J.S.Sharma pp.195-212, *Environmental Management in Petroleum Industry*

Art, H W, (1971), *Atmospheric salts in the functioning of a maritime forest ecosystem.* Unpublished Ph.D. Thesis, Yale University, School of Forestry and Environmental Studies, New Haven, Connecticut, pp 135

Art, H W, Bormann, F H, Voigt, G K, and Woodwell, G M, (1974), *Barrier island forest ecosystem:* Role of meteorologic nutrient inputs, Science 184: 60-62

Aubertin, G M, and M.P.Aubertin, (1981), Assessment of Non-traditional Controls on Ambient Air Quality. Publ. No. 81-07. Institute of Natural Resources, State of Illinois, Chicago, IL, pp 284.

Aylor, D E, (1975), *Deposition of particles of regweed pollen in a plant canopy.* J.Appl.Meteorol. 14: 52-57.

Bach, W. (1972), Atmospheric Pollution, McGraw-Hill, New York, pp144

Bache, D.H. (1979), Particle transport within plant canopies – I, A framework for analysis. Atmos. Environ.13:1257-1262.

Bennett, J.H. and A.C.Hill. (1975), *Interactions of air pollutants with canopies of vegetatioin,* In J.B.Mudd and T.T.Kozlowski, eds., Responses of Plants to Air Pollution. Academic Press, New York, pp.273-306.

Bennett, J.H. and AC.Hill. (1973), *Absorption of gaseous air pollutants by a standardized plant canopy.* J.Air Pollu. Control Assoc. 23:203-206.

Bennett,J.H.,A.C.Hill, and D.M.Gates. (1973), A model for gaseous pollutant sorption by leaves. J.Air Pollu. Control Assoc. 23:957-962.

Bormann, F.H., P.R.Shafer, and D.Mulcahy. (1958), *Fallout on the vegetation of New England during the 1957 atom bomb test series.* Ecology 39:376-378.

Boyce, S.G. (1954), The salt spray community. Ecol. Monogr. 24:29-67.

Chakrabarti,U K, Environmental Impact Assessment, In S.K.Wahi,A.K.Agnihotri,J.S.Sharma (Eds) Environmental Management in Petroleum Industry Wiley Eastern pp.85-89,

Chamberlain, A.C. (1967), *Deposition of particles to natural surfaces.* In P.H.Gregory and J.L.Monteith, eds., Airborne Microbes. 17th Symp.Soc. Gen. Microbiol., Cambridge Univ. Press, London, pp.138-164.

Chamberlain, A.C. (1970), Interception and retention of radioactive aerosols by vegetation. Atmos. Environ. 4: 57-78.

Chamberlain, A.C. (1975) , The movement of particles in plant communities. In J.I.Monteith (Ed.),Vegetation and the Atmosphere, Vol. I. Academic Press, New York, pp.155-203.

Chand, K M K, An Approach to Environmental Impact Assessment, In S.K.Wahi,A.K.Agnihotri,J.S.Sharma (Eds), Environmental Management in Petroleum Industry, Wiley Eastern pp.23-27

Chandhuri, A B, (1993), Tree and the Environment Ashish Publishing House, New Delhi,

Clayton, J.L. (1972), Salt spray and mineral cycling in two California ecosystems.Ecology 53: 74-81.

Comprehensive Environmental Impact Assessment, (1993), Tamilnadu Petroproducts Limited, Madras; p 485.

Costantini, A. and A.E.Rich. (1973), *Comparison of salt injury to four species of coniferous tree seedlings when salt was applied to the potting medium and to the needles with or without an anti-transpirant.*

Phytopathology 63:200. Deposition of 2.75, 5.0 and 8.5 um particles to plant and soil surfaces. Environ. Polu.12:293-305.

Dinesh, R S, Emissions during Drilling, Production, Storage and LPG Plant Operations, In S.K.Wahi, A.K.Agnihotri, J.S.Sharma pp. 263-270, *Environmental Management in Petroleum Industry*

Dochinger, L.S. (1972) , Can trees cleanse the air of particulate pollutants? Intl. Shade Tree Conf. Proc. 48:45-48.

Eaton, T.E. (1979), *Natural and artificially altered patterns of salt spray across forested barrier island.* Atmos.Environ. 13: 705-709.

Edmonds, R.L. and C.H.Driver. (1974), *Dispersion and Deposition of spores of Fomes anosus and fluorescent particles.*Phytopathkology 64:1313-1321.

Elder F. and C. Hosler. (1954).*Ragweed pollen in the atmosphere.* Report, Dept of Meteorology, Pennsylvania State Univ., University Part, PA.

Environmental Health Science Centre, (1975), The Role of Plants in Environmental Purification. Environ. Health Sci. Ctr., Oregon State Univ., Corvallis, OR, 34 pp.

Environmental Impact Assessment of Lube Plant Expansion In Environmental management Petroleum Industries, M/s Madras Refineries Ltd. Madras. Neeri. Nagpur - 440 020.

Erisman, J W, and Draaijers, G P J, (1995), Deposition Processes and Measurement Techniques In.*Studies in Environmental Science*, 63, Elsevier.

Fritschen, L.J., C.H. Driver, C. Avery, J. Buffo, R.Edmonds, R.Kinerson, and P.Schiess. (1970), Dispersion of air traces into and within a forested area (3).

Report No.OSDO1366, College of Forest Resources, Washington Univ., Seattle, W A, 53 pp.

Garland, J.A. (1977), The dry deposition of sulfur dioxide to land and water surfaces.Proc. Royal Soc. London 354: 245-268.

Garland, J.A. and J.R. Branson. (1977) , The deposition of sulfur dioxide to pine forest assessed by a radioactive tracer method. Tellus 29:445-454.

Garland, J.A. and S.A.Penkett. (1976), Absorption of peroxyacetylnitrate and ozone by natural surfaces.Atmos. Environ. 10:1127-1131.

Graustein, W.D. (1978), Measurement of dust input to a forested watershed using $^{87}Sr/^{86}$ Sr rations.

Geol. Soc. Am. Abst. 10:411, Gregory, P.H. (1971), The leaf as a spore trap.

In T.F. Preece and C.H. Dickinson, eds., Ecology of Leaf Surface Microorganisma. Academic Press, New York 640 pp.

Gregory, P.H. (1973), The Microbiology of the Atmosphere. Wiley, New York, 377 pp.

Hanson, G.P. and L.Thorne. (1972), Vegetation to reduce air pollution, Lasca Leaves 20: 60-65

Heck, W W, and Brandt, C S, (1977), The Effects of Air Pollution, Academic Press, New York

Heichel, G.H. and L.Hankin. (1972), Particles containing lead, chlorine and bromine detected on trees with an electron microprobe. Environ. Sci. Technol. 6: 1121-1112.

Heichel, G.H. and L.Hankin. (1976).*Roadside coniferous windbreaks as sinks for vehicular lead emissions.* J.Air.Pollu. Control Assoc. 26:767-770.

Heisler, G.M.(1975), How trees modify metropolitan climate and noise.In Forestry Issues in Urban America.

Proc. 1974 National Convention of Society of American Foresters, New York, pp.103-112.

Helmke, P.A., W.P.Robarge, M.B.Schoenfield, P.Burger, R.D.Koons, and J.E.Thresher.(1984)

Impacts of Coal Combustion on Trace Elements in the Environment: Wisconsin Power Plant Impact Study.

Publ. No. EPA-600-53-84 070. U.S.Environmental Protection Agency Environmental Research Lab, Duluth, ME.

Helvey,J.D.(1971), A summary of rainfall interception by certain conifers of North America.

In Proc. Biological Effects in the Hydrological Cycle. U.S.D.A. Forest Service, Washington, DC,pp.103-113.

Hill, A.C. (1971), Vegetation: A sink for atmospheric pollutants. J. Air Pollu. Control Assoc. 21:341-346.

Hill, A.C. and E.M.Chamberlain Jr. (1974), *The removal of water solulble gases from the atmosphere by vegetation.* Atmospheric-Surface Exchange of Particulate and Gaseous Pollutants Symp. Richland, W A, Sept. 4-6, 1974, 12pp.

Ingold, C.T. (1971), *Fungal Spores*. Clarendon Press, Oxford, 302 pp.

Jashnani, I. (1988), A Study of the Feasibility of Using Trees to Reduce Polllutants Resulting from the Proposed Coal Conversion of Unit No.2 H.A.

Wagner Power Plant, Engineering and Computer Services, 10451 Twin Rivers Road. Columbia, MD, 63 pp.

Jensen, K.F. (1975), Sulfur content of hybrid poplar cuttings fumigated with sulfur dioxide.

U.A.D.A. Forest Service, Res.Note No.NE-209, Upper Darby, PA, 4 pp.

Johnson, W B, (1976), Air Pollutants, Their Transformation and Transport A.C.Stern, (Ed)

Kabel, R.L. (1976), Natural removal of gaseous pollutants.3rd Symp. Atmospheric Turbulence, Diffusion and Air Quality. Amer. Meteorological Soc., Oct. 19-22, 1976, Raleigh, NC.

Kable, R.L., R.A.O'Dell, M.Taheri, and D.D.Davis. (1976), A preliminary model of gaseous polutant uptake by vegetation.

Centre for Air Environment Studies, Publ. No.455-76, Pennsylvania State Univ., University Park, PA, 96 pp.

Kapoor, R K, and Gupta, V K, (1990), Atenuation of Air Pollution by Green Belt-Optimisation of Density of Tree Plantation

In:S.E.Schwartz and V.G.N.Sligh(Eds) P.No.1265-1275 Percipitatich Scavengtng and Atmosphere Surpace Exchange

Kapoor, R K, and Gupta, V K, (1992), Attentuation of Air Pollution by Greenbelt In J.B.Shukla, T.G.Hallam and V.Capasso (Eds) p.29-56

Kapoor, S, Sources of Noise Pollution in Oil Industry, In Environmental Management Petroleum Industries Wiley Eastern, p.445

Keller, T.(1978), How effective are forests in improving air quality? Eighth World Forestry Conference, Jakarta, Indonesia, Oct. 16-28, 1978, 9 pp.

Khan F.I. and Abbasi, S.A. (1997), Risk Analysis of a Chloralkali Industry Situated in a Populated Area . Process Safety Progress (USA), 172-184.

Khan F.I. and Abbasi, S.A. (1998), *DOMIFECT – A New Software for the Study of Domino Effects During Accidents* Environmental Modelling and Software (USA), 13 163-177.

Khan F.I. and Abbasi, S.A. (1998), Rapid Quantitative Risk Assessment of a Petrochemical Industry Journal of Cleaner Production (USA), 6 9-22.

Khan F.I. and Abbasi, S.A. (1999), HAZDIG – A New Software for Studying Hazardous Dispersion Journal of Loss Prevention in Process Industries (UK), in press.

Khan F.I. and Abbasi, S.A.(1999), Modelling and Simulation of Heavy Gas Dispersion Journal of Loss Prevention in Chemical Process Industries (UK), in press.

Khan, F.I. and Abbasi, S.A. (1998), Inherently Safer Design Based on Rapid Risk Analysis Journal of Loss Prevention in Process Industries (UK), II 361 - 372.

Khan, F.I. and Abbasi, S.A. (1998), Risk Assessment in Chemical Process Industries Discovery Publishing House, New Delhi, pages 359.Kovacs, M, (1985), Pollution Control & Conservatioin Ellis Horwood Limited, Wes Sussex, London.

Krishna, S, Mudan, *FacilityInitialRiskScreeningTechnique* In S.K.Wahi, A.K.Agnihotri, J.S.Sharma (Eds)

Environmental Management in Petroleum Industry, Wiley Eastern pp.23-27

Langer, G. (1965), Particle deposition and re-entrainment from coniferous tree. Part II. Experiments with individual leaves. Kolloid Z.Z.Polym. 204:119-124.

Little, P. (1977), Deposition of 2.75, 5.0 and 8.5um particles to plant and soil surfaces. Environ. Pollu. 12: 293-305.

Little, P. and M.H.Martin (1972), A survey of zinc, lead and cadmium in soil and natural vegetation around a smelting complex. Environ. Pollu. 241-254

Martin, A. and F.R.Barber (1971), Some measurements of loss of atmospheric sulfur dioxide near foliage.Atmos. Environ. 5:345-352.

Martin, W.E. (1959), The vegetation of Island Beach State Park, New Jersey.

Ecol. Monogr. 29: 1-46.

McCure, D.C., D.H. Silbkerman, R.H. Mandl, L.H.Weinstein, P.C.Freudenthal, and P.A.Giardina. (1977)

Studies on the effects of saline aerosols of cooling tower origin on plants. J. Air Polu. Control Assoc. 27: 319-324.

Moser, B.C. (1979), Airborne salt and spray techniques for experimentation and its effects on vegetation.

Phytopathology 69: 1002-1006. Murphy, C.E. Jr., T.R., Sinclair, and K.R.Knoerr (1977)

An assessment of the use of forests as sinks for the removal of atmospheric sulfur dioxide.

J. Environ. Qual. 6:388-396, Neuberger, H., C.C. Hosler, and C. Koemond (1967) Vegetation as an aerosol filter.

In S.W. Tromp and W.H. Weihe, eds., Biometeorology 2. Pergamon Press, New York, pp. 693-702.

Oak Ridge National Laboratory (1969), Progress report in postattack ecology. Interim Progress Report N. ORNL-TM-2466. Oak Ridge, TN,60pp

Oosting, H.J. (1945), Tolearnce to salt spray of plants of coastal dunes. Ecology 26: 85-89.

Oosting, H.J. and W.D. Billings (1942), Factorsz affecting vegetatioinal zonatic on coastal dunes.Ecology 23:131-142.

Padmanabhamurty, B, and Satapathy, K L, (1996), *Efficacy of Screens and Vegetation in Mitigating Vehicular Traffic Noise Indian* Journal of Environmental Protection, 16 129-134.

Page, A.L. and A.C.Chang (1979), *Contamination of soil and vegetation by atmospheric deposition of trace elements.* Phytopathology 69: 1007-1011.

Podgorow, N.W. (1967), Plantings as dust filters.Lets. Khoz. 20: 39-40.

Prithvi Raj Singh, Petrochemical Industry and Environmental Issues In S.K.Wahi,A.K.Agnihotri,

J.S.Sharma (Eds) , Environmental Management in Petroleum Industry Wiley Eastern pp.23-27

Rana, K S, Oil Pollution: Its Impact on Aquatic Ecosystem In S.K.Wahi, A.K.Agnihotri, J.S.Sharma pp.195-212

Environmental Management in Petroleum Industry

Rao, D N, Petroleum Production Operations: An Ecological Perspective (In) S.K.Wahi,A.K.Agnihnotri,J.S.Sharma pp.373-374, Environmental Management in Petroleum Industry

Wiley Eastern, Rao, D N, Air Pollutants:Nature, Sources and Meteorological Relations In S.K.Wahi, A.K. Agnihotri, J.S.Sharma, Environmental Management in Petroleum Industries

Wiley Eastern, pp. 371-372,

Rao, D N, Air Pollution and Plant Productivity

In S.K.Wahi,A.K.Agnikhotri,J.S.Sharma Environmental Management in Petroleum Industry, Wiley Eastern, pp.343-369, Rao, D N,

Petroleum Production Operations, In Ecology and Environmental Pollution Control

Rao, D N, Plants and Air Pollutant Mixtures, In S.K.Wahi, A.K.Agnikhotri, J.S.Sharma, Environmental Management in Petroleum Industr y Wiley Eastern, pp.317-342

Rao, D N, Plants and Particulate Pollutants In S.K.Wahi,A.K.Agnikhotri,J.S.Sharma pp.291-315 Environmental Management in Petroleum Industry Wiley Eastern, pp.291-315

Rao, D N, Vegetation in Industrial Environment In S.k.Wahi,A.K.Agnihotri,J.S.Sharma Environmental Management in Petroleum Industry Wiley Eastern ,pp. 373-374

Rasmussen, K.H., M.Taheri, and R.L.Kabel. (1975), Global emissions and natural processes for removal of gaseous polutants. Water Air Soil Pollu. 4: 33-64

Rauner, J.L. (1976), Deciduous forests. In J;L;Monteith, ed;l Vegetation and the Atmosphere. 2.Academic Press, New York, pp. 241-264

Raynor, G.S., M.E. Smith, I.A.Singer, L.A.Cohen, and J.V.Hayes (1966) The dispersion of ragweed pollen into a forest.

Proc. 7th National Conf. Agricultural Meteorology, Aug. 29-Sept. 1, 1966. Rutgers Univ., New Brunswick, NJ.

Raynor, S. (1967), *Effects of a forest on particulate dispersion.* In C.A. Mawson ed., Proc. USAEC Meteorological Information Meeting, Chalk River Nuclear Laboratories, Chalk River, Ontarion, Canada, Sept. 11-14, 1967, pp.581-586.

Rich, S. and N.C. Turner (1972), Importance of moisture on stomatal behavior of plants subjected to ozone. J.Air. Pollu.Control Assoc. 22: 369-371.

Rich, S., P.E. Waggoner, and H.Tomlinson. (1970), Ozone uptake by bean leaves. Science 169: 79-80.

Roberts, B.R. (1971), Foliar absorption of gaseous air pollutants. Am. Nursery 133: 44-45

Roberts, B.R. (1974), Foliar sorption of atmospheric sulfur dioxide by woody plants. Environ. Pollu. 7: 133-140

Roberts, B.R. and C.R., Krause. (1976), Changes in ambient SO_2 by rhododendron and pyracantha. Hort Sci. 11:111-112.

Rogers, H.H., H.E. Jeffries, and A.M. Witherspoon. (1979), Measuring air pollutant uptake by plants: Nitrogen dioxide. J.Environ. Qual. 8: 551-557.

Romney, E.M., R.G. Lindberg., H.A.Hawthorne, B.G. Bystrom, and K.H. Larson (1963), Contaminatiion of plant foliage with radioactive fallout. Ecology 44:343-349.

Rosinki, J. and C.T. Nagamoto (1965), Particle deposition on and re-entrainment from coniferous trees. Part J. Experiments with trees. Kolloid Z.A. Polym. 204:111-119.

Roy, R K and Sharma, S C, (1997), Green Belt for Minimizing Industrial and Urban Pollution Encology 11, 8-12

Russell, I.J. (1974), *Some factors affective beta particle dose to tree populations in the eastern New England area from stratospheric fallout to 1974.* Report No.CH-3015-13, Atomic Energy Commission, Chicago, IL, 47pp

Russell, I.J. and C.E.Choquette. (1974), Scale factors for foliar contaminatioin by stratospheric sources of fission products in the New England area.

Report No.CH-3015-13, Atomic Energy Commission, Chicago, IL, 47 pp.

S.A.Abbasi and E.V.Ramasami (1999), Biotechnological Pollution Control Systems

Orient Longmens (UPIL), Hyderabad; pages 237., S.A.Abbasi, P.Krishnakumari, and F.I.Khan (1999) Hot Topics

Oxford University Press, New Delhi: pages 357., Salisbury, F.B. and C.W.Ross. (1978) , Plant Physiology.

Wadsworth, Belmont, CA, 422pp. Sanjay Bhutani, Management of Noise Pollution

In S.k.Wahi,A.K.Agnihotri,J.S.Sharma, Environmental Management in Petroleum Industry, Wiley Eastern, pp.417-427

Sanjay Bhutani, Management of Noise Pollution In Environmental Management Petroleum Industries, Wiley Eastern,p.427

Sharma, B K, and Kaur, H, (1995), Environmental Chemistry,(Second Edition), Goal Publishing House,Meerut

Sharma, J S, and Agnihotri, A K, Concept of Air Pollution in Petroleum Industry , In S.K.Wahi,A.K.Agnihotri,J.S.Sharma (Eds), Environmental Management in Petroleum Industry Wiley Eastern pp.107-128

Sharma, J S, and Chaudhary, D R, Oil Field Air Pollution in Upper Assam,India: A Case Study In S.K.Wahi, A.K.Agnihotri, J.S.Sharma (Eds) Environmental Management in Petroleum Industry Wiley Eastern pp.107-128

Sharma, J S, Flaring practices in Petroleum Industry Environmental Perspective In S.K.Wahi,A.K.Agnihotri,J.S.Sharma (Eds) Environmental Management in Petroleum Industry Wiley Eastern pp.129-153

Sharma, S M, Minimising Environmental Liabilities for Oil Field Wastes In S.K.Wahi, A.K.Agnihotri, J.S.Sharma, pp.253-262 *Environmental Management in Petroleum Industry*

Sheih, C.M. (1977), Application of a statistical trajectory model of the simulation of sulfur pollution orver northeastern United States.Atomos. Environ. 11: 173-178.

Sheih, C.M., M.L. Wesely, and B.B. Hicks. (1979), A guide for estimating dry deposition velocities of sulfur over the eastern United States and surrounding regions.

Argonne National Laboratory Report No.ANL-RER-79-2, 55pp

Singh, M P, Recent advances in risk assessment In S.K.Wahi,A.K.Agnihotri,J.S.Sharma (Eds) Environmental Management in Petroleum Industry Wiley Eastern pp.23-27

Singh, R P, Impact of Drilling Activity on Environment In S.K.Wahi, A.K.Agnihotri, J.S.Sharma PP. 271-287 Environmental Management in Petroleum Industry, Singh, S P, (1986), Planting of Trees B.R.Publishing Corporation,Delhi.

Sivasamy, N, and Srinivasan, V, Environmental Polution and its Control By Trees The Hindu, 1997

Slinn, W.G.N. (1975), Dry deposition and resuspension of aerosol particles - A new look at some old problems.

Proc. Conf. Atmosphere-Surface Exchange of Particles and Gases, ERDA Conf. Series, No. CONF-740921, Washington, DC, pp.1-40

Slinn, W.G.N. (1976), Some approximations for the wet and dry removal of particles and gases from the atmosphere.

Atmos. Sciences Dept., Battelle Memorial Institute, Pacific Northwest Laboratory, Richland, WA.

Smith, W H, (1990) Air Pollution and Forests *Publisher: Springer – Verlag New York*, Inc., 175 Fifth Avenue, New York, *New York 10010, USA*

Smith, W.H. (1971), Lead contamination of roadside white pine. For.Sci. 17: 195-198

Smith, W.H. (1973), Metal contaminatin of urban woody plants. Environ. Sci. Technol. 7:631-636.

Smith, W.H. (1976), Lead contamination of the roadside ecosystem. J. Air polu. Control Assoc. 26: 753-766.

Smith, W.H. (1979), Urban vegetation and air quality.

In Proc. National Urban Forestry Conference, Washington, DC, Nov. 13-16, 1978, U.S.D.A. Forest Service, Washington, D.C. and State Univ. of New York, Publ. No. 80-003 Syracuse, NY, pp.284-305

Smith, W.H. and B.J.Staskowicz .(1977), Removal of atmospheric particle by leaves and twigs of urban trees: Some preliminary observations and assessment of research needs. Environ. Mamt. 1:317-328.

Smith, W.H. and L.S. Dochinger .(1975), Air Pollution and Metropolitan Woody Vegetation. Pinchot Institute, consortium for Environmental Forestry Research, Publ. No. PIEFR-PA-1. U.S.D.A. Forest Service, Upper Darby, PA, 74 pp.

Smith, W.H. and L.S.Dochinger (1976), Capability of metropolitan trees to reduce atmospheric contaminants.

In H. Gerhold, F. Santamor, and S. Little, eds., Proc, Better Trees for Metropolitan Landscapes, U.S.D.A. Forest Service, Gen. Tech; Report No. NE-22, Upper Darby, PA, pp. 49-59.

Smith, W.H.(1970)a.Technical review: Trees in the city. J. Am. Inst. Planners 6: 429-436.

Smith, W.H.(1974), Air pollution – Effects on the structure and function of the temperate forest ecosystem.Environ. Pollu. 6: 111-129.

Smith,W.H.(1970)b. *Salt contamination of white pine planted adjacent to an interstate highway.* Plant Dis. Reptr. 54: 1021-1025

Steubing, L. And R. Klee. (1970), Comparative investigations into the dust filtering effects oflbroad leaved and coniferous woody vegetation.

Agnew. Bot. 4: 73-85, Thorne, L. and G.P. Hansen. (1972), Species differences in rates of vegetal ozone absorption.Environ. Pollu. 3:303-312.

Townsend, A.M. (1974), Sorptionof ozone by nine shade tree species. J.Am. Soc. Hort. Sci. 99:206-208.

U. S. Environmental Protectiion Agency (1976)a. Open Space as an Air Resource Management Measure. I. Sink Factors. U.S.E.P.A. Publ. No. EPA-450/3/76g.028a, Research Triangle Park, NC.

U.S.Environmental Protection Agency (1976)b. Open Space as an Air Resource Management Measure, II. Design Criteria. U.S.E.P.A. Publ. No. EPA450/3/76-028b, Research Triangle Park, NC.

U.S.Envrrinomental Protection agency (1976)c. Open Space as on Air Resource Management Measure. III. Demonstration Plan (St. Louis, MO). U.S.E.P.A. Publ. No. EPA-450/3-76/028c, Research Triangle Park, NC.

Umesh Chandra, S F H, Rizvi and Uniyal, A K, Inductively Coupled Plasma In Environmental Management Petroleum Industries Wiley Eastern,p.459-460 Varshney, C K, Ecological Considerations in Environmental Planning

In S.k.Wahi,A.K.Agnihotri, J.S.Sharma Environmental Management in Petroleum Industry Wiley Eastern, pp.401-413

Varshney, C K, Role of Plants in Indicating, Monitoring and Mitigating Air Pollution In S.k.Wahi,A.K.Agnihotri,J.S.Sharma Environmental Management in Petroleum Industry Wiley Eastern, pp.383-400

Velchamy, S, Singh, S M, and Negi, S S, Solid Waste and Sludge Management in Oil Industry In S.K. Wahi, A.K.Agnihotri, J.S.Sharma Ed. Environmental Management in Petroleum Industry Wiley Eastern, pp.213-219,

Waggoner, P.E. (1971) Plants and polluted air.Bioscience 21:455-459.

Waggoner, P.E. (1975), Micrometeorological models. In J.L. Monteith, ed;l Vegetation and the Atmosphere.I. Academic Press, New York, pp.205-228.

Warren, J.L. (1973), Green space for air pollution control. School of Forest Resources, Tech. Rep. No. 50, North Carolina State Univ., Raleigh, NC, 118 pp.

Wedding, J.B., R.W. Carlson, J.H.Stukel, and F.A. Bazzaz (1975), Aerosol deposition on plant leaves. Environ. Sci. Tech. 9:151-153.

Wells, B.W. and I.V.Shunk (1938), Salt spray: An important factor in coastal ecology. Torr. Bot. Club Bull. 65:485-492.

White, E.J. and F. Turner (1970), Method of estimating income of nutrients in catch of airborne particles by a woodland canopy. J.Appl.Ecol. 7:441-461.

Whittaker, R.H. and G.M.Woodwell. (1967), Surface area relations of woody plants and forest communities.Am. J. Bot. 8: 931-939

Witherspoon, J.P. and F.G.Taylor, Jr. (1969), Retention of a fallout simulant containing ^{134}Cs by pine and oak trees. Health Phys. 17:825-829.

Wood, F.A. and D.D. Davis. (1969), Sensitivity to ozone determined for tree. Pennsylvania State Univ., Sci. Agr. 17:4-5

Woodcock, A.H. (1953), Salt nuclei in marine air as a function of altitude and wind force. J. Meteorol. 10:362-371.

Zinke, P.J. (1967), Forest interception studies in the United States. In Forest Hydrology, Pergamon Press, Oxford, England, pp. 137-160.